SALLI

COLLECTED READINGS

DAVID B. LOTT, EDITOR

Fortress Press
Minneapolis

SALLIE MCFAGUE
Collected Readings

Copyright © 2013 Fortress Press. All rights reserved. Except for brief quotations in critical articles or reviews, no part of this book may be reproduced in any manner without prior written permission from the publisher. Visit http://www.augsburgfortress.org/copyrights/contact.asp or write to Permissions, Augsburg Fortress, Box 1209, Minneapolis, MN 55440.

Unless otherwise noted, scripture quotations are from the New Revised Standard Version Bible, copyright © 1989 by the Division of Christian Education of the National Council of Churches of Christ in the USA, and are used with permission.

Chapter 20, "Falling in Love with God and the World: Some Reflections on the Doctrine of God," originally appeared in *Ecumenical Review* 65, no. 1 (2013): 17–34. Used by permission of World Council of Churches and Wiley Blackwell.

Cover design: Tory Herman

Cover image © iStockphoto / Aptyp_koK

Library of Congress Cataloging-in-Publication Data is available

Print ISBN 978-0-8006-9988-8

eBook ISBN 978-1-4514-6517-4

The paper used in this publication meets the minimum requirements of American National Standard for Information Sciences—Permanence of Paper for Printed Library Materials, ANSI Z329.48-1984.

Manufactured in the U.S.A.

This book was produced using PressBooks.com, and PDF rendering was done by PrinceXML.

SALLIE MCFAGUE

CONTENTS

Introduction   vii
    David B. Lott
Bibliography   xvii
Prologue: A Religious Autobiography   xix

Part I. The Language of Theology: Parables, Metaphors, and Models

1. A Trial Run: Parable, Poem, and Autobiographical Story   3
2. Parables as Metaphors   17
3. Creeds: Models or Dogmas   25
4. God as Mother, Lover, and Friend   33
5. A Meditation on Exodus 33:23b   61

Part II. Theology and Spirituality: Metaphorical, Ecological, and Kenotic Approaches

6. Metaphorical Theology   69
7. Metaphors, Models, and Concepts   85
8. Theology of Nature: Remythologizing Christian Doctrine   95
9. Consider the Lilies of the Field   107
10. The Ecological Model and Christian Spirituality   127
11. How Shall We Live? Christianity and Planetary Economics   139
12. A Spirituality for the Whole Planet / Kenotic Theology   155

Part III. Constructing Theology: God, Humans, and the World

13. The Christian Paradigm   167
14. Sin: The Refusal to Accept Our Place   179
15. Human Existence in the Spirit   195
16. Christ and the Ecological Economic Worldview   201
17. God and the World   211
18. "The Dearest Freshness Deep Down Things": The Holy Spirit and Climate Change   227

19. Who Are We Human Beings? 241
20. Falling in Love with God and the World: Some Reflections on 247
    the Doctrine of God

Index of Names and Subjects 267

Introduction
David B. Lott

> *Christian theology is the attempt to think about God and the world—who God is and who we are—in light of what the tradition has claimed in the past and what we must say in the present. Every Christian is a theologian; each of us has a theology. That is, each of us has a picture, a set of assumptions, usually not conscious, of how we think God and the world are related. And all of us can and do express through our words and actions who we think God is and who we think we are. These unconscious or implicit theologies are very powerful. They control many of our decisions and actions; we rely on them as justification for what we do personally and as a nation. Theology matters.*
> —Sallie McFague (2008:5)

Sallie McFague has spent the entirety of her long teaching and publishing career exploring the relationship between God and the world, showing us that theology indeed matters. This is, as she says, what theologians do. Yet, in McFague's case, it has led her to explore how God and the world are inseparable from one another: how God is implicated as we seek to understand the world and how the world is revealed as God's body. This fascinating exploration is traced in eight books, each of which represents a segment of a theological pilgrimage that begins in exploring the nature of theological language and is now culminating in an understanding of Christian discipleship as the practice of restraint. Using McFague's own words, this volume follows her journey. It is an attempt to survey the terrain she explores, following her steps across an undiscovered landscape from one point to another.

Reading Sallie McFague's major books in order, from 1975's *Speaking in Parables* to 2013's *Blessed Are the Consumers*, is indeed like taking a trip with an eloquent, observant companion. In the preface to *Life Abundant* (2001), she writes, "I have written each of my books in an effort to make up for deficiencies in the last one." These self-perceived deficiencies are surely apparent to the author in the way they are not to the reader, as her ever-probing mind is moving on to the next step in the journey, taking steps she did not foresee as she wrote each prior volume. The ostensibly freeform nature of this trek is hinted at in *Super, Natural Christians* (1997), where she suggests that the metaphor of the hike is a better one than that of the map to describe our relationship to the natural world. This same "hike" metaphor may also be applied to her theological project. As carefully crafted as each of her books is, there is no suggestion that she is employing some sort of theological GPS unit to plot a predetermined path. Nor is she content to stop in one place, as if each book were some final destination. Rather, all her writing continually asks, "Where to, next?" and immediately whisks the reader onto a new path, one continuous with what has been previously explored before, yet uncovering new and distinct terrain.

McFague is not simply a companion or a guide; more than that, her writing demonstrates that she is a dedicated teacher, through and through. She repeats ideas in her books in order to instill them better within her readers. Stories and illustrations recur from volume to volume, often employed in very different ways from their original use. Like words shouted across a vast canyon, they echo back in varying tones, highlighting ideas and concepts one may not have heard before. Inasmuch as she describes her overall theological project as a "constructive" one, there is also a sense in which hers is also a practical theology, dedicated not so much to the arts of ministry, as the term is usually applied, but to "what we must say in the present" about God and the world, for the ways that speech serves "as justification for what we do personally and as a nation." And, for McFague, this has meant considering how our understandings of God—including the language and metaphors we use to speak about God—shape how we regard the natural world and the human impact upon it, particularly in terms of environmental protection and thriving, nuclear arms, and economic justice. For this, she is one of the most essential North American Christian theologians of the late twentieth and early twenty-first centuries.

Biographical Sketch

Born in 1933 in Quincy, Massachusetts, Sallie McFague graduated from Smith College with a Bachelor of Arts in Literature, followed by a Bachelor of Divinity from Yale Divinity School. At Yale University she earned master's and doctoral degrees in theology. Yale University Press published her doctoral dissertation, *Literature and the Christian Life*, in 1966. She taught briefly at both Smith and Yale Divinity School, and served as editor for the journal *Soundings* from 1967 to 1975, but her academic career began in earnest in 1970 when she joined the faculty at Vanderbilt Divinity School. She taught there for thirty years, including five years as dean of the Divinity School, and was named Carpenter Professor of Theology in 1980. Since 2000, she has served as Distinguished Theologian in Residence at Vancouver School of Theology in British Columbia.

Bits of her biography have emerged in her books, mainly as illustrations of her arguments. In "A Religious Autobiography," from *Life Abundant* (which serves as this book's prologue), we learn about her youthful religious devotion and Episcopalian upbringing, the influence of Karl Barth, H. Richard Niebuhr, and Gordon Kaufman on her thinking, of her life in Nashville and Vancouver, and of her "conversion" experiences. These provide some shape and sense to the theological journey traced through her books. Yet McFague, unlike some theologians of her generation—and quite a few in later generations—is not interested in using her writing for autobiographical pondering and probing. While experience is key to much of her theological understanding, her focus is on the contours of things earthly and divine; her theology is personal but not individualistic. Instead, experience becomes a way to steer away from both needless abstraction and self-indulgent irrelevancy.

The ways in which experience informs a theology that matters is what has led McFague to explore the role of the metaphorical in our theological endeavors. This is a salient feature of her work. Her first major book, *Speaking in Parables: A Study in Metaphor and Theology* (1975), underscores her training in literature. As much a work of literary analysis as of theological interpretation, it not only explores biblical parables but also religious poetry and religious autobiography understood as parabolic forms. Here we are introduced to the basic theological hermeneutic informing all her work, which is grounded in the ordinary and the everyday. McFague explores the epistemological function of metaphors, writing, "Metaphor is a way of *knowing*, not just a way of communicating. In metaphor, knowledge and its expression are one and the same" (4). She concludes: "A theology that takes its cues from the parables never reaches its object, but in language, belief, and life as metaphor, story, and living engagement we are sent off in its direction. It is a theology for skeptics and for our time" (181).

Her next volume, *Metaphorical Theology: Models of God in Religious Language* (1982), is her most explicitly theoretical work. It is here that she takes her earlier work on metaphor and parable and translates this into the full-blown theological method that has informed all her subsequent work. In the preface, McFague observes that as the language of theology has moved from the imagistic to the conceptual, it has spawned countless idolatries and irrelevancies. To revitalize theology for our time, McFague suggests that we replace the patriarchal model of God as father with one of God as friend. In this work McFague, who is often grouped with other feminist theologians of her generation, makes her most explicit statements about feminist thought. (Elsewhere in her work, she deals with such matters mostly implicitly or in passing.)

Models of God: Theology for an Ecological, Nuclear Age, which followed in 1987, is her most celebrated book (it received the American Academy of Religion Award of Excellence in 1988), and the culmination of her work on metaphors and models. To her earlier criticism of the patriarchal theological model she adds analyses of other imperialistic and triumphalist models that she sees as contributing to a growing nuclear threat and the degradation of the environment. And she undertakes her first extended look at the God-world relationship and suggests the metaphor of the world as God's body. A brilliantly constructed work, it culminates with three chapters that consider God in terms of the models of mother, lover, and friend, and each of these in terms of God's love, activity, and ethic. In so doing, she begins to explore how God's presence to and among us is mediated via universal immanence and worldly transcendence, melded into what she later refers to as "immanental transcendence."

The Body of God: An Ecological Theology (1993) is perhaps the closest McFague has come to offering something resembling a systematic theology. It is, as she writes in the preface, "an attempt to look at everything through one lens, the model of the universe or the world as God's body" (vii), a model that she first introduced in *Models of God*. It takes her concern for embodiment in more explicit directions, and once more uses scientific approaches as a theological resource. Moving through what she describes as "the overlapping circles—the common creation story, the world as God's body, and the Christic paradigm" (xii), McFague offers here a radically incarnational theological vision that sets the stage for the nature spirituality and deepening environmental concern that marks the second half of her publishing career.

The organic, ecological model that McFague introduces in *The Body of God*—that is, a model based on an understanding that "supports both radical individuality and difference while at the same time insisting on radical interdependence of all the parts" (28)—becomes the groundwork for the direction she pursues in her subsequent books, which take a decided cosmological perspective and attend especially to issues related to nature, the environment, and spirituality. In "A Religious Autobiography," she describes this shift as at first vocational, but then also spiritual. *Super, Natural Christians: How Christians Should Love Nature* (1998) is her first effort to explicate this new nature spirituality. Here, however, she pulls back a bit from the panentheism that she began to embrace earlier in order to take a more appreciative look at the world as it is. (*Panentheism* is seeing everything in God and God in everything—radical immanence *and* transcendence—as opposed to *pantheism*, in which God is identical with the world.) She pushes back against the "subject-objects" approach to nature traditionally taken by Western Christians, arguing that it is overly anthropocentric and androcentric, setting humans over against nature. Instead, she exhorts us to a "subject-subjects" perspective as "a way to think and act that integrates God, nature, and human beings" (3), exploring works by nature writers for illustration. She concludes that "A Christian nature spirituality is . . . determinedly realistic: it begins and ends with a hymn to the things themselves. . . . A Christian nature spirituality is also determinedly hopeful because it believes that the creator of these wonderful, ordinary creatures is working in, through, and on behalf of us all" (178).

This hopeful realism turns more urgent in *Life Abundant: Rethinking Theology and Economy for a Planet in Peril* (2001), which moves beyond a contemplation of what it means for Christians to love nature to the imagining of what it means for us to assure an "abundant life" for all. To the ecological theological model she here adds an ecological economic model, arguing that just as we have been so imbedded in imperialistic, patriarchal models of God, so do we unthinkingly embrace assumptions about market capitalism and its attendant consumerism that militate against our announced love of nature and care for "the least of these." Our lives are filled with such material abundance, which symbolizes the "good life" in Western society, that it is hard for us to imagine what a sustainable "good life" might mean for the rest of creation, much less humans of lesser means and fewer possessions. And so McFague not only reconsiders our contemporary practices and context, but uses this organic economic model to reinvigorate her theological project, urging us to a radical rethinking so that we might live differently.

A New Climate for Theology: God, the World, and Global Warming (2008) is, as the title suggests, McFague's most topical book, using the climate-change crisis that emerged during the first decade of the twenty-first century as the impetus for deepening and broadening the perspective offered in *Life Abundant*. Steeped again in economic and scientific approaches, it often renews some of the key ideas of her earlier books. For instance, the ecological anthropology offered here ponders again the implications of Western radical individualism and ecological illiteracy. She once more discusses prevailing models of God—deistic, dialogic, monarchical, and agential—in order to reiterate the model of the world as God's body and radical incarnationalism, reminding us, "God is with us as the source and power of all our efforts to live differently" (77). Here, however, the earlier exhortation to "think differently" is employed to develop what she calls an "urban ecotheology," pressing us to reconsider our notions of nature and to embrace urban environments, where living differently, in sustainable ways, is especially necessary to address the growing challenge of global warming. *A New Climate* also introduces the element of *kenosis*, which McFague defines as "self-limitation so that others may have place and space to grow and flourish" and "the way God acts toward the world and the way people should act toward one another and toward creation" (136).

While McFague says she first considered writing on kenoticism as early as 1970, it is at the heart of McFague's latest book, *Blessed Are the Consumers: Climate Change and the Practice of Restraint* (2013). Religious autobiography has long been an interest of McFague's—nearly every one of her books devotes some pages to it by way of illustration—and here she develops her kenotic theology by examining closely the autobiographical writings of three Christian "saints" who especially model kenotic lives: John Woolman, Simone Weil, and Dorothy Day. In "A Religious Autobiography," McFague took note of four "conversion experiences" in her life, the fourth of which is acquaintance with God—coming to know that God is love. *Blessed Are the Consumers* suggests a fifth conversion experience (or, at least, a second phase of that fourth conversion): experience of God and the world as radically kenotic. She now interprets the Trinity not as a union of three static entities but as a circle dance of self-emptying love. Hence, God is not seen as a "being" (even the highest) but as the loving activity that pulses through the universe. Likewise, the understanding of redemption changes from a theory of a sacrificial, substitutionary atonement to a view of Jesus' life and death as the mirror reflecting God's own self-emptying love for others (and hence also, the kind of living to which disciples are called). Here her theological vision may be understood as not just Christian but as having an interfaith value also, as it supports a theme common to most religions that "loving one's neighbor is tantamount to loving God" (xiii). The final essay in this volume of collected readings, "Falling in Love with God and the World: Some Reflections on the Doctrine of God," continues this theme of the kenotic and suggests that it may well continue to be at the heart of any future books that emerge from the remarkable mind of Sallie McFague.

Outline of This Book

Any collection such as this is necessarily selective. Thus this book does not pretend to be a definitive compilation from McFague's writings but only an interpretive presentation of her work. It does, however, present an impressionistic portrait of her and her theological project—something like a contemporary photo montage where as one steps away from numerous small pictures, the mind's eye itself creates a larger representation of its main subject. As noted earlier regarding our relationship to the natural world, this book should not be regarded as a map but enjoyed as a hike, not directionless but one among several ways to navigate a journey through McFague's theological project. To set the direction for this book, I have been guided by McFague's work in metaphorical approaches.

The book opens with the aforementioned "A Religious Autobiography," where McFague describes the four "conversion experiences" of her life and attempts to give an account of her own journey (at least up to 2001). This sets the stage for helping the reader understand how her work has gone through phases represented in the selections that follow. Part 1, "The Language of Theology: Parables, Metaphors, and Models," focuses on metaphor and models themselves, showing how these function in discourse, not only theological discourse, but literary and scientific discourse as well. Drawing primarily from her first three books, it sets up the hermeneutical basis for her more explicitly theological writings and represents the "head theology" that predominated in McFague's thinking before her "third" conversion experience. The brief closing essay, "A Meditation on Exodus," suggests also something of McFague's biblical hermeneutic and the creative potential of her approach.

In part 2, "Theology and Spirituality: Metaphorical, Ecological, and Kenotic Approaches," the metaphorical hermeneutic introduced in part 1 becomes the basis from which McFague has developed particular approaches to doing theology—specifically what she calls "metaphorical" theology. But this metaphorical approach over time makes room for additional, complementary models—the organic model of theology, the ecological model of economics, and the kenotic. In addition, it provides a path to fresh ways to practice both spirituality and ethics. While *Metaphorical Theology* and *Models of God* are again represented, the focus is more on her subsequent books, and traces how her theological approach has developed over time.

Part 3, "Constructing Theology: God, Humans, and the World," demonstrates how these theological approaches may be applied to central Christian themes such as the doctrine of God, anthropology, sin, Jesus, the Spirit, salvation, and cosmology. Again drawing from a range of books, it also suggests some ways in which McFague's views on these particulars have shifted over time. The final selection, a new essay titled "Falling in Love with God and the World," provides a sense of McFague's most current thinking at the time this collection is being assembled and thus is a fitting conclusion and "summing up" for the whole.

The essays included herein have been lightly edited, primarily to remove cross-referencing unnecessary to this new context and many of the textual notes. Readers are encouraged to revisit these pieces in their original contexts in order to obtain this information. References to McFague's books are keyed by date and page to the bibliography that immediately follows this introduction.

Acknowledgments

I am grateful first to the staff of Fortress Press for their invitation to edit this volume, and for their efforts to help me gather the various chapters from books whose original electronic files disappeared many years ago. In particular I thank Scott Tunseth and intern Kate Crouse, who handled the heavy lifting of scanning many, many pages of aged books into word-processing files. Michael West, who served as editor for all of McFague's works from *The Body of God* on, was a helpful conversation partner as I assembled this collection, providing perspective few others could have. My partner, Robert Huberty, provided editorial and other support as I worked slowly to form this into a volume worthy of its subject and worthwhile to serious students of theology. The ecumenical lectionary study group I attend weekly here on Capitol Hill in Washington, D.C., was also both forebearing and encouraging as I repeatedly brought McFague's thoughts to bear upon the week's preaching texts. For this and their ongoing friendship, this marvelous group of pastors, priests, and laity deserve mention by name: Rose Beeson, David Deutsch, Bill Doggett, Rebecca Justice ("Justi") Schunior, Cara Spaccarelli, Andy Walton, and Michael Wilker.

And of course, I am especially grateful to Sallie McFague, who has been utterly supportive and encouraging to my efforts as I conceptualized and assembled this project. The fast friendship and trust we have built through this work is the sort of lovely and unexpected gift that an editor only occasionally gets to experience in this work of publishing. Yet beyond this friendship, she has also bestowed to me—and to the world—a sustainable theological vision that provides realistic hope for an abundant life with God, creation, and one another.

Bibliography

This complete listing of Sallie McFague's books, of which she is the sole author, is ordered according to year of original publication. References to McFague's books in the text and notes are keyed to this bibliography.

Literature and the Christian Life. 1966. New Haven: Yale University Press.
Speaking in Parables: A Study in Metaphor and Theology. 1975. Philadelphia: Fortress Press.
Metaphorical Theology: Models of God in Religious Language. 1982. Philadelphia: Fortress Press.
Models of God: Theology for an Ecological, Nuclear Age. 1987. Philadelphia: Fortress Press.
The Body of God: An Ecological Theology. 1993. Minneapolis: Fortress Press.
Super, Natural Christians: How We Should Love Nature. 1997. Minneapolis: Fortress Press.
Life Abundant: Rethinking Theology and Economy for a Planet in Peril. 2001. Minneapolis: Fortress Press.
A New Climate for Theology: God, the World, and Global Warming. 2008. Minneapolis: Fortress Press.
Blessed Are the Consumers: Climate Change and the Practice of Restraint. 2013. Minneapolis: Fortress Press.

Prologue: A Religious Autobiography

In this personal reflection from Life Abundant *(2001), Sallie McFague gives us a glimpse into her own religious and theological development up to the period just prior to her retirement from Vanderbilt Divinity School. Listening carefully, readers will hear the four "conversion experiences" described here echoed in the twenty-plus selections that follow this prologue. As such, just as "A Trial Run" (ch. 1, below) set the stage for her book* Speaking in Parables, *this essay anticipates the themes and ideas to be explored in this volume.*

Source: 2001:3–14

For many years I have taught a course on religious autobiography; it was the first course I taught, and I am still teaching it. Why? Because I am very interested in people who try to live their faith, who have what I would call a "working theology," a set of deeply held beliefs that actually function in their personal and public lives. Augustine, John Woolman, Sojourner Truth, Dietrich Bonhoeffer, Dorothy Day, and Martin Luther King Jr. are a few of these people. Each of them struggled to discern God's action in and through their lives and then to express that reality in everything they did. Their theologies became embodied in themselves; as disciples of Christ they became mini-incarnations of God's love. We call such people "saints," reflections of God, images of God with us in the flesh. They are intimations of what it means to be "fully alive," living life from, toward, and with God. They are examples to the rest of us of what a Christlike life is. They fascinate because in them we see God and the human in intimate connection, human lives showing forth different facets of divine power and love.

While it may seem outrageous to suggest, I believe each of us is called to this vocation, the vocation of sainthood. Each Christian is asked to examine his or her life with the goal of discerning the action of God in it and then to express God's power and love in everything. Each of us is expected to have a working theology, one that makes a difference in how we conduct our personal lives and how we act at professional and public levels. Becoming a mature

Christian means internalizing one's beliefs so that they are evident in whatever one says or does. Made in the image of God, humans are called to grow into that image more fully—to become "like God," which for Christians means becoming like Christ, following Christ. And following Christ means following One who, like us, was flesh and bones, of the earth, earthy. It means that Christian saints focus on God's work of helping to make all of us, every creature on the planet, fully alive. Christian sainthood is, it appears, a very mundane—a worldly, earthly—business.

For all the years I have been teaching the course in religious autobiography, it never occurred to me to write my own. Actually, I wasn't ready. I believe I might be now. I want to see how a few beliefs which I now hold undeniably can function as a working theology for the ecological and justice crises facing our planet in the twenty-first century. A bare-bones theology, a few beliefs carefully thought through and actually functioning at personal and public levels, may be more significant than a comprehensive, systematic, but loosely embraced theology. What is one prepared to live? What beliefs are livable; that is, what beliefs will support the flourishing of life?

I want to use my own history as a case study for other Christians who are also trying to integrate their beliefs and their actions at the deepest level, who are trying to be whole, mature Christians functioning effectively in the twenty-first century on planet earth. The story I will share will be brief, narrow, and focused. It is meant as a pedagogical tool for others and hence will ignore all kinds of personal data (family, schooling, relationships, etc.), which undoubtedly in a full autobiography would be relevant but will be passed over here.

I have had four "conversions," four experiences of such importance that they changed my thinking about God and my behavior. The first, which came in two stages, occurred when I was around seven years old. One day while walking home from school the thought came to me that some day I would not be here; I would not exist. Christmas would come, and I would not be around to celebrate it; even more shocking, my birthday would occur, and I would not be present. It was not an experience of death—and the fear of it; rather, it was an experience of non-being: I simply would not exist. For months, indeed years, I could not get this thought out of my mind; I was fascinated and terrified by it. Eventually, it began to turn into a sense of wonder that I *was* alive—and so were myriad other creatures. Over decades this wonder has stayed with me, growing stronger and deeper until now I believe that one of the most profound religious emotions is wonder at and gratitude for life in all its incredible shapes, colors, and sizes. Along with Annie Dillard I now exclaim, "My God what a world.

There is no accounting for one second of it," and along with Alice Walker I notice the color purple in fields when I pass by.[1] That early experience of nonbeing has eventuated into praise to God for all beings fully alive.

The second stage of my seventh-year conversion occurred one day when the teacher asked the class, "What name will you write more than any other in your life?" Being an eager student, I immediately raised my hand to answer. Fortunately, the teacher did not call on me; had she done so, I would have been red with embarrassment. The correct answer was, of course, one's own name, but I was going to answer, "God." That incident stayed with me as I gradually discerned its meaning. I have decided I was not wrong: "God" is the name beneath, with, and in each of our names. As I have come to realize that we all live and move and have our being in God, the names of each person, species, creature, and element are superimposed over God's name. God *is* reality; God is the source of the reality of each of us. Panentheism—seeing the world as *in* God—puts God's "name" first, but each of our names are included and preserved in their distinctiveness within the divine reality. My early experience of God's name as primary, the experience of divine transcendence and preeminence, would stay with me and grow.

It lay dormant, however, during my teenage years growing up in Boston as a member of a conventional Episcopal church. At most, God was the Great Moralizer, the upholder of proper appearances and conduct. My second conversion occurred at college while reading Karl Barth's *Commentary on Romans*. Suddenly the transcendence of God took on a whole new meaning for me. I began to have a glimmer of what the word "God" meant. My boxed-in, comfortable, tribal notion of God was split wide open and like a cold, bracing mountain wind, the awesome presence of the divine brushed my life. That evening I walked home from the library in a daze; I had seen something I would never forget: that God is God and nothing else is. My teacher and mentor, H. Richard Niebuhr, would call it "radical monotheism," and Paul Tillich described it as the Protestant Principle. It is Christianity in its "Protestant" or prophetic mode and a necessary component, I believe, of any theology. For years, however, it would keep me from recognizing and growing into my early sense of wonder at life and its grounding in God (the "Catholic" side that every theology also must have). It created a dualism in my belief and actions that sent me on a long detour, a detour in which the world was not *in* God and God was not *with* the world. The child's love of nature was set aside for the budding theologian's dedication to the transcendent—and distant—God.

Eventually, I found a way back (or one was given to me, as I now see it). The way back was through nature—I became a hiker. I did not find God in nature, but I found a sense of belonging, of being the "proper size" in the forest. Whenever I got on a trail, I immediately had a sense of proportion, of fitting in, of being neither too big nor too small, but "just right" in relation to the trees above me, the bushes and flowers beside me, and the earth under my feet. I felt *in* nature; it surrounded me; I was part of it. It felt like coming home. After many years, this experience on the trail came to symbolize how we (all of us creatures) fit into God's world, each with space and a place. What had been an experience of overwhelming and distant transcendence became one of equally awesome but now immanent and intimate transcendence. God's magnificence, God's preeminence, God's "Godness" was manifest *in and through and with* the earth and all its creatures. I learned this first through nature; eventually, I would see it as what Christians call "incarnation"—God with us here and now for the flourishing of all living beings. Nature can seduce us with its beauty and right order to love and glorify God. This is the way it happened to me.

My third conversion occurred when I was teaching theology at a divinity school. I had several books published and was progressing nicely up the career ladder. There was just one problem: most of my theology was still in my head. It wasn't bad theology; in fact, it was pretty good. It just didn't actually function in my life and I didn't hold to my beliefs with much fervor. I was a theologian but I didn't have a vocation. However, around 1980 I read an essay by another theologian, Gordon Kaufman, in which he claimed that, given the nuclear and ecological crises facing our planet, theology could no longer proceed with business as usual. It must deconstruct and reconstruct its central symbols—God, Christ, human being—from within this new context.[2] What would Christians say about God and the world if they took the planetary ecological situation as our interpretive lens? How different would Christian faith be if the well-being of human beings were not the only criterion? What would Christianity look like from a cosmological rather than just an anthropocentric perspective?

I believed that Kaufman was dead right. I revamped my teaching and research agendas in this direction and settled down to learning something about cosmology, evolutionary biology, and ecological science—about which I knew nothing. It has been a deeply instructive exercise, given me some "ecological literacy," and shown me the tiny niche that my work can fill for the planetary agenda. It also refashioned my sense of who we are in the scheme of things. My sense on the hiking trail that we humans fit into nature, can feel comfortable in our proper place, was confirmed by my readings. We do indeed fit here, but not at the top of the heap as we have supposed. Rather, we fit as one species among millions of others on which we depend for the air we breathe and the food we eat and for whom we are increasingly responsible. What I learned about our place in the scheme of things has become central to my belief that a paradigm shift in our consumer lifestyle will be critical to our well-being as well as our planet's.

This third conversion, while intellectual and theological, was certainly vocational as well. I believed that teaching and writing books that attempt to help people, especially Christians, shift from an anthropocentric to a cosmological paradigm—a way of being in the world that supports the flourishing of all life—is a form of activism. I saw it as a way in which my beliefs, which were increasingly becoming more defined and deeply held, could be embodied. I believed that this kind of work was a form of Christian activism.

But there was still a piece missing. That piece was me. I have always been intrigued by Dietrich Bonhoeffer's comment that he began as a theologian, became a Christian, and finally grew into a "contemporary."[3] I think what he meant was that he started as an academic Christian, became a practicing Christian, and finally became an embodied, "present" one. In other words, God finally became daily and immediate to him: God's presence was the *milieu*, the "world" within which he lived when imprisoned during World War II. Certainly from his letters one gains the sense of a man whose faith became immediate, present, and functional in the daily horrors and infrequent joys of prison life. He had no use for the distant, metaphysical God of his own past nor the God-of-the-gaps invoked by prisoners during air raids. Rather, for him God was the incarnate Christ, present with him in his suffering during interrogations by the Nazi officials, but also present when he could sit in the sun, watch an anthill, or eat a piece of fruit. The embodied, present God accompanied Bonhoeffer in his daily life, whatever that life brought. This God had gradually been fashioning Bonhoeffer in the divine image, into an embodied, present Christian who lived his faith.

My fourth conversion has been something like Bonhoeffer's sense of becoming contemporary with God. Finally, after years of talking *about* God (what theologians are paid to do!), I am becoming acquainted *with* God. This conversion has occurred quite deliberately: I engaged a spiritual director and have undertaken a daily pattern of meditation. I am doing what is called "practicing the presence of God," setting aside time for relating to God. To say that it has been instructive would be a gross understatement; it has been revelatory. Revelation, as I now see it, is God's loving self-disclosure, and that is what I have experienced. I am meeting *God* and God is *love*. How outrageous as well as platitudinous that sounds! I can scarcely believe I am writing it, let alone intending to publish it. Why am I doing so? Simply because it is true; it is what has happened, is happening, to me.

Let me back up and try to flesh this out a little. When I was young I recall hearing the grown-ups whispering in the kitchen on holidays—usually the women preparing dinner. I was convinced that they were talking about things that mattered, what life was all about, how everything fit together. I could not have articulated it that way then, but I recall from a very early age having a sense of the mystery of things and my ignorance about all of it. I wanted to find out; I thought the whispering women were talking about it (I am sure now they were talking about things never discussed openly in the 1940s—cancer, divorce, mental illness, unwanted babies, etc.). Gradually, over the decades separating my six-year-old self from my sixty-plus-year-old self, the mystery has been revealed to me—or so it seems, at least. I quote from an entry in my journal: "I feel as though I finally understand what life is about. It is, quite simply, acknowledging how things are—living in the truth. And the truth is that God is the source and sustainer of everything." Since I have undertaken the daily practice of prayer, I have gradually felt my center, the center of my being, shifting from myself to God. From the burdensome task of trying to ground myself in myself, I have let go and allowed God to become the One in and for whom I live.

I hasten to add two qualifications. First, I am a newcomer to living in this reality—I know little about it except the undeniable belief that it *is* reality, mine and that of everything else. Second, trying to live in God's reality in no way detracts from *my* reality; in fact, it enhances and fulfills it. I feel more "me" than at any other time in my life. I am also more aware of the distinctiveness and concrete particularity of other things: faces are more luminous, the color purple in fields is brighter.

The overwhelming emotion that I have experienced from this revelation of the mystery of things—from meeting God and knowing that God is love—is similar to Ebenezer Scrooge's on Christmas Day. He kicked up his heels, exclaiming, "I didn't miss it after all!" I feel this way. In the sixth decade of my life I have been invited on a new journey, which seems like a great adventure, perhaps the greatest adventure of which human beings are capable.

Some Reflections

Several things have already become clear to me about this journey. It becomes immediately evident that one learns as much about oneself and the world as one does about God. In prayer a reversal occurs; we do not talk about God and the world but begin to see ourselves and the world in God. We begin to see human life and the world from the divine perspective, from a broader and more inclusive point of view than we are otherwise capable of holding. We begin to recognize who we are in the scheme of things from the perspective of the Creator and Redeemer of everything that is. We are no longer the center (the definition of sin); we know God is the Center (a definition of salvation).

Another thing that is becoming clear to me is that God is always available; the problem is, we are not. Whereas I used to think God was distant (because transcendent), now I realize that God is "ubiquitous," an old, quaint way of saying that God is everywhere all the time. As I become aware of God's presence in my life, I realize that there is nothing special about this—I am not special to be experiencing God's presence and it is not remarkable for God to be present. God is available all the time to everyone and everything. *We* have to become conscious of God's presence. At one level, it is no different from any important relationship: one has to pay attention to the other, listen, and be open. To say God is always present is simply to acknowledge that God is reality, the breath, the life, the power, the love beneath, above, around, and in everything. This is divine transcendence *immanently* experienced; it is the magnificence and awesomeness of God *with us*.

This brings me to a further insight from "the neophyte's notebook." It is alright to be excessive: one can't love God *too much*. It's a relief to finally find the proper object of insatiable desire. Augustine and Thomas were right: our hearts are restless until they rest in God, and we were made to know and enjoy God forever. One doesn't have to hold back; the *sanctus* is the proper primary prayer; we were made to glorify God—and it feels good to do so. But once again, it is not an either/or—God or the world. The incarnation has taken on a whole new meaning for me: it means God is forever and truly the God with and for the flesh, the earth, the world. Many of the saints who speak about loving God know that it is easier to love God than the neighbor. Hence, the best test, as Teresa of Avila shrewdly suggests, is to stick with the neighbor: "And be certain that the more advanced you see you are in love for your neighbor the more advanced you will be in the love of God."[4] The briefest of my credos, then, might be: "We live to give God glory by loving the world and everything in it."

Third, this adventure is showing me how deeply interconnected are the active and contemplative dimensions of the Christian life. I learned this first from teaching the religious autobiography course: all the people we read were social activists. None of them were hermits or New Agers, interested only in their own individual spiritual development. On the contrary, they knew they had to be deeply rooted in God in order to do their justice work in the world. Dorothy Day could never have lasted decades in New York's Bowery ministering to the homeless, the alcoholics, and the destitute without a deep spiritual life. Like Bonhoeffer's God, Day's was immediate, present, and functional—the power that guided and sustained her. We misinterpret God's love when we think it is merely for our comfort or even our spiritual growth. If the saints give us a lesson, it is that God's presence in our lives should turn us into workers for an alternative world.

Finally, these initial reflections have suggested to me that working for an alternative world is a prime directive for Christian living. Do I mean another, supernatural world? Does practicing the presence of God mean leaving this world as so much Christian asceticism and fundamentalism advocate? By no means (as the incarnation insists), but it does mean trying to live *differently* in our one and only world. My reflections coalesce around this point: what I have learned about who God is, who we are, and where we fit into the scheme of things tells me that the one thing needful in a theology for twenty-first-century North American middle-class Christians is an alternative view of the abundant life from that of our consumer culture. *Life Abundant* is about this reconstruction. We will take as our context for revisioning theology the well-being of our planet and all its creatures, seeing that project against the deterioration of nature and the injustice to poor people that the religion of our time—consumerism—is bringing about. If one believes that "the glory of God is all creatures fully alive," then our current worldview and its lifestyle are wrong. It is more than that: it is sinful and evil, for it is contrary to God's will for creation.

This sounds like a universal and universalizing project. Actually, it isn't. I will be interpreting this problem and its alternative through a narrow lens: the little bit I know, the few beliefs I hold undeniably. For many years I have been aware that most good (coherent, interesting, plausible) theology grows from a central insight—one possible, deeply held, and thoroughly embodied statement about God and the world. A few examples: for Paul it was being made righteous by God through Christ; for John it was the Word made flesh; for Thomas it was the nature/supernature relationship; for Schleiermacher it was the feeling of absolute dependence; for Barth it was the radical transcendence of God; for the liberation theologians it is the preferential option for the poor. None of these is wrong, but all of them are partial. There is no such thing as a complete theology; there are only piecemeal theologies, the best efforts of human beings to state what they have found to be undeniable through their experience of God and as members of the Christian community. It is as if a tiny bit of God is available to each creature, whatever aspect of God that creature needs and can absorb. Most of us cannot absorb very much of the infinite Divine Being. At most we might come to reflect a smidgen of it in our thinking and actions. No one has ever seen God, so what more can we expect? But a tiny bit is enough; that is, enough if it is deeply held, well understood, and carefully argued—and if it is open to the many other bits from other Christians as we all struggle to discern God's will for our world.

As I come to the end of these reflections on my religious journey, I will try to summarize them at the level closest to my experience. . . . [H]ere I want to suggest the heart of my theology, the core that informs the whole.

We live and move and have our being in God. God is closer to us (to every iota of creation) than we are to ourselves. God is the breath of our breath, the love with which we love, the power that sustains our work. When we become aware of God, who is the Alpha and Omega, as the source and goal of everything and of all life, love, and power, then we become channels for these realities, both in our own lives and for others. We become available to be "saved" (restored to health and happiness) and to help "save" others. Salvation means living in God's presence, in imitation of divine love for the world. Each of us can love only a tiny fragment of the earth, but that is our task.

I am slowly learning to live and think and act within the divine *milieu*. I sense the world (and myself) becoming ordered by that gracious Presence. I am beginning to see things within that Light and everything seems different. Things are neither chaotic nor ordered in relation to me and my wants. Everything is ordered by God and in relation to God. Reality "makes sense," not according to worldly standards (nor mine), but in terms of the love that created everything and wants it to flourish. Ecologically, theologically, and personally it makes sense: the world is characterized by radical relationality ordered by and to the Power in the universe, who is love. It is the reality in which all are to live together in community to glorify God and to share with each other. Such reality has order and harmony; the disorder and confusion come when we fail to acknowledge this order and try to reorder things around ourselves.

From my growing acquaintance with God has come confirmation of my earliest religious experiences: gratitude for life and glory to God. Pierre Teilhard de Chardin said that from the time he was a child he had two passions: a passion for the world and a passion for God, and his lifelong goal was to bring these two together.[5] I think my journey has been similar: the "Catholic" sacramental appreciation of the world joined with the "Protestant" prophetic witness to divine transcendence. The key to their unity, of course, is the incarnation which, in its profound simplicity, means "God with us," God with the world and the world within God. The incarnation, it seems to me, is not merely or solely about Jesus. It is more radical than that, although for Christians Jesus is the paradigm of both God with us and the world within God. The incarnation reveals God as *always* with us and our being *defined* as within God. The incarnation is the solution to the "two worlds problem": the problem of how to love God and the world. There is only one world, a world that God loves. Since God loves it, we not only *can* but *should*. In fact, loving the world (not God alone), or rather, loving God *through* loving the world, is the Christian way.

The above paragraphs are a summary of my most deeply held beliefs. This theological core has implications for Christian discipleship in twenty-first-century North America. The Christian way (according to this view) inevitably leads to an understanding of salvation as deification, becoming like God. Made in God's image, we are to grow into that reality by doing what God does: love the world. Jesus Christ is the incarnation of God because he did that fully—his mind, heart, and will were one with God's love for the world. We see this in his ministry to the outcast, oppressed, and sick as well as in his death on a cross in defiance of the powers of greed, hatred, and domination. But we also are called to this vocation: Christian discipleship is loving the world. As we see in the story of Jesus and the stories of the saints (all Christians who try to do this), it is not easy or pleasant. While appreciating the color purple is one dimension of passion for the world, identifying with its sufferings is another.

Such identification is, I believe, increasingly essential for favored North American Christians who, along with other Westerners, are experiencing the highest level of the "good life" that any human beings ever have. The context in which we experience this consumer abundance, however, is one of a widening gap between the well-off and the poor of the world, as well as an increasing deterioration of the "resources" (the natural world) that fund our abundance. We cannot, in good conscience, "love the world"—its snowcapped mountains and panda bears—while at the same time destroying it and allowing our less well-off sisters and brothers to sink into deeper poverty. Hence, I believe Christian discipleship for twenty-first-century North American Christians means "cruciform living," an alternative notion of the abundant life, which will involve a philosophy of "enoughness," limitations on energy use, and sacrifice for the sake of others. For us privileged Christians a "cross-shaped" life will not be primarily what Christ does for us, but what we can do for others. We do not need so much to accept Christ's sacrifice for our sins as we need to repent of a major sin—our silent complicity in the impoverishment of others and the degradation of the planet. In Charles Birch's pithy statement: "The rich must live more simply, so that the poor may simply live."[6] While not all North American Christians are "rich," most of us are avid consumers, and few Christian churches have suggested alternative visions of abundant living. We should be doing so. Christians have the obligation not just to live differently themselves, but to recommend an alternative to the paradigm of unlimited consumption. Can an alternative life be good, be abundant? I believe it can be but only within God's ordering of reality, in which right relations (what is good for the planet) becomes our standard.

Since the world, according to the incarnation, is where God dwells, it is God's "house," and we should abide by God's house rules. The house rules for the whole earth are right relations among all creatures, relations governed in basic ways by economics. What God's house rules are—in terms of ecological and economic imperatives—is one of the major tasks of Christian discernment. I am suggesting that the context within which North American Christians should undertake such discernment is a cruciform one: the recognition that a *different* way of living in the world is called for rather than the dominant consumer model.

Notes

1. Annie Dillard, *Pilgrim at Tinker Creek: A Mystical Excursion into the Natural World* (New York: Bantam, 1975), 269; Alice Walker, *The Color Purple* (New York: Washington Square, 1978), 178.

2. Gordon Kaufman, *Theology for a Nuclear Age* (Philadelphia: Westminster, 1985).

3. Eberhard Bethge, "Turning Points in Bonhoeffer's Life and Thought," in Peter Vorkink, ed., *Bonhoeffer in a World Come of Age* (Philadelphia: Fortress Press, 1968), 79.

4. Teresa of Avila, *The Interior Castle*, trans. Kieran Kavanaugh and Otilio Rodriguez (New York: Paulist, 1979), 100.

5. Pierre Teilhard de Chardin, *Writings in Time of War*, trans. Rene Hague (London: Collins, 1968), 14.

6. Charles Birch, Nairobi World Council of Churches Assembly, 1975.

PART I

The Language of Theology: Parables, Metaphors, and Models

1

A Trial Run: Parable, Poem, and Autobiographical Story

Sallie McFague's first major book, Speaking in Parables *(1976) introduces her early concern with exploring theological discourse and how that arises out of various literary forms. She notes at the outset of the book's introduction, "The purpose of theology is to make it possible for the gospel to be heard in our time" (1). Given that McFague rarely uses such "gospel" language in her later work, this statement sounds surprisingly traditional, even quaint, as does the noninclusive language for both God and humans that marks the book—a decided departure from what is yet to come. Using Sam Keen's story of the peach-seed monkey to represent autobiographical story is also unusual (she later prefers to highlight figures such as John Woolman and Dorothy Day), but it is interesting that she employs it here as a kind of negative example, demonstrating metaphorical failure. This first chapter of* Speaking in Parables *nevertheless provides a good précis of her initial concerns, many of which recur in her later works. For instance, Gerard Manley Hopkins's "God's Grandeur" makes repeated appearances over the years (including in chapter 18, below). Thus the exploration of metaphor found here remains vital and helpful for understanding her later theological development.*

Source: 1976:10–25

A trial run is a worthwhile enterprise. Many books use the first five chapters to give historical background, then refute other views, and only in the final chapter (usually called "Prolegomena to Some Theological Directions") is there a clue given to what the author has been up to. I would rather attempt a trial run, which, full of holes and unsubstantiated assertions, nevertheless gives the reader some clue as to how the theory might shake down in practice. In this brief chapter we will do no more than look in some detail at a few examples of literary genres that have been used for religious reflection. The stress in this chapter ... is on detail, for the crucial point here is to persuade the reader with a few well-known examples from Christian letters that parabolic theology is not a theory to be *applied to* literary genres of the Christian tradition but a kind of reflection that arises *from* them. Such persuasion will be effective only if the details of a parable or a poem can be shown to substantiate, even to demand, such an approach.

Theological discourse, and especially "God-talk," during what has been called the "absence" or the "death" of God, is, as we all know, in trouble. Richard Rubenstein, the Jewish theologian, states the problem this way:

> Contemporary theology reveals less about God than it does about the kind of men we are. ... Today's theologian, be he Jewish or Christian, has more in common with the poet and the creative artist than with the metaphysician and physical scientist. He communicates a very private subjectivity.[1]

And Sam Keen says that

> for the moment, at least, we must put all orthodox stories in brackets and suspend whatever remains of our belief-ful attitude. Our starting point must be individual biography and history. If I am to discover the holy, it must be in *my* biography and not in the history of Israel. If there is a principle which gives unity and meaning to history, it must be something I touch, feel, and experience.[2]

Several similar chords are struck in these two statements: the insistence that theology be existential, personal, sensuous; the wariness with which both Rubenstein and Keen approach talk *about God*; an intimation that a way out of the dilemma may be through the language and methods of the poet and storyteller. Their insistence on existential, sensuous, religious reflection that tells stories about *human life* and only by implication speaks of God is not as radical as it might at first blush seem, for it is an old and vibrant tradition in Western Christendom. We see it everywhere in the Old and New Testaments—in the history of Israel in its covenant with God and the many little stories that reflect that big one (Abraham and Isaac, the exodus from Egypt, Saul and David, and so on) and in the story of Jesus of Nazareth, which again is the central story reflected in many little stories, principally the parables. Worldly stories about human beings in their full personal, historical, bodily reality is also the "way" of Augustine's *Confessions*, of Dante's *Divine Comedy*, of John Donne's religious sonnets, of John Bunyan's *Pilgrim's Progress*, of Milton's *Paradise Lost*, of John Woolman's *Journal*, of George Herbert's sacramental poetry, of Kierkegaard's work as an author, of T. S. Eliot's "Wasteland," of Teilhard de Chardin's letters and writings from the trenches. There are many indications that the *kind* of theological discourse Rubenstein and Keen are groping for is not only appropriate to the Judaic-Christian heritage, but is *called for* by it.

In order to get a few more solid clues to the nature of such discourse, let us look at three examples of religious reflection all concerned with God-talk, a parable, a poem, and an autobiographical story: the parable of the Prodigal Son, Gerard Manley Hopkins's poem "God's Grandeur," and Sam Keen's story of the peach-seed monkey.

The Prodigal Son

[11] And he said, "There was a man who had two sons; [12] and the younger of them said to his father, 'Father, give me the share of my property that falls to me.' And he divided his living between them. [13] Not many days later, the younger son gathered all he had and took his journey into a far country, and there he squandered his property in loose living. [14] And when he had spent everything, a great famine arose in that country, and he began to be in want. [15] So he went and joined himself to one of the citizens of that country, who sent him into his fields to feed swine. [16] And he would gladly have fed on the pods that the swine ate; and no one gave him anything. [17] But when he came to himself he said, 'How many of my father's hired servants have bread enough and to spare, but I perish here with hunger! [18] I will arise and go to my father, and I will say to him, "Father, I have sinned against heaven and before you; [19] I am no longer worthy to be called your son; treat me as one of your hired servants. [20] And he arose and came to his father. But while he was yet at a distance, his father saw him and had compassion, and ran and embraced him and kissed him. [21] And the son said to him, 'Father, I have sinned against heaven and before you; I am no longer worthy to be called your son.' [22] But the father said to his servants, 'Bring quickly the best robe, and put it on him; and put a ring on his hand, and shoes on his feet. [23] And bring the fatted calf and kill it, and let us eat and make merry;

[24] for this my son was dead, and is alive again; he was lost, and is found.' And they began to make merry.

[25] "Now his elder son was in the fields; and as he came and drew near to the house, he heard music and dancing. [26] And he called one of the servants and asked what this meant. [27] And he said to him, 'Your brother has come, and your father has killed the fatted calf, because he has received him safe and sound.' [28] But he was angry and refused to go in. His father came out and entreated him, [29] but he answered his father, 'Lo, these many years I have served you, and I never disobeyed your command; yet you never gave me a kid, that I might make merry with my friends. [30] But when this son of yours came, who has devoured your living with harlots, you killed for him the fatted calf!' [31] And he said to him, 'Son, you are always with me, and all that is mine is yours. [32] It was fitting to make merry and be glad, for this your brother was dead, and is alive; he was lost, and is found.'" (Luke 15:11-32)

A parable is an extended metaphor. A parable is not an allegory, where the meaning is extrinsic to the story, nor is it an example story where, as in the story of the Good Samaritan, the total meaning is within the story. Rather, as an extended metaphor, the meaning is found only within the story itself although it is not exhausted *by* that story. At the same time that a parable is an aesthetic whole and hence demands rapt attention on itself and its configurations, it is open-ended, expanding ordinary meaning so that from a careful analysis of the parable we learn a new thing, are shocked into a new awareness. *How* the new insight occurs is, of course, the heart of the matter; it is enough to say at this point that the two dimensions—the ordinary and the extraordinary—are related intricately *within* the confines of the parable so that such "God-talk" as we have in the Prodigal Son is an existential, worldly, sensuous story of *human life.*

The shock, surprise, or revelatory aspect—the insight into fatherly love—is carried in the parable of the Prodigal Son by the *radicalness* of the imagery and action. This parable, like many others, is economical, tense, riven with radical comparisons and disjunctions. The comparisons are extreme; what is contrasted, however, is not this world versus another world, but the radicalness of love, faith, and hope *within* this world. The setting is worldly but the orientation or "frame" of the story is radical. The radical dimension provides the context, which disrupts the ordinary dimension and allows us to see it anew as reformed by God's extraordinary love. What is "seen," however, is not something "spiritual" (God's love "in itself," whatever that would be), but the homely and familiar in a new context—ordinary life lived in a new context, the context of radical, unmerited love. That love—and God himself—are nowhere directly mentioned in the story; the perception of divine love is achieved through stretching the surface of the story with an extreme imagery of hunger and feasting, rejection and acceptance, lost and found, death and life.

The pattern of extreme contrasts runs throughout the entire parable, from the father's willingness to divide his property without question and the son's decision to take "*all* he had" and go into a "*far* country" where he "*squandered* his property in *loose* living" to the extraordinary developments upon the son's return. The imagery of life and death dominates the parable at its beginning, middle, and end: the most radical dichotomy sets the tone for the other extreme images. At the outset of the parable the son treats the father as if he were dead, for, as Gunther Bornkamm mentions, a son has the right of disposal of property only after a father's death.[3] The extremism is also evident in such phrases as "he had spent *everything*," "a *great* famine arose," "no one gave him *anything*." His job, feeding swine, is of course the worst possible one since it brought him into direct contact with unclean animals; he, however, was so close to starvation he would gladly have eaten the swine's food. Verse 17 is the turning point of the parable, and, characteristically, it is an absolute about-face ("but he came to himself"); his repentance countenances no rationalizations. The surrealistic or "absurd" part of the story, what makes verse 20, with the undignified and poignant image of the father spying the boy from a distance (how many times, we wonder, had he watched that road during those long months?) and running to embrace him (older Near Easterners did *not* run).[4] The "compassion" of the father is expressed in the distinctive New Testament usage of a word that means, "love from the bowels." When the boy starts to give his repentance speech exactly as rehearsed, the father cuts him short and changes the unspoken words to their opposite—the son is not to be considered a servant but an honored guest. The extraordinary love and graciousness of the father for the boy is entirely without grounding in anything the boy has done or said—even his repentance speech is cut short. Then in breathless succession more unmerited gifts are heaped upon the prodigal: the best robe (the ceremonial robe which in the East is a mark of high distinction), a ring (a signet ring is a sign of authority), shoes (a luxury worn only by free men, not slaves), a fatted calf (in a land where meat is rarely eaten). All of this happens because, and here the main imagery of the parable emerges again, the lost is found, the dead is alive. The latter part of the parable—the refusal and rejection by the elder son—is dealt with in the same way, through lavish, extraordinary, "absurd" generosity.

One *could* paraphrase this parable in the theological assertion "God's love knows no bounds," but to do that would be to miss what the parable can do for our insight into such love. For what *counts* here is not extricating an abstract concept but precisely the opposite, delving into the details of the story itself, letting the metaphor do its job of revealing the new setting for ordinary life. It is the play of the radical images that does the job. If we want to talk about what this parable has to say about God, we must do so in terms that do not extrapolate from that moment when the father, waiting these many months, finally sees his son, and we must do so in terms that dig into the details *of* that moment. Thus the radical contrasts and the concrete images are not embellishments but are the meaning, for there is no way to the meaning except through them.

Dan Via talks about the "in-meaning" and the "through-meaning" of metaphors: meanings that are united inseparably as form and content, body and awareness. "The human organism is a body that thinks, and in all thinking the mind unites with a figure—language—of its own devising."[5] "A body that thinks": this description of human life would satisfy Rubenstein and Keen, it is the assumption of all metaphorical language, and it is also basically and radically Christian. The modern post-Cartesian split of mind and body is radically anti-Christian; meaning and truth for human beings are embodied, hence *embodied language,* metaphorical language, is the most appropriate way—perhaps the only way—to suggest this meaning and truth. The multiplication table, and, we might add, the conceptual clarity of doctrinal creeds or theological propositions, are not *more* true for human beings than are the myth of the fall or the parable of the Prodigal Son. Metaphorical language is a mirror of our own constitution: the unity of body and soul, outer and inner, familiar and unfamiliar, known and unknown. Metaphorical language conveys meaning through the body of the world. It makes connections, sees resemblances, uniting body and soul—earthly, temporal, ordinary experience with its meaning. But the "meaning" is not there to be read off conceptually; we only get at the meaning through the metaphor.

Metaphorical or imagistic language has the peculiar quality of both expressing and communicating at the same time. *Glossolalia,* speaking in strange tongues, expresses but does not communicate; logical or highly conceptual language communicates precisely but is not highly expressive. Only metaphorical language, because it sets the familiar in a new context, does both—it can express more than the familiar and yet at the same time communicate, since it uses terms known to us. The kingdom (the unfamiliar) is a coin, which a woman lost and found; it is a valuable pearl. *New* meaning is generated by making words mean more than they ordinarily do: this, in fact, is the definition of metaphor. But at the same time it is an entirely indirect mode. There are no explicit statements about God; everything is refracted through the earthly metaphor or story. Metaphor is, I believe, the heart of the parabolic tradition of religious reflection as contrasted with the more propositionally oriented tradition of regular or systematic theology.

The insistence on embodied language, on the indirection of metaphor, on the intimate relations of the ordinary and the extraordinary *within* the parable does not mean that "nothing is said about God" in a parable and in theological reflection based on parables. But it does mean that we must be precise when we speak of *how* assertions are made about God in parables. They are made not in direct propositions but with what Philip Wheelwright calls "soft focus" or "assertorial lightness." This is the case because, as Wheelwright says, "the plain fact is that not all facts are plain."

> "The Lord whose oracle is at Delphi," said Heraclitus referring to Apollo the god and symbol of wisdom, "neither speaks nor conceals but gives signs." . . . There are meanings of high, sometimes of very high importance, which cannot be stated in terms strictly defined. . . . Plain speech may sometimes have conceptual exactitude, but it will be inaccurate with respect to the new thing that one wants to say, the freshly imagined experience that one wants to describe and communicate.[6]

Such "assertions" can *only* be made lightly or in soft focus. Thus parables are not only, as I have maintained, a deformation of ordinary life by placing that life in the context of the new and extraordinary, but they also tell us, though indirectly, something about the new and extraordinary context. The parables make ontological as well as existential "assertions"—they tell us something about God as well as something about our life—but the assertions about God are made lightly, indirectly, and cannot be extricated finally and completely from the story which expresses or, better, "images" them.

God's Grandeur

The world is charged with the grandeur of God.
   It will flame out, like shining from shook foil;
   it gathers to a greatness, like the ooze of oil

> Crushed. Why do men then now not reck his rod?
> Generations have trod, have trod, have trod;
>   And all is seared with trade; bleared, smeared with toil;
>   And wears man's smudge and shares man's smell: the soil
> Is bare now, nor can foot feel, being shod.
>
> And for all this, nature is never spent;
>   There lives the dearest freshness deep down things;
> And though the last lights off the black West went
>   Oh, morning, at the brown brink eastward, springs—
> Because the Holy Ghost over the bent
>   World broods with warm breast and with ah! Bright wings.[7]

At first glance this poem by Gerard Manley Hopkins seems miles removed from the parable of the Prodigal Son: it appears to be "about" God, or at least about nature, rather than about human life. But note that it speaks of God *only* in his grandeur, that is, it speaks of him only sacramentally through his effects—the world is charged with the grandeur *of* God—and it speaks of nature and human beings inextricably involved with each other, ecologically, symbiotically united—nature wears our smudge and shares our smell. The theme of the poem is the renewal of the world, a renewal that is not merely natural but is from the providential, life-giving hand of God. As with the Prodigal Son we discover this theme only *through* the metaphors of the poem, only through its *own* intrinsic details.

"God's Grandeur" is of course a sonnet, with the first eight lines laying out the situation and the sestet giving the resolution, and as with most sonnets the last two lines hold a special revelatory surprise. It is a highly intricate poem and we can do no more than suggest a few of the intricacies, but it is important to indicate some of them, for my thesis is that the *details* are the meaning of the poem.

    l.1 "Charged" suggests the modern image of electricity (and more generally of potency) but the word also has overtones of responsibility as in "charged with a responsibility"; therefore the image is both impersonal and personal.

    l.2 "Flame out" picks up the electricity image from l.1 and also implies movement outward, the enveloping power of flame to consume all. In his notes on the poem, Hopkins writes of "shook foil": "I mean foil in the sense of leaf or tinsel . . . Shaken gold-foil gives off broad glares like sheet lightning and also, and *this is true of nothing else*, owing to its zigzag dents and creasings and network of small many cornered facets, a sort of fork lightning too."[8] The image of shook foil is one of glory, brilliance, light, and power: God's grandeur in nature is unmistakable, *obvious*.

l.3 The outward shining movement is now contracted, it "gathers to a greatness" like the "ooze of oil," and a shift of tone is implied in the ambiguous sound of the "o's" here.

l.4 Crushed: golden spurts of oil spatter out. The grandeur of God is so obvious it could hit you in the eye. So why do men not see it, why do they not "reck his rod"—a phrase that recalls the "charged" of l.1. The responsibility of nature to show forth God's grandeur is mirrored in man's responsibility to *see* the grandeur in nature.

ll.5-8 The topic changes to men and what they have done to nature and the new subject is carried by the mechanical image of the treadmill ("have trod, have trod, have trod") and the nasty "s" sounds—seared, smeared, smudge, shares, smell, soil, shod. Here are some nice ecological and anti-pollution overtones in 1877: man cannot *feel* the earth or, by implication, perceive God in nature, since he wears shoes.

l.9 The sestet opens with the renewal of nature. The power for renewal appears to be within nature—the instress or pressure of God comes immanently, not as a *deus ex machina* but from the incredible resources of renewal with which God has endowed the world.

l.11 "Last lights off the black West" envisions a total catastrophe, a Hiroshima of civilization, the setting of the sun for the last time.

l.12 The reversal begins: a new day, a gradual lessening of "black" to "brown," a new morning "springs"—a lively physical movement, and also a new spring following the winter (a suggestion of the cycle of fertility-nature cults).

ll.13-14 All the foregoing happens *because* of the Holy Ghost (it is not a fertility cult or an entirely immanent occurrence). Here in the image of the dove, as solicitous as a mother bird with her warm breast, recalling Genesis 1 in "broods," the Holy Ghost manifests the power of a second creation carried by the exclamation, "with ah! Bright wings." It is not just the warmth of the nest of creation but the glory and unexpected possibilities implied in the image of the bird's wings rising radiantly against the rising sun. These images of radiance recall, of course, the opening images of the poem and bring us back to the grandeur of God shining in the world.

It is useful to recall that Hopkins was a follower of Duns Scotus, with his skepticism about the range of theological reason. Nowhere in this poem does Hopkins talk directly *about* God: the language is imagistic and metaphorical at all times—electricity, flame, tinfoil, oil, morning, dove, and wings. There is no way to the "theology," if you will, except through the poetry, and this is not, I believe, just precious aestheticism. For, just to take that last metaphor of the bird and plumb its intrinsic meanings—creation, rebirth, nest, comfort, care for the *bent* world, and finally *bright* wings—is a lesson in the appropriateness of metaphorical theological language for a human being—"a body that thinks." Hopkins's poem is an existential, sensuous story of human beings in relation to God, a panoramic story of the violations of God's world by them and God's renewal of it. What one "gets" from this story, this poem, is not new information that can be catalogued but *new insight* into what we might call the gracious power of God in the world or better, his powerful graciousness. A deep probing of the metaphors of the poem puts us in touch with the graciousness of God's power as it impinges on and renews our familiar world; we feel we understand somewhat better, in terms that matter to us—personal, worldly, concrete terms—what such a notion might mean.

The Peach-Seed Monkey

Once upon a time when there were still Indians, Gypsies, bears, and bad men in the woods of Tennessee where I played and, more important still, there was no death, a promise was made to me. One endless summer afternoon my father sat in the eternal shade of a peach tree, carving on a seed he had picked up. With increasing excitement and covetousness I watched while, using a skill common to all omnipotent creators, he fashioned a small monkey out of the seed. All of my vagrant wishes and desires disciplined themselves and came to focus on that peach-seed monkey. If only I could have it, I would possess a treasure which could not be matched in the whole cosmopolitan town of Maryville! What status, what identity, I would achieve by owning such a curio! Finally I marshaled my nerve and asked if I might have the monkey when it was finished (on the sixth day of creation). My father replied, "This one is for your mother, but I will carve you one some day."

Days passed, then weeks and, finally, years, and the someday on which I was to receive the monkey did not arrive. In truth, I forgot all about the peach-seed monkey. Life in ambience of my father was exciting, secure, and colorful. He did all of those things for his children a father can do, not the least of which was merely delighting in their existence. One of the lasting tokens I retained of the measure of his dignity and courage was the manner in which, with emphysema sapping his energy and eroding his future, he continued to wonder, to struggle, and to grow.

In the pure air and dry heat of an Arizona afternoon on the summer before the death of God, my father and sat under a juniper tree. I listened as he wrestled with the task of taking the measure of his success and failure in life. There came a moment of silence that cried out of testimony. Suddenly I remembered the peach-seed monkey, and I heard the right words coming from myself to fill the silence: "In all that is important you have never failed me. With one exception, you kept the promises you made to me—you never carved me that peach seed monkey."

Not long after this conversation I received a small package in the mail. In it was a peach-seed monkey and a note which said: "Here is the monkey I promised you. You will notice that I broke one leg and had to repair it with glue. I am sorry I didn't have time to carve a perfect one." Two weeks later my father died. He died only at the end of his life.[9]

When we move from Hopkins's poem to Sam Keen's story of a peach-seed monkey, we seem to be in another world again. There is no grandeur of God crackling and flaming here, but an atmosphere, which is described, as *post-Christian* and *death of God*. Keen sees no possibility of using the metaphors and stories and myths of the tradition: he must start with his own story and see if from that "there is anything in my experience which gives it unity, depth, density, dignity, meaning, and value—which makes graceful freedom possible."[10] This is his central question and I do not think it wrong or inappropriate when dealing with Keen's radically personal and subjective, anti-traditionalist, anti-God-talk story of the peach-seed monkey to keep in mind the compassion of the father for the son in the parable of the Prodigal Son and the warmth and bright wings of the dove brooding over the bent world in

Hopkins's poem. In all three cases, I believe, we are concerned with human confidence in the foundations of being *as told in the human story.*

Keen has himself analyzed his story of the peach-seed monkey. He says that for him the peach-seed monkey is a symbol for "all the promises, which were made to me and the energy and care which nourished and created me as a human being."[11] It became for him translucent to another reality—"my sense of the basic trustworthiness of the world and my consequent freedom to commit myself to action."[12] He can become through the story a receiver and a maker of promises; this gives a unity of past, present, and future for him and hence gives him a "story," identity. Keen does not believe the peach-seed monkey is only history; one like it lies in each person's biography and, as he says, "in the depth of each man's biography lies the story of all men."[13] In the depths of this story of the peach-seed monkey lies Keen's sense of the holy and the sacred: the basic solicitude of life, which makes graceful freedom possible. Keen would not call this God-talk, nor shall we; but whatever it is, it is certainly in the same tradition as the Prodigal Son and "God's Grandeur." Keen's story is not of the same caliber as the others. The fact that he added an "explanation" is the giveaway: the peach-seed monkey is really a symbol, not a metaphor—that is, it "stands for" something (and he tells us what that something is). The correlation in a symbol is much tighter than in a metaphor—one thing stands for another thing—and it loses the multilayered, rich, and always partly ambiguous or "soft" focus of a metaphor. The fact that Keen sees his life as a story and events in it within a context of graciousness reveals his sensitivity to the necessity of dealing with religious insight indirectly, but his straight talk *about* the meaning of the story of the peach-seed monkey suggests a failure of nerve and a wish to take shortcuts. His analysis makes the story little more than an illustration of what he obviously can say more directly in discursive language. But the desire is there in Keen and in many others for a secular, indirect, low-key way of dealing with the graciousness experienced in ordinary life.

The language of a people is their sense of reality; we can live only within the confines of our language. If that language is one-dimensional, as Herbert Marcuse puts it, if it is jargon, the jargon of technocracy, of Madison Avenue, of politics—or of theology—then we lead one-dimensional lives, meaningless lives, lives within language that has ceased to express our depths for it is not capable of expressing anything but the limits of what we *already* know and feel. It is no longer open to or suggestive of any reality beyond itself, and hence we have no means of renewing ordinary life and language, of seeing it in new contexts. Our ability to express the deeper dimensions of human existence is determined by the metaphorical aliveness of our language, and that language in turn is controlled by the vision of reality we hold. The teller of the parable of the Prodigal Son, Hopkins, and, to some extent, Keen beheld a vision of reality that demanded a breakthrough beyond one-dimensional, univocal language—it demanded metaphor, for such is always the route out of established meaning to new meaning; and metaphor in turn became the proper vehicle for the expression and communication of what they beheld—it is the language for "a body that thinks."

For many of us the language of the Christian tradition is no longer authoritative; no longer revelatory; no longer metaphorical; no longer meaningful. Much of it has become tired clichés, one-dimensional, univocal language. When this happens, it means that theological reflection is faced with an enormous task—the task of embodying it anew. This will not happen, I believe, through systematic theology, for systematic theology is second-level language, language which orders, arranges, explicates, makes precise the first-order revelatory, metaphorical language. How the renovation of basic Christian language will take place will not, I suspect, be unlike the "way" we see in the tradition of religious reflection we have been analyzing. It will be through the search for new metaphors—poems, stories, even lives—which will "image" to us, in our total existential unity, the compassion of the father, the bright wings of the bird, the trustworthiness of a world in which parents keep promises to their children.

Contemporary poems, novels, and autobiographies can serve as imaginative re-creations, "deformations," of the old, allowing us to see the old in a new setting and thus to see it anew. What is at stake here is not simply the renewal of Christian symbols and traditional language—it is not the problem of translating what old symbols "say" into contemporary language—but the more basic hermeneutical task of understanding the creative imagination as that which uniquely allows us to see and say the conceptually imperceivable and inexpressible. . . . what we could call in other words the relationship between parable and theology—the word of address and words oriented toward serving the hearing of that address. Although the way from parable to theology, Robert Funk says, is "circuitous and tortuous,"[14] still the language of the imagination was at our beginning, and in spite of the rocky path, it will be always an ingredient in all our theology or we will abdicate our task—the service of helping God's word to be heard.

> It appears that history has brought theological language full circle: having begun with the poetry of parable, metaphor, simile, and aphorism, it seems that theology is being thrust back upon the

language of its infancy. The reason may be that just as faith could not be presupposed then, it cannot be presupposed now. In such a context the redeeming word must lay its own foundation: by its power as word it must be able to bring that world into being in which faith is possible, indeed necessary. Only then is it possible for theology to extrapolate conceptually from faith's experience of the world as redeemed. If, in the intervening centuries, theology has grown less and less solicitous of its ownmost origin, it is now being forced to renew itself at its source—or perish.[15]

Notes

1. Richard L. Rubenstein, *After Auschwitz: Radical Theology and Contemporary Judaism* (New York: Bobbs-Merrill, 1966), x.

2. Sam Keen, *To a Dancing God* (New York: Harper & Row, 1970), 99.

3. Gunther Bornkamm, *Jesus of Nazareth*, trans. Irene and Fraser McLuskey with James M. Robinson (London: Hodder and Stoughton, 1960), 126–27.

4. Dan O. Via Jr., *The Parables: Their Literary and Existential Dimension* (Philadelphia: Fortress Press, 1967), 172.

5. Ibid., 83.

6. Philip Wheelwright, *The Burning Fountain: A Study in the Language of Symbolism* (Bloomington: Indiana University Press, 1968), 86.

7. *Poems and Prose of Gerard Manley Hopkins* (London: Penguin, 1953), 27.

8. Ibid., 219.

9. Keen, *To a Dancing God*, 100–101.

10. Ibid., 99.

11. Ibid., 101.

12. Ibid.

13. Ibid., 103.

14. Robert W. Funk, "The Parables: A Fragmentary Agenda," in *Jesus and Man's Hope*, II, ed. Donald G. Miller and Dikran Y. Hadidian (Pittsburgh: Pittsburgh Theological Seminary, 1971), 300.

15. Robert W. Funk, "Myth and The Literal Non-Literal," in *Parable, Myth and Language*, ed. Tony Stoneburner (Cambridge, Mass.: The Church Society for College Work, 1968), 63.

2

Parables as Metaphors

This selection from chapter 4 of Speaking in Parables *fleshes out some of the ideas introduced in the previous chapter regarding parables, and gives a sense of McFague's developing biblical hermeneutic. Whereas earlier she delved into the parable of the Prodigal Son, in this chapter she focuses more on the parable of the Wedding Feast (Matt. 22:1-10). It is here also that she introduces us to her early christological concept of Jesus as "the parable of God"—that is, "the distinctive way the transcendent touches the worldly—only in, through, and under ordinary life" (3). This christological turn evidences her demurral from her early theological influence, Karl Barth, and initiates her later, more expansive theological concern for immanental transcendence.*

Source: 1976:72-80

Parables have not always, or usually, been viewed as metaphors. Historical criticism tended to focus on "what a parable meant" in its historical context (C. H. Dodd and Joachim Jeremias). This approach is perhaps an advance over Jülicher, whose "one-point" interpretation tended to reduce the parables to their ideational possibilities, evidencing little if any appreciation for them as metaphors, in other words, as nonreducible entities. A metaphor is neither reducible to one point nor is its "meaning" foreclosed in some historical moment: it is rather generative of *new* meanings in the plural. C. H. Dodd's definition of Jesus' parables does point to other possibilities.

> At its simplest the parable is a metaphor or simile drawn from nature or common life, arresting the hearer by its vividness or strangeness, and leaving the mind in sufficient doubt about its precise application to tease it into active thought.[1]

The emphasis on strangeness, doubt, and teasing into active thought preclude the reduction of the parabolic form to one point or to a purely historical interpretation. Amos Wilder indicates the same direction when he conceives of the parable as a metaphor in which "we have an image with a certain shock to the imagination which directly conveys vision of what is signified."[2]

But before we can speak directly of the "certain shock to the imagination" which the parable form effects, we must look at its setting—not its historical setting (a question for the New Testament scholars to debate) but its setting as an aesthetic object. As an extended metaphor, the parable is an aesthetic object—and we shall have more to say about this—but, it seems to me, an aesthetic object of a special sort. For to a greater degree than other aesthetic objects, such as an Eliot poem or a Tolstoy novel, the setting of the parable is triangular. The components of the triangle are source or author (Jesus as narrator), the aesthetic object (the parable narrated), and the effect (the listeners to whom the parable is narrated). This triangle pattern points to the original situation of the parables: *Jesus* told *stories* to *people*. All three factors should operate in any analysis of the parables, for they cannot be abstracted from their source or from their listeners. As Norman Perrin points out, there are three kinds of interpretation involved in any *textual* criticism: historical, literary, and hermeneutical; that is, criticism of *who* tells or writes, *what* is told or written, and to *whom* the text is directed.[3]

The parables present a special case, however, for the point of Jesus' parables is not mere illumination, aesthetic insight, or secret wisdom. There is a stress in the parables on confrontation and decision, an emphasis not evident in most other aesthetic objects. "The parables of Jesus were directed to a specific situation, the situation of men and women confronted by the imminence of the interruption of God into their world."[4] Hence, while the three components of the interpretative triangle are crucial, there is an emphasis on the third, on the listeners, though, as we shall see, the power of the confrontation occurs only because of *who* told the parables and *what* is being told to them.

The first component of the triangle, Jesus as narrator, is perhaps the most difficult. We are all well aware of the pitfalls of the Intentional Fallacy, the deleterious effects on the integrity of the aesthetic object through interpretation by means of the "intentions" of the artist. And we have no desire to fall into that trap, not because it is unfashionable but because if we take the parable as metaphor seriously, attention must be focused on the parable itself and not on its authority or source. Two qualifications can be made, however. First, it does matter, in the instance of the biblical parables, that Jesus and not someone else told them. They are, as Perrin points out, "highly personal texts," which express "the vision of reality of their author," and that vision "cannot be contemplated except in dialogue with their creator."[5] The "voice" which calls us (as Walter

Ong would put it) in the parables is the voice of Jesus.[6] The best way to his vision is through the parables, for, as New Testament scholars agree, the parables not only are Jesus' most characteristic form of teaching but are among the most authentic strata in the New Testament. Hence our attention should not be diverted from the parables to the intentions of their author, for it is only by giving extraordinary attention to the parables themselves that we hear that voice and understand that vision.

Second, Jesus is related to the parables obliquely, not directly. . . . [T]he attention of the listeners is directed not toward the speaker nor toward "religious" questions, but toward two "logics" of comporting oneself with reality. As Robert Funk points out, Jesus, as the speaker of the parable, brings the new "logic" near and in this sense the parable can be considered as "the self-attestation of Jesus, i.e., as the inverbalization of Jesus as the word," but the self-attestation is hidden and indirect—"the parable is an oblique invitation on the part of Jesus to follow him. Since Jesus belongs to the situation figured in the parable, it is he who has embarked upon this way, who lives out of the new 'logic'."[7] In summary, then, it is necessary to attend in a New Testament parable to Jesus as the speaker of the parables, but this can and ought to be done in a way that not only retains their integrity as aesthetic objects but in fact pushes us to focus on the parables themselves.

A second component of the triangle, the listeners, is as essential for a just appreciation of the situation of the parables as is Jesus as narrator. In fact, extraordinary attention is being paid to the listeners by current biblical scholarship: the heart of the new hermeneutic project is, as we have seen, not the interpretation *of* the parables, but the interpretation of the listeners *by* the parables. . . . [T]he way in which the hearers "hear" the parable, whether they align themselves with the old "logic" of everydayness or with the new "logic" of grace, interprets them. They are interpreted, understood, defined by their response. And this emphasis by current scholarship on the hearers is not merely an attempt to make the parables "relevant" to today's people; the parables in the New Testament are set in deeply controversial contexts—they are told in response to questions, accusations, demands, and are meant to involve the listeners directly as participants. Implied in parable after parable is the question, "And what do *you* say? What will *you* do?" In fact, . . . the structure of the story—its two "logics"—is predicated on the basis of bringing the listeners, indirectly, to a decision. But again, as with Jesus the speaker, the importance of the role of the listeners does not turn our attention away from the parable but toward it. For we need not and ought not commit the Affective Fallacy at this point—interpreting the parable by means of its effect on the listeners. Rather, concern with the effect forces us back to the parable itself, for if we are to gain *new* insight, if the parable is to work its effect, there is no way to accomplish this but through maximum attention to its own givens, to the parable as metaphor.

We are brought, then, to the parable itself as the way to hear the voice it embodies and the challenge it presents to us. The two central features of the parable as aesthetic object are its realism and its strangeness. In Jesus' parable of the Wedding Feast the realistic story is primary, and this is true of all of Jesus' parables. They are about people getting married, wayward sons, widows on limited incomes, migrant workers, doctors and patients, fools and wise men, and so on. The commonness of the parables, their secularity and mundanity, has been acknowledged and appreciated by all, and it is such an obvious trait that we might be inclined to overlook its importance. But it is special when compared with other bodies of religious literature where gods and their doings (the Greeks), hierarchies of aeons and quasi-deities (the Gnostics), wise sayings and admonitions (the Buddhists) predominate. The Sermon on the Mount, a collection of Jesus' sayings and teachings, is throughout metaphorical—the teaching is evoked in terms of salt losing its savor, lamps under bushels, temple gifts versus brotherly reconciliation, plucked-out eyes and dismembered bodies, an eye for an eye, coats and cloaks, treasures eaten by moth and rust, lilies of the field, birds of the air, pearls before swine, loaves and stones, fishes and serpents. The list of New Testament metaphors seems endless and little needs to be said about the extensiveness and commonness of biblical imagery. But it does need to be stressed that it is *there* and is the *dominant* language of the New Testament.

This realism is not the same as Homeric realism—it is not mere surface detail, all in the "foreground." Rather it is realism "fraught with background," as Erich Auerbach puts it, and this "background," in both the Old Testament and the New, is the "way" the Judaic-Christian tradition has handled the matter of speaking of the divine. *The only legitimate way of speaking of the incursion of the divine into history, or so it appears to this tradition, is metaphorically.* Metaphor is proper to the subject matter because God remains hidden.[8] The belief that Jesus is the word of God—that God is manifest somehow in a human life—does not dissipate metaphor but in fact intensifies its centrality, for what is more indirect—a more complete union of the realistic and the strange—than a human life as the abode of the divine? Jesus as the word is metaphor par excellence: he is the parable of God.

It is entirely natural or inevitable, then, that the realism of the parables is of a special sort, that it provides again and again "that certain shock to the imagination" which Amos Wilder mentions. The way this shock is conveyed initially is the assumption of the parables that important things happen and are decided at the everyday level. The parables again and again indicate that it is in the seemingly insignificant events of being invited to a party and refusing to go, being jealous of a younger brother who seems to have it all his way, resenting other workers who get the same pay for less work, that the ultimate questions of life are decided.

> The "field" which the parable thus conjures up is not merely this or that isolated piece of earthiness, but the very tissue of reality, the nexus of relations, which constitutes the arena of human existence where life is won or lost.[9]

The "shock," in the first instance, consists in realizing, say in the parable of the Wedding Feast, that one's casual refusal to accept a gracious invitation apparently has something to do with whether one lives or dies. How can this be? But such is the nature of metaphor, of the parables as metaphors, and of the underlying assumption in the Bible of how the divine and the human orders are related. But the particular *way* that the parable works the relation between the two dimensions is the crucial question, and it is on this that we must now focus. A parable, an extended metaphor, works the relation between the ordinary and the extraordinary in the same way as a metaphor. An allegory is translucent to its reality—it is a form of direct communication that assumes that the reader or listener already knows about the reality being symbolized. Metaphor, on the contrary, is indirect, attempting to bring about new insight by framing the ordinary in an extraordinary context. That is to say, "the certain shock to the imagination" is *seeing the familiar in a new way*; the stress in a parable is not seeing something completely unfamiliar, or something "religious." One does not see "the divine" directly in a parable at all.

Thus in the parable of the Wedding Feast we are at no point "taken out" of the story into a "religious" world; the shock or new insight of the parable is in being brought to see that everyday situation—the wedding feast and its guest list—in a new way: invitation not by merit but by a gracious lack of concern about merit. The invitation by grace *is* brought to light, glimpsed, pointed to by means of cracks in the realism of the story—exaggeration, hyperbole, dislocations (the refusal of all the worthy guests to come, the shameful treatment and unmerited murder of the servants, the closing invitation to the people of the streets to come to the feast). The whole movement of the story not only is kept within its own confines at every point but returns the reader who would participate fully in it and be illuminated by it again and again to the story itself.

This is to say that as an indirect mode, metaphor does not, like discursive language, direct attention to "the thing" but directs it elsewhere in such a way that "the thing" is glimpsed. If this is the case, only fuller attention to the "elsewhere" will provide further illumination of "the thing." Christianity is necessarily and always wedded to indirection. It is also a way of knowing which delimits spectator knowledge, primarily because what is being offered is not information one can store but an experience. It is a truism to say that art is not kinetic; it does not force anyone to make a decision, to *do* anything. Kierkegaard was right when he insisted on the hiatus between the aesthetic and the ethical, a hiatus that can be bridged only by an agent. But it is also true that those who have followed the movement of the two "logics" of the parable of the Wedding Feast find themselves provoked, stimulated, edged into a decision about which "logic" will be their own. In a sense, the parable has trapped them; it starts off on ordinary ground and catches them off balance as it switches "logics" mid-way. The parable does not teach a spectator a lesson; rather it invites and surprises a participant into an experience. This is its power, its power then and now to be revelatory, not once upon a time, but every time a person becomes caught up in it and by it.

A parable of Jesus is not only an interesting story; it is a call to decision issued from one who in some way or other is himself a parable, or, as Christians believe, *the* parable of God. It is, then, not just another work of art; we have stressed the aesthetic nature of the parable not merely because parables have been debased into allegories and homilies but because of the religious significance of the aesthetic quality of parables. The crucial point is that a parable is metaphorical at every level and in every way—in language, in belief, in life. To say that it is metaphorical in language is obvious—the multitude of familiar images employed by the New Testament to evoke that great unfamiliar, the kingdom of God, needs little elaboration. The kingdom is never defined; it is spoken of in metaphorical language. But there is a deeper sense in which parables are metaphoric. A parable is an *extended* metaphor—the metaphor is not in discrete images that allow for a flash of insight (a purely aesthetic or intellectual "Aha!"), but it is a way of believing and living that initially seems ordinary, yet is so dislocated and rent from its usual context that, if the parable "works," the spectators become participants, not because they want to necessarily or simply have "gotten the point" but because they have, for the moment, "lost control" or as the new hermeneuts say, "been interpreted." The secure, familiar everydayness of the story of their own lives has been torn apart; they have seen another story—the story of a mundane life like their own moving by a different "logic," and they begin to understand (not just with their heads) that another way of believing and living—another context or frame for their lives—might be a possibility *for them.*

The impact of the parables is directly tied to their qualities as aesthetic objects, their insistence that insight be embodied, incarnated; but the uncanny and unnerving aspect of the New Testament parables is that the peculiar insight they are concerned with, believing in a loving God who upsets the logic of the familiar, must be embodied, incarnated in human *lives*, not in the head alone but in and through the full scope and breadth of a human life. If this is the parabolic way it is necessarily metaphoric, necessarily indirect, because it is concerned not with what we believe, know, or are, but what we are in the process of believing, knowing, and becoming *in our lives.* Parables are not, then, riddles that give privileged knowledge to those who solve them. They are not primarily concerned with knowing but with doing (understood as deciding on a way of life based on new insight). Thus, to emphasize the parable as aesthetic object does not mean resting in whatever insight it may give us, but rather, while recognizing that its *power* to bring to decision derives from its aesthetic qualities, we must not forget that the goal of a parable is finally in the realm of willing, not of knowing. In a parable we are, as Perrin says, confronted by Jesus' vision of reality and challenged to decide what we will do about it.

> To read a parable of Jesus is ultimately to be confronted by Jesus' vision of reality. As an aid to this, we can and we should consider the nature and function of metaphor and of metaphorical language, we can and we should consider such literary aspects as the movement of the plot, the function of disclosure scenes, the Unjust Steward as a picaresque rogue, and so on. But ultimately what matters is the vision of reality of the author and the challenge of that vision of reality to ourselves.[10]

Notes

1. C. H. Dodd, *The Parables of the Kingdom* (New York: Scribner, 1961), 16.
2. Amos N. Wilder, *The Language of the Gospel: Early Christian Rhetoric* (New York: Harper & Row, 1964), 80.
3. Norman Perrin, "Historical Criticism, Literary Criticism, and Hermeneutics: The Interpretation of the Parables of Jesus and the Gospel of Mark Today," *Journal of Religion* 52 (1972): 361–75.
4. Ibid., 365.
5. Ibid., 370–71.
6. Walter J. Ong, "Voice as Summons for Belief: Literature, Faith, and the Divided Self," *Literature and Religion*, ed. Giles B. Gunn (New York: Harper & Row, 1971), 68–86.

7. Robert W. Funk, *Language, Hermeneutic and Word of God: The Problem of Language in the New Testament and Contemporary Theology* (New York: Harper & Row, 1966), 197.
8. Ibid., 154.
9. Ibid., 155–56.
10. Perrin, "Historical Criticism," 374.

3

Creeds: Models or Dogmas

In McFague's second book, Metaphorical Theology *(1982), she deepens her exploration of metaphor to work more with models, which she defines as "systematic and relatively permanent metaphors" that serve as a "critical link between parables . . . and conceptual language, which orders, analyzes, and criticizes the images of a tradition in a logical and comprehensive fashion. . . . like metaphors, [they] retain the tension at the heart of all religious language and, like concepts, [they] order the images of a tradition so that they may become an intelligible path for life" (103). The argument she offers in this volume is filled with theoretical explications too complex to detail here, including a lengthy section that shows how scientific models may help us understand and critique theological models. However, this concern for theological models leads to obvious questions of how Christian confessional statements function as theological discourse, particularly in our contemporary context. Her earlier exploration of the parables of the kingdom of God and her christological interpretation of Jesus as the parable of God become a means to critique the ways in which creeds attempt to define God using a single, hierarchal model that may lead to idolatrous and oppressive understandings and practices. (For more on models, see chs. 6 and 7, below.)*

Source: 1982:111–17

The Apostles' Creed (and to a lesser extent, the Nicene Creed) is probably recited by more Christians with greater frequency than any other confession of faith. Sunday after Sunday it is repeated by Christians around the world, many of whom have little comprehension of its momentous assertions, let alone its power or its oddity. It is a majestic statement summing up the central beliefs of Christian faith in a narrative of amazing economy; in form it is trinitarian, its three articles specifying the work of the Father, Son, and Holy Spirit. All of heaven and earth is included in it, but it is neither general nor abstract; rather, it is comprised of concrete images and events that tell the story of the world in

Christian perspective from beginning to end. Its power lies in the metaphors and models that people repeat over and over again: "God the Father Almighty maker of heaven and earth," "Jesus Christ his only Son our Lord," "descended into hell," "communion of saints," "forgiveness of sins," "resurrection of the body," and "life everlasting." These phrases have been the ones by which Christians describe and interpret their religious experience; moreover, they constitute the language *in* which Christians experience religiously, for the language is not only shaped by experience but shapes it as well. In fact, the language of the creed may become so ordinary and accepted that its oddity is forgotten: occasionally one is aware of its strangeness, but usually it is recited with the same equanimity with which one reads a newspaper.

When we notice some of the phrases from the Nicene Creed, the situation changes, for the form is less narrational and more abstract, the language less imagistic and more conceptual: "all things visible and invisible," "the only-begotten Son of God," "God of God, Light of Light, Very God of Very God, begotten, not made, being of one substance with the Father." We realize something new here, that a point is being emphasized concerning the relationship between the Father and the Son, and that this point is being pressed by means of concepts intended to be as precise as possible. We should also note, however, that while the key phrase, "being of one substance with the Father," is clearly philosophical, conceptual language, many of the other phrases are still metaphorical or contain metaphors. At the very least, then, the church's main creeds are a fascinating mix of metaphorical and conceptual language in basically narrative form. The focus of their content, moreover, is *relationship*, not only the relationship of the Father to the Son and to the Holy Spirit, but also the relationship of God to the world, to its creation and salvation.

The evolution of these creeds and the controversies surrounding their development, most notably the trinitarian formula and the subsequent controversy ending in the Chalcedonian formula (451 CE), are incredibly complex and beyond our concern here. Suffice it to say that these controversies defined, as precisely as possible with available philosophical concepts, two key relationships: the relationship among the "persons" of the Godhead ("one substance, three persons") and the relationship between the divine and the human in Jesus Christ ("one person with or in two natures"). The overarching relationship of the creeds, and the reason for their concern with the above relations, is the one between God and humanity; the creeds were concerned with salvation above all else. Whether the credal understanding of this relationship is faithful to the root-metaphor of Christianity—the kingdom of God made known in the parables and Jesus as parable of God—is a highly complex question. We do not presume to answer that question definitely, although we must deal with it in attempting to analyze this translation language as emergent from and related to its metaphorical, parabolic base.

Are the creeds models or dogmas? Do they, as Augustine says, "fence a mystery," or do they pose as explanations of it and hence reduce it to literal statements? Is credal language open-ended, relative, tensive, iconoclastic, and indirect or is it absolutistic, possessive, static, literalistic, and idolatrous? The verdict is mixed. To be sure, many characteristics of models are evident in credal language. We notice immediately that two of the major images—"Father" and "Son"—are concrete, detailed models which simplify in an intelligible way what are otherwise impregnable mysteries, that is, God and Jesus of Nazareth. These models are well-known, common ones with great potential for exploitation since we all have a vast network of commonplaces associated with paternal and filial behavior. Nescience immediately becomes knowledge, silence is broken, we can speak, *not* because we know now who God is or who Jesus is but because we know about fathers and sons. These models are also comprehensive and systematic: they provide a grid of interpretation for all of "heaven and earth." If God is Father, then he is "begetter" or creator of all that is, including human beings, who as creatures are "children"; he is also sustainer, provider, and governor of the world and, through his Son, he restores and reconciles his children when they fall away from him through sin and rebellion. An entire theology *in nuce* is present in these models. That these models are interrelated is evident: "Father" is the dominant model spawning subsidiary models of "Son" (not, the creeds insist, in subordination, but Father comes first, while Son comes second), "children," "creation," "rebellion," "reconciliation," as well as others. Many models emerge and they are related to one another intrinsically and naturally, creating a pattern of interpretation from the beginning of the world to its fulfillment. The models provide explanation for doctrine, or, more accurately, the theory emerging from the creeds of the relationships involved is exemplified in terms of models. The theory is not illustrated by the models but the models are exemplars of it: one does not have doctrine *and* models in the creeds, but doctrine *in* models. There is little attempt, even in the Nicene Creed, to expurgate models; rather, *conceptual and metaphorical language lie side by side.*

Above all else, the creeds focus not on describing human and divine natures, but on modeling relationships of various kinds: within the Godhead, between divinity and humanity in Jesus Christ, between God and humanity. This is a controversial assertion, since the creeds have been criticized as adopting the substance language of Greek philosophy, and by so doing, describing divine and human activity in terms of static, substantial divine and human natures. The criticism is valid to the extent that the conceptual framework does veer in this direction, but the form of the creeds is still narrational and hence dynamic. Moreover, and of greater significance, the conceptual language is, at base, relational because of the centrality of the models of father, son, and children—relationships, not natures.

Finally, the creeds powerfully shape feelings and attitudes due to their models, not to their conceptual elements. It is no surprise that the central model of the creeds, the paternal one, has singularly influenced religious emotions and behavior, for, even if Freud had not told us so, we know from our own experience that relations with fathers embrace a highly complex mix of pleasure, pain, and guilt.

In sum, we can say, I believe, that credal language manifests many characteristics of interpretation by means of models. Serious questions must nevertheless be raised. While the creeds focus on relationships, the root-metaphor of Christianity—the kingdom of God and the relationship of reorientation based on security in God alone—appears in a somewhat skewed form. One does not expect it to appear in the same form in the creeds as in the parables (for translation languages necessarily change the form), but the critical marks of metaphorical theology—a relationship between God and humanity of a certain quality and tension of a certain kind—should be evident if continuity between the parabolic base and its interpretation is to be maintained.

While this issue is highly complex and undoubtedly involves many factors, one problem with the credal language appears to be the hegemony of the paternal model. In my opinion, it undercuts both the *content* and the form of metaphorical theology. It undercuts the *content* of the relationship with God as one based not on merit but on grace because paternal imagery alone is not capable of modeling this pattern. The commonplaces associated with paternal imagery move between the poles of domination and providence and, more often than not, tend toward reward through merit rather than toward acceptance through compassion. As we shall see, one of the advantages of including maternal models for the divine-human relationship is that traditionally maternal love has more frequently been associated with unmerited care than has paternal love.[1] Parental models alone of either a paternal or maternal cast are, however, not sufficient to serve as the only models in a metaphorical theology. The problem here, as in most areas where models are critical, is the reluctance or refusal to use many—complementary and varied—models.

It is this reluctance or refusal that also points to the way in which the paternal model undercuts the *form* of metaphorical theology. It is not this model in particular that is the problem but its hegemony, its status as *the* interpretive grid for Christian faith, which elevates it to an absolute, literalistic, and virtually idolatrous position. Credal language is both deceptive and powerful; hence, the temptations to idolatry are strong. It is deceptive because it looks like literal language: "I believe in God, the Father Almighty, maker of heaven and earth; And in Jesus Christ his only Son our Lord." It appears to be a straightforward assertion defining the nature of God as father and Jesus Christ as son, as well as the relationship between them. That "definition" is by means of *one model* and, as we have seen, it is a model carrying heavy emotional freight. The temptation to possess God in this language, to identify the relationships described as enclosed in this language, is almost irresistible. While Ian Ramsey's comment on Arius's literalization of the trinitarian formula may not be entirely fair to Arius, it does identify a tendency not only common among patristic theologians but among us moderns as well.

> In effect, Arius said: "Sons come after fathers," so that if we talk of Jesus in terms of worship, we cannot escape some degree of subordination if we are to use the words meaningfully. So did Arius idolize what is only a model, and run it to death. . . . Arius did not realize that words like "son" and "father" only provided models.[2]

While it is necessary to remember that creeds emerged in the fight against heresies and hence, understandably, tend in the direction of definiteness, it is even more necessary to recall their limitations. Augustine is not alone in his awareness of the inadequacy of all language to express divine reality. Karl Rahner has said that dogma is the beginning, not the end, of theological reflection and all sensitive users of religious language agree with him. J. F. Bethune-Baker, a patristics scholar, says "all attempts to explain the nature and the relations of the Deity must largely depend on metaphor, and no one metaphor can exhaust those relations. Each metaphor can only describe one aspect of the nature of being of the Deity, and the inferences which can be drawn from it have their limits when they conflict with the inferences which can be truly drawn from other metaphors describing other aspects."[3] This obvious but often overlooked reminder lies at the base of our criticism of credal language as usually understood (whatever its intentions) as nonmetaphorical. Seldom is it recognized as tentative, open, relative, indirect, and tensive. The metaphorical "is and is not" is forgotten and identification takes place. God *is* Father, Jesus Christ *is* Son, and we *are* children. The appropriateness of these models as relative and helpful aids for interpreting the divine-human relationship is changed into an assertion of their literal and exclusive truth.

The verdict, then, on credal language is complex: credal language is a mix of models and concepts, in some ways a translation language in continuity with its parabolic base, but skewed due to its excessive reliance on *one* model, which is neither adequate to express the new relationship introduced by Jesus of Nazareth nor free from the idolatry which is the fate of any exclusive model. A central insight concerning the kingdom of God from the parables and Jesus as parable is that *it cannot be defined,* either imagistically or conceptually. It is a *relationship* modeled in the parables and in Jesus of Nazareth; hence, this relationship and not "God the father" (or "God the mother," or any other model) is the root-metaphor of Christianity. Many models will be necessary to intimate what it means to live in such a relationship with God and with others, but as an *event* which will take many forms at various times in different peoples' lives, it is not an "object" whose nature can be described.

By contrast, atonement theories have had quite a different history from that of credal statements on God and Christ. . . . [T]here are several such theories and the four main ones—ransom, deification, satisfaction, and moral influence—all are models. In atonement theories, not only have the concepts never moved very far from the models in which they were first expressed, but, even more significantly, all the models have survived and some combination of two or more of them is often embraced together. Even here, though, when *one* model is absolutized—the prime example on the contemporary scene being the satisfaction model—the result has been as disastrous as in the creeds. Generally, however, with atonement theories the church has realized that its models incur inconsistencies and moral difficulties at the conceptual level; that the "negative analogy," that part of a model not meant to apply, enters at a particular point when the exploitation of details becomes overambitious. It is then necessary to pull back, to realize, for instance, that the appropriateness of interpreting Christ's work as "satisfaction" does not mean that something objective is done *to* us without internal transformation, and to balance that model with "moral influence," stressing change in heart as an intrinsic part of genuine reconciliation. Atonement theory has been, from one point of view, a "muddle" contrasted with the neatness of the Nicene and Chalcedonian formulas. From another point of view, atonement theory is a good illustration of metaphorical theology, for it has allowed for multiple and alternative models, an obvious admission of the relative, tensive, and indirect character of theological reflection.

Notes

1. The monarchial model is closely associated with the patriarchal in the Christian tradition and one finds that the models of king, lord, father, husband, and judge mutually affect one another, so that "father," which *can* be interpreted in the direction of person-to-person reconciliation, is more often seen in hierarchical terms as dominance and control by the divine in relation to the human.

2. Ian T. Ramsey, *Religious Language: An Empirical Placing of Theological Phrases* (New York: Macmillan, 1967), 184–85.

3. J. F. Bethune-Baker, *Introduction to the Early History of Christian Doctrine*, 9th ed. (London: Metheun & Co., 1957), 160.

4

God as Mother, Lover, and Friend

Sallie McFague closes Metaphorical Theology *with a critique of the model of God as father, demonstrating how feminist theology has sought new, more inclusive models of God, and offering up the model of God as friend as a possible alternative. This search forms the core of her third book,* Models of God *(1987), which extends the work on theological language begun in her first two volumes with a new urgency in light of nuclear and environmental threats. The need for present-day models that better express the God-world relationship in terms of immanental transcendence here becomes more pressing. As she writes in the book's preface, "I have come to see patriarchal as well as imperialistic, triumphalistic metaphors for God in an increasingly grim light: this language is not only idolatrous and irrelevant—besides being oppressive to many who do not identify with it—but it may also work against the continuation of life on our planet" (ix). Thus, in an attempt at remythologizing the God-world relationship, she experiments with models of God as mother, lover, and friend in terms of three key questions: "What sort of divine love is suggested by each? What activity, work, or doctrine is associated with each? And what does each imply concerning the conduct of human existence?" (xiii). The four excerpts in this section offer first her rationale for experimenting with these particular models, and then each model is discussed in terms of one of the aforementioned questions, as a way to give a sense of the whole of this marvelously crafted argument, perhaps McFague's most influential writing to date.*

Sources: 1987:78–87; 101–109; 137–46; 174–80

Our task is to suggest an imaginative picture of the relationship between God and the world that will express the saving presence of God in our present. That saving presence we have interpreted as a destabilizing, inclusive, nonhierarchical vision of fulfillment for all of creation. If what is sought is a likely account of the relationship between God and world, is there value in looking at the cosmos as God's bodily presence in all times and places?

If we accept that picture, will the metaphors of mother, lover, and friend, be suitable ones for God's relationship to the world? [First,] we need to deal with some preliminary issues regarding personal metaphors. Throughout our discussion so far we have assumed divine personal agency. The analogy of self:body::God:world rests on this assumption, but we must now ask about its viability.

Two questions are central in any discussion of personal metaphors for understanding the God-world relation: Why use any personal metaphors? Why use these particular ones? Not all religious traditions use personal metaphors, or at least they do not use them to the degree the Judeo-Christian tradition does. Some mystical religions, as well as those intimately involved in nature's cycles, are far less personalistic in their imagery. If our task is to suggest imagery that will overcome the distance between God and the world while underscoring the immanence of God in the world, is it not counterproductive to continue using personal metaphors? This is a very serious question and is not a concern solely in our present ecological, nuclear crisis. To many people for a long time, the notion of a personal God has seemed incredible, for it appears to support the notion of a being existing somewhere whose only way to act on the world is to intervene in its affairs. It is not possible to trace here the modern history of this issue, but the remote God of the deists was certainly a first step away from an interventionist, personal God, and both Schleiermacher's turn to the self as the place where the presence of God is felt and Hegel's near-identification of God and the world are part of the history. These patterns were picked up by Bultmann's refusal to talk of God and divine activity except as implications of human states and by Tillich's wariness about personal images of God and his preference for "Being-itself" as the primary designation. One can see the direction that the issue of a personal God has taken during the past two centuries, by bringing to mind the embarrassment that such a "primitive" concept of God appears to present, as well as the genuine bewilderment it causes when we try to conceive the activity of such a God in a world that is understood as an evolutionary, causal nexus permitting no interference by outside agents. Is not a personal God both an anachronism from the childhood of humanity, best now discarded, and an impossibility in a time when agency, whether divine or human, is understood to take place in a highly complex ecological, evolutionary matrix of multiple agents, a matrix characterized by chance and necessity? Would it not be better, as Gordon Kaufman suggests, to conceive of God in terms of the multifarious physical, biological, and historico-cultural conditions that have made human existence possible, rather than in quasi-personal terms? Kaufman finds that the political, personal images of the tradition undergird militaristic and passive attitudes, whereas the familial images are too individualistic to function effectively in our evolutionary, ecological world. At most, Kaufman says, one can speak of the "hidden creativity" or "unpredictable grace" that works in and through the incredibly complex physical, biological, and historico-cultural matrix that has resulted in our present situation. I agree thoroughly with much of what Kaufman says and especially with his comment that "devotion to a God conceived in terms other than these [the physical, biological, historico-cultural matrix] will not be devotion to God, that is, to that reality which has (to the best of our understanding) in fact created us."[1] We must understand God and the activity of God in the world in a fashion that is not just commensurate with an ecological, evolutionary sensibility but intrinsic to it. I disagree with Kaufman's position, however, in that I do not believe that the reduction of the personal God to hidden creativity or unpredictable grace is desirable or necessary.

It is not desirable because, as I suggested earlier, any imaginative picture attempting to unseat the triumphalist, royal model must be at least as attractive as it is. It must be an understanding of the God-world relationship that will move people to live by it and work for it; it must come from a place deep within human experience. It is no accident that much of the tradition's most powerful imagery does come from this place. It is imagery reflecting the beginning and continuation of life, imagery of sex, breath, food, blood, and water, as in the second birth, the breath of the Holy Spirit, bread and wine, the blood of the cross, the resurrection of the body, and the water of baptism. This language continues to be powerful because images arising from the most basic level of physical existence—the level of our tenuous hold on existence and what is needed to keep it going—are images of life and death. I am not suggesting that there are some sacred, permanent metaphors that can replace the royalist, triumphalist model; but there may be a place to look for metaphors that goes even deeper than the political arena, from which most long-term models of the God-world relationship in the West have come. In the political arena the concern is with how we govern our lives; a deeper question is how we live at all and how well we live. Metaphors of mothers, lovers, friends, and bodies come from this level, as does the classic model of father understood as parent. If the imagery of mothers, lovers, friends, and bodies proved credible for picturing the God-world relation, it would certainly also be attractive, for it is unmatched in power: it holds within it the power not of mere kings but of life and death.

But although it may not be desirable to do away with personal imagery for God, it may still be necessary. How can personal metaphors be credible in our time? Do they not presuppose an external, interventionist understanding of the relationship between God and the world? Many apparently do not think so, for besides a movement during the last two centuries away from the model of personal agency for God there has been a countervailing movement toward it. Hence, another way to see the theological history of the past two centuries is as a movement toward taking the human self and the relationship between the self and the body, as a, if not the, prime model for imaging God and God's relationship to the world. It is not just mystics like Teilhard de Chardin or process theologians like Charles Hartshorne who press this case but a surprising range of theologians from a variety of perspectives. Much of the reason for this shift lies in the current understanding of persons not as substantial individuals, separated from one another and from the world, who enter into relationships of their own choice, but as beings-in-relationship of the most radical and thoroughgoing nature. The model . . . is not of a machine with separate parts relating externally but of an organ with all aspects intrinsically and internally related. The human person is the most complex organ known to us, and it exists as an embodied whole within an incredibly rich organic complex of mutually interrelated and interdependent parts, aspects, and dimensions. To be a person, therefore, is not to be a being related externally to other individual beings but to be part of—and to the best of our knowledge, the most sophisticated, complex, and unified part of—an organic whole that embraces all that is. If, then, we speak of God in personal metaphors, we will not be speaking of a being that is related externally to the world, as, for instance, a king to his realm, but we will be conceiving God on the model of the most complex part of the whole that is the universe—that is, on the model of ourselves. There are several points to make in support of the personal model for the God-world relationship: it is the one we know best; it is the richest; and the kind of activity of God in the world it suggests is both credible in our time and needed by it.

It is perhaps simplistic to put weight on the fact that the personal model is the one we know best, but cases against the model often overlook that fact. It is the only metaphor we know from the inside: there is nothing we can say about God with the help of any other model that has the same credibility to us, because there is no other aspect of the universe that we know in the same way, with the privilege of the insider. The tradition says we are the *imago Dei*, and that inevitably means we imagine God in our image. Presumably, if dolphins or apes have inklings of a higher reality, they imagine it after the model they know best—themselves. That is said not in jest but to bring home why personal metaphors, those modeled on human beings as we understand them today, are suitable for us. Another way to make this point is to consider the alternative to a personal model. Nonpersonal metaphors would be either metaphors from nature (other animals or natural phenomena such as the sun, water, sky, and mountains) or concepts from one or another philosophical tradition (such as "Being-itself," "substance," and "ground of Being"), which at some level are also, of course, metaphorical. We are limited in the ways we can model the God-world relationship, and although we should certainly include a wide range of metaphors from many sources, to exclude the one we know best or to make it secondary to ones we know less well seems foolish.

It would also be unwise for another reason: it is the richest model available to us. This is not anthropocentric hubris but simply a recognition that since we are the most complex, unified creature we know, with what to us are mysterious and fathomless depths, we are the best model. Given the nature of heuristic, metaphorical theology, that is not to say that God *is* a person or that personal language describes or defines God. It is to say, rather, that to speak of God with the aid of or through the screen of such language is better than some other ways of speaking. It is, for instance, more interesting, illuminating, and richer to speak of God as a friend than as a rock, though "A mighty fortress is our God" has a place in talk about God. Its place, however, is a limited one, and the rock metaphor does not begin to suggest the potential for elaboration that the metaphor of a friend does. To speak of God's saving presence in our present only with the help of images about rocks and wind, or with any other natural metaphors, is to overlook the richest source we have—ourselves.

Finally, the strongest argument for personal metaphors in our time is that the current understanding of personal agency allows personal metaphors to reflect a view of God's activity in the world as radically relational, immanental, interdependent, and noninterventionist. Current theological attention to the issue of divine activity in the world is considerable and varied, but there is widespread agreement that the understanding of the self, both in relation to its own body (as embodied self) and in relation to others (as profoundly embedded in and constituted by those others), is a helpful and illuminating model. The evolutionary, organic complex is widely considered the context in which to interpret personal agency—with the agent as part of an intricate causal network that both influences it and is influenced by it—and this allows for an understanding of personal presence credible within the new sensibility. Moreover, it is the model for God's activity in the world that we need today, for to imagine God as the personal presence in the universe who epitomizes personhood, that is, *who has intrinsic relations with all else that exists*, is to possess a highly suggestive model for God's saving presence. If, on the model current today, a person is defined in terms of relationships, then, as Schubert Ogden says, God is "the Thou with the greatest conceivable degree of real relatedness to others—namely, relatedness to *all* others—is for that very reason the most truly absolute Thou any mind can conceive."[2] If personhood is defined in terms of intrinsic relations with others, then to think of God as personal in no sense implies a being separate from other beings who relates externally and distantly to them, in the way that the king-realm personal model suggests. On the contrary, it suggests, I believe, that God is present in and to the world as the kind of other, the kind of Thou, much closer to a mother, lover, or friend than to a king or lord. The intrinsic, interdependent relationships we know most about are also the most intimate, interpersonal ones: they are the ones that begin, support, and nurture life.

This defense of the personal model for understanding the God-world relationship has brought us finally, then, to the issue of the particular metaphors of mother, lover, and friend. If one accepts the personal model, one must ask which personal models are most appropriate for expressing the saving power and presence of God in our time. Although most personal metaphors in the Judeo-Christian tradition have come from the political arena, an understanding of the gospel as a destabilizing, inclusive, nonhierarchical vision of fulfillment for all of creation should look elsewhere. It should look to that level of human experience concerned with the beginnings, continuation, and support of life, the level not of how we govern our lives but of how we live at all and the quality of that life. In an understanding of the gospel for a holistic, nuclear age, when the continuation and the quality of life must be seen as central, we need to return to the most basic realities of existence and to the most basic relationships, for metaphors in which to express that understanding. The symbols of sex, food, water, breath, and blood (all that makes it possible for embodied life to begin and continue) and the relationships of mothers (and fathers), lovers, and friends (those most basic of all relationships, which more than any others contain potential for expressing the most profound fulfillment)—it is from such sources that metaphors for God's saving presence in our time should be drawn.

In particular I would make a case for experimenting in our time with mother, lover, and friend as three models that have been strangely neglected in the Judeo-Christian tradition. All three models represent basic human relationships; indeed, one could say that the three, along with the model of father, represent the most basic human relationships. Hence, if one is going to employ a personal model for God, it makes sense to consider these three seriously. And they have been considered seriously in most religious traditions, for the simple reason that when people are attempting to express the inexpressible, they use what is nearest and dearest to them: they invoke the most important human relationships. One basic human relationship, that of father, has received massive attention in our tradition; the others have been, at best, neglected and, at worst, repressed. There are traces of them in Scripture and the tradition, but they have never become, or been allowed to become, major models.

Yet I hope that it has become evident that, given the kind of understanding of the gospel appropriate for a holistic, nuclear age, they may well be the most illuminating personal metaphors available. In different ways all three models suggest forms of fundamental intimacy, mutuality, and relatedness that could be a rich resource for expressing how in our time life can be supported and fulfilled rather than destroyed. They are all immanental models, in contrast to the radically transcendent models for God in the Western tradition. As we have seen, part of the difficulty with the dominant model of God is its transcendence, a transcendence undergirded by triumphalist, sovereign, patriarchal imagery that contributes to a sense of distance between God and the world. The relatedness of all life, and hence the responsibility of human beings for the fate of the earth, is supported by models of God as mother, lover, and friend of the world.

Moreover, these metaphors project a different view of power, of how to bring about change, than the royal model. It is not the power of control through either domination or benevolence but the power of response and responsibility—the power of love in its various forms (agape, eros, and philia) that operates by persuasion, care, attention, passion, and mutuality. The way of being in the world which these metaphors suggest is close to the way of the cross, the way of radical identification with all which the model of servant once expressed. It is a way of being with others totally different from the way of kings and lords.

A final question remains before we close out the case for personal models and especially for the ones chosen. Are they perhaps too intimate and too individualistic? We have already touched on the issue of intimacy: the more intimate, in the sense of the closer to the most basic realities of human existence, the better. An ascetic strain, however, has kept Christianity from acknowledging the physical and often sexual basis of many of its most powerful symbols, and its wariness in dealing with maternal and erotic language for God arises from this same puritanism. Part of the task of a heuristic theology is to consider what has not been considered, especially if the possibilities for illuminating certain aspects of the God-world relationship are great, as I believe they are in the metaphors of mother and lover. (The model of friend is less problematic in this regard, but as we will see, there have been other reasons for its neglect.)

The charge that these metaphors may be individualistic just at a time when radically relational, inclusive metaphors are needed is a serious one. It would be unanswerable if the metaphors had to be interpreted as suggesting a one-to-one relationship between God and individual human beings. Admittedly, in a context where God's saving power is understood as directed to specific individuals (who are also perceived as independent entities), speaking of God as mother, lover, and friend only accentuates the already particularistic understanding of salvation. But a radically inclusive view of the gospel means that the basic relationship between God and all others cannot be one-to-one; or rather, that it is one-to-one only as it is inclusive of all. The Gospel of John gives the clue: for God so loved the *world.* It is not individuals who are loved by God as mother, lover, and friend but the world. This means that we do not have to interpret these personal metaphors as suggesting a one-to-one relationship between God and individual human beings: we can use the metaphors that have the greatest power and meaning to us in a universal way, and in fact, only as we apply them universally can they also pertain individually. As mother to the world, God mothers each and all: the divine maternal love can be particular only because it is universal. If we understand God's saving presence as directed to the fulfillment of all of creation—with each of us part of that whole—we participate in God's love not as individuals but as members of an organic whole, God's body. Therefore, metaphors that could indeed be individualistic become radically socialized when applied to the world. Moreover, they have the potential for becoming politicized as well, for as the *imago Dei,* we are called to mother, love, and befriend the world, both other human beings and the earth. Whether or not we are in our own personal lives mothers or fathers, or have a lover or even a friend, is not important: these most basic of loves lie deeply within us all. The model of God as mother, lover, and friend of the world presents us with an ethic of response and responsibility toward other human beings and other forms of life, in which our deep parental, erotic, and companionable instincts can be socialized and politicized.

In summary, the personal models for the God-world relationship have been defended as the ones we know best, as the richest, and as credible and needed in our time. The particular metaphors of mother, lover, and friend, which come from the deepest level of life and are concerned with its fulfillment, have been suggested as illuminating possibilities for expressing an inclusive, nonhierarchical understanding of the gospel. It has been claimed that the object of this gospel is not individuals but the world, and it has been proposed that the world—the cosmos or universe—be seen as God's body. We have attempted to imagine the resurrection promise of divine presence—"Lo, I am with you always"—as a worldly reality, as the presence of God in the body of our world. In this, we have imaged God as both caring deeply for that world and calling us to care as well. This imaginative picture is radically different from that of a risen, ascended king in relationship with his realm but remarkably appropriate to an understanding of the story of Jesus of Nazareth as a surprising invitation to the last and the least, expressed in his parables, table fellowship, and cross. That destabilizing, inclusive, nonhierarchical vision of fulfillment can be perceived as continuing when we conceive of the world as God's body to which God is present as mother, lover, and friend of the last and the least in all of creation.

THE LOVE OF GOD AS MOTHER: AGAPE

Hidden away in the third volume of Paul Tillich's *Systematic Theology* is the suggestion that the symbolic dimension of the "ground of being" "points to the mother-quality of giving birth, carrying, and embracing, and, at the same time, of calling back, resisting independence of the created, and swallowing it."[3] He goes on to say that the uneasy feeling that many Protestants have about the first statement about God—that God is the power of being in all being—arises from the fact that their consciousness is shaped by the demanding father image for whom righteousness and not the gift of life is primary. What the father-God gives is redemption from sins; what the mother-God gives is life itself. But there is another reason that one might feel uneasy about Tillich's suggestion, for it implies divine resistance to independence for created being, whereas Western thought has prized its image of independent individuals who are saved one by one, either by their own moral choices or by divine grace. But what if the power in us, that which gives us our very existence, is not primarily judging individuals but calling us back, wanting to be more fully united with us, or as Tillich graphically puts it, wanting to "swallow" us? Our first reaction is fear of the maternal maw and a cry that we are independent; owing nothing to anyone, ready to face the consequences of our own actions.

But Tillich's symbolic suggestion for imaging the ground of being, the depths of divinity, as mother-love, which both gives life to all and desires reunification with all life, is helpful as we attempt to answer the question of the kind of love implied in the model of God as mother. We have characterized this love as agape, but that designation needs considerable qualification since the usual understanding of agape sees it as totally unmotivated, disinterested love. Obviously, if God as the power of being, God as mother, calls us back and wants to be reunited with us, her love is not totally disinterested. But one must ask, why should we *want* it to be? The discussions on the nature of divine love, principally in Protestant circles and principally motivated by the desire to expunge any trace of need or interest on the part of God toward creation, paint a picture of God as isolated from creation and in no way dependent on it. As C. S. Lewis says, God is "at home in the land of the Trinity," presumably finding relations with the other "persons" sufficiently satisfying so that, needing nothing, God "loves into existence wholly superfluous creatures."[4] Discussions about agape as definitive of divine love have, unfortunately, usually focused on redemption, not creation, and as a result have stressed the disinterested character of God's love, which can overlook the sin in the sinners and love them anyway. In other words, even though we are worthless, we are loved—but disinterestedly. Needless to say, this is a sterile and unattractive view of divine love and a view that most of us would not settle for even as a description of human love. If, among ourselves, we want to be loved not in spite of who we are but because in some sense we are valuable, desirable, and needed, then is this not the case also with divine love? If God's creative love is agapic love, then is it not a statement to created beings: "It is good that you exist!"?[5] Agape has been characterized as the love that gives (usually in contrast with eros as the love that takes), and as such it belongs with the gift of life, creation. If it is considered in that context instead of the context of redemption, it need not be disinterested; in fact, it should not be.

As "interested," divine agape cannot be isolated from the other forms of love, eros and philia. If, with Tillich, one understands love as the "moving power of life," as that "which drives everything that is towards everything else that is," then elements of need, desire, and mutuality are evident in all forms of love.[6] An understanding of love as unifying and reuniting is basic to an interpretation of Christian faith as destabilizing, inclusive, nonhierarchical fulfillment for all. It is the love that underscores the interdependence of life in all its forms, the desire to be with other beings in both their needs and their joy. Nonetheless, the *depth* of divine love can be characterized as agapic, for the distinctive feature of this love is its impartiality, its willing of existence and fulfillment for all being.

God as the giver of life, as the power of being in all being, can be imaged through the metaphor of mother—and of father. Parental love is the most powerful and intimate experience we have of giving love whose return is not calculated (though a return is appreciated): it is the gift of *life as such* to others. Parental love wills life and when it comes, exclaims, "It is good that you exist!" Moreover, in addition to being the gift of life, parental love nurtures what it has brought into existence, wanting growth and fulfillment for all. This agapic love is revolutionary, for it loves the weak and vulnerable as well as the strong and beautiful. No human love can, of course, be perfectly just and impartial, but parental love is the best metaphor we have for imaging the creative love of God.

An important caveat is necessary at this point: the parental model in its siding with life as such is not "pro-life" in the sense of being antiabortion. This is the case because of two features of our model: it is concerned with all species, not just human beings (and not with individuals in any species), and it is concerned with the nurture and fulfillment of life, not just with birth. On the first point: whereas we as biological or adoptive parents are interested in only one species—our own—and with particular individuals within that species, God as the mother of the universe is interested in all forms of life. One indication of human pride is our colossal ego in imagining that of the millions of forms of life in the universe, we are the only ones that matter. Why should our birth, nurture, and fulfillment be the only concern of the power that gives life to all life? God as mother, on the side of life as such, does not therefore mean on the side of only one species or on the side of every individual human birth (or every individual birth in any other species). This first point on the goodness of creation, "It is good that you exist!" must be followed immediately by the second: the household or economy of the universe must be ordered and managed in a way so as to bring about the nurture and fulfillment of life—and again, this cannot mean every individual life that could be brought into existence. In a closed ecological system with limits on natural resources, difficult decisions must be made to insure the continuation, growth, and fulfillment of the many forms of life (not just one form and not all its individuals). Population control, both for our own species and other species, is one such decision. The balance between quantity and quality of life is one that a contemporary sensibility must keep to the forefront. To be on the side of life means participating in the decisions necessary to keep that balance. It cannot mean being "pro-life" in terms of one species or in terms of unlimited numbers, for such a perspective would in the long run mean being against life in its many and varied forms.

Let us now consider our model in more detail: the model of parental love for God's agapic, creative love. Why is this a powerful, attractive model for expressing the Christian faith in our time? If the heart of Christian faith for an ecological, nuclear age must be profound awareness of the preciousness and vulnerability of life as a gift we receive and pass on, with appreciation for its value and desire for its fulfillment, it is difficult to think of any metaphors more apt than the parental one. There are three features basic to the parental model, which will give flesh to this statement: it brings us closest to the beginnings of life, to the nurture of life, and to the impartial fulfillment of life.

Much of the power in the parental model is its immediate connection with the mystery of new life. Becoming a biological parent is the closest experience most people have to an experience of creation, that is, of bringing into existence. No matter how knowledgeable one is biologically, no matter how aware that human beings by becoming parents are simply doing what all animals do in passing life along, becoming a biological parent is for most people an awesome experience, inspiring feelings of having glimpsed the heart of things. We are, after all, the only creatures who can think about the wonder of existence, the sheer fact that "things are," that the incredible richness and complexity of life in all its forms has existed for millions of years, and that as part of the vast, unfathomable network of life, we both receive it from others and pass it along. At the time of the birth of new life from our bodies, we feel a sense of being co-creators, participating at least passively in the great chain of being. No matter how trite and hackneyed the phrases have become—"the miracle of birth," "the wonder of existence," and so on—on becoming a parent one repeats them again and again and joins the millions of others who marvel at their role in passing life along.

There are other ways of being parental besides being a biological parent, and I want to stress this point at the outset, because much of the case for the models of mother (father), lover, and friend rests on their extensions beyond their physical and immediate base. One can, of course, be an adoptive parent as well as a biological one, but even more important for our purposes is that all human beings have parental inclinations. All human beings have the potential for passing life along, for helping to bring the next generation (of whatever kind of beings) into existence, nurturing and guiding it, and working toward its fulfillment. These tendencies are so basic, widespread, and various that it is difficult to catalogue all the ways they are expressed. Some of the ways that come most readily to mind, such as in teaching, medicine, gardening, and social work, are only the tip of the iceberg, for in almost any cultural, political, economic, or social activity, there are aspects of the work that could be called parental.

Having made this point, however, let us return to the base of the model, in the physical act of giving birth. It is from this base that the model derives its power, for here it joins the reservoir of the great symbols of life and of life's continuity: blood, water, breath, sex, and food. In the acts of conception, gestation, and birth all are involved, and it is therefore no surprise that these symbols became the center of most religions, including Christianity, for they have the power to express the renewal and transformation of life—the "second birth"—because they are the basis of our "first birth." And yet, at least in

Christianity, our first birth has been strangely neglected; another way of saying this is that creation, the birth of the world and all its beings, has not been permitted the imagery that this tradition uses so freely for the transformation and fulfillment of creation. Why is this case?

One reason is surely that Christianity, alienated as it always has been from female sexuality, has been willing to image the second, "spiritual," renewal of existence in the birth metaphor, but not the first, "physical," coming into existence. In fact, as we shall see, in the Hebraic-Christian tradition, creation has been imaginatively pictured as an intellectual, aesthetic "act" of God, accomplished through God's word and wrought by God's "hands" much as a painting is created by an artist or a form by a sculptor. But the model of God as mother suggests a very different kind of creation, one in keeping with the world as God's body but not one that the central tradition has been willing to consider. And it is clearly the parent as mother that is the stronger candidate for an understanding of creation as bodied forth from the divine being, for it is the imagery of gestation, giving birth, and lactation that creates an imaginative picture of creation as profoundly dependent on and cared for by divine life. There simply is no other imagery available to us that has the power for expressing the interdependence and interrelatedness of all life with its ground. All of us, female and male, have the womb as our first home, all of us are born from the bodies of our mothers, all of us are fed by our mothers. What better imagery could there be for expressing the most basic reality of existence: that we live and move and have our being in God?

If the symbol of birth were allowed openly and centrally into the tradition, would this involve a radical theological change? Would it mean a different understanding of God's relation to the world? . . . [T]he simple answer is yes, the view associated with birth symbolism would be different from the distant, anthropocentric view in the monarchical model: it would be an intimate view, inclusive of the cosmos, but not one that identifies God and the world. By analogy, mothers, at least good ones, encourage the independence of their offspring, and even though children are products of their parents' bodies, they are often radically different from them.

The power of the parental model for God's creative, agapic love only begins with the birth imagery. Of equal importance is the ability of the model to express the nurturing of life and, to a lesser extent, its impartial fulfillment. It is at these levels that the more complex theological and ethical issues arise, for the divine agapic love that nurtures all creatures is a model of justice at the most basic level of the fair distribution of the necessities of life, and divine agapic love impartially fulfilling all creation is a model of *inclusive* justice. In our understanding of Christianity as a destabilizing, inclusive, nonhierarchical vision of fulfillment for all, the parental model of God is especially pertinent as a way of talking about God's "just" love, the love that attends to the most basic needs of all creatures. It is important to look more closely at the way the model expresses the nurture and inclusion of all of life.

Parents feed the young. This is, across the entire range of life, the most basic responsibility of parents, often of fathers as well as of mothers. Among most animals it is instinctual and is often accomplished only at the cost of the health or life of the parent. It is not principally from altruistic motives that parents feed the young but from a base close to the one that brought new life into existence, the source that participates in passing life along. With human parents, the same love that says, "It is good that you exist!" desires that existence to continue, and for many parents in much of the world that is a daily and often horrendous struggle. There is, perhaps, no picture more powerful to express "giving" love than that of parents wanting, but not having the food, to feed their starving children.

The Christian tradition has paid a lot of attention to food and eating imagery. In fact, one could say that such imagery is probably at the center of the tradition's symbolic power: not only does the New Testament portrait of Jesus of Nazareth paint him as constantly feeding people, and eating with outcasts, but the church has as its central ritual a eucharistic meal reminiscent of the passion and death of Jesus and suggestive of the eschatological banquet yet to come. Christianity may be reticent in regard to birth imagery, especially as associated with natural, female processes, but it has shown no comparable reluctance to use the experience of eating as a symbol of spiritual nourishment. In fact, as many have pointed out, the Christian Eucharist has obvious overtones of cannibalism! But the power of the food imagery is precisely in not fearing the physical connection, for the use of food as a symbol of the renewal of life must be grounded in food's basic role as the maintainer of life. Unfortunately, however, although the power of food imagery has been preserved in Christianity, the practical truth that food is basic to all life has often been neglected. A tradition that uses food as a symbol of spiritual renewal has often forgotten what parents know so well: that the young must be fed.

A theology that sees God as the parent who feeds the young and, by extension, the weak and vulnerable understands God as caring about the most basic needs of life in its struggle to continue. One can extend nurture to include much more than attention to physical needs, but one ought not move too quickly, for the concern about life and its continuation that is a basic ingredient in the sensibility needed in our time has too often been neglected by

Christianity in its interest in "spiritual" well-being. An evolutionary, ecological sensibility makes no clear distinction between matter and spirit or between body and mind, for life is a continuum and cannot flourish at the so-called higher levels unless supported at all levels. God as parent loves agapically in giving, with no thought of return, the sustenance needed for life to continue. This is creative love, for it provides the conditions minimally necessary for life to go on.

Finally, God as parent wants *all* to flourish. Divine agapic love is inclusive and hence a model of impartial justice. This is a difficult point to make without falling back into the old view of agape as disinterested; moreover, parental love can model the impartiality of divine love only in a highly qualified way. Yet it is central to the essence of agapic love to stress that it is impartial, or as I would prefer to say, inclusive. This is a better way to express what is at stake than to call the love disinterested, which suggests that God's love is detached, unconcerned, or perfunctory. In fact, the opposite is intended, for agapic love functions in spite of obstacles and in this way can be love of *all*, whatever the barriers may be. God as mother is parent to *all* species and wishes all to flourish. We can reflect this inclusiveness in the model of parent only in partial and distorted fashion, for as parents we tend by instinct to focus on our own species and on particular individuals within that species. To be sure, when we extend the model beyond its physical base to include our parental inclinations toward human children not our own, as well as toward life forms not our own, a measure of impartiality, of inclusiveness, emerges, but only as a faint intimation of divine agape. It is imperative to recognize when a model falters. This one falters here.

With most recent understandings of agape, however, our model would have faltered long ago, for if divine love is seen as totally different from all forms of love that we know, as entirely "giving" whereas human love is only "taking," no human love will serve as a metaphor for God's love. But we have maintained that dimensions of divine agapic love, especially those involved in the creating and sustaining of life, can be modeled with great power by parental love. What this model or any model cannot do is express the mystery that *all* are included, even the last and the least.

THE ACTIVITY OF GOD AS LOVER: SAVING

One of the most impressive features of the Judeo-Christian tradition is its understanding of sin and evil. Often more convincing than its proposed solutions to these issues is its analysis of them. One way to characterize the classic Christian analysis of sin and evil is as anthropological, radical, and tragic: human beings, while not responsible for all the evil in the cosmos, are responsible for much of it, yet even their sin, as far-reaching as it is, cannot account for the profoundly tragic character of existence. In other words, the classical view underscores the deeply ambivalent situation that most sensitive people acknowledge: that the magnitude of human evil both private and public is enormous, but that it occurs in a situation so flawed that one feels as much victim as perpetrator. It is Christianity's acknowledgment of the mystery surrounding the issues of sin and evil—that they are in the final analysis beyond our comprehension and our ability to redress—that continues to be persuasive.

An understanding of sin and evil within the context of our model of God as lover of the world will not only retain but deepen this classical perspective. For the world God loves and finds valuable, and would have us love and find valuable, is an incredibly complex ecological whole that even if we want to love it rightly, we often do not know how to. The sheer immensity of the household of God, the unfathomable number of phenomena that need to be kept in some sort of balance, means that the ancient notion of a flawed universe in which evil powers and principalities operate takes on new significance. We realize that, even when we are motivated by the best of intentions, our efforts to be sensitive to the needs of some parts of God's body, some species of flora and fauna, will inevitably mean the deterioration and demise of others. We exist in a no-win situation, in a way that an ecological sensibility brings home to us more profoundly than an individualistic one does: one can imagine that certain (elect) individuals will be saved—and can hope that one is part of that company—but when the vision of salvation is an inclusive one of fulfillment for all, it is evident that many individuals and some species will be sacrificed for others. There is, then, a tragic aspect to our model: if we see ourselves and every other creature as parts of the body of God and if we see that body as the universe in all its complexity which has evolved over eons of unrecorded and recorded time, then we will realize that, whatever salvation means, it must take into account the organic solidarity of our actual situation. We cannot be loved apart from that state of affairs, and given its immensity, complexity, and intricacy, not all phenomena can reach the same degree of fulfillment, since many will have to suffer or to be sacrificed for others. Far from being a sentimental view, the model of God as lover, as understood in an ecological context, is painfully tough-minded. One is reminded of Jonathan Edwards's notion of the "consent to being," an acknowledgment that one's own puny existence is not the center of things, for each of us is part of a scheme so awesome, mysterious, and enormous that, at a profound level, we can only "consent" to the state of things.

If the ecological context produces a deepening of the situation in which human sin occurs, the nuclear threat does so even more. To live permanently with nuclear knowledge, with the knowledge forever of how to destroy ourselves and other life, is to go beyond the temptation the serpent in the garden of Eden offered human beings. He told them they could be "like God, knowing good and evil" (Gen. 3:5b). Nuclear knowledge, the special serpent of our time, tempts us to be like God not merely by knowing good and evil but by exercising ultimate power over good and evil. We have a tempter no other generation has had: we face the temptation to end life, to be the un-creators of life in inverted imitation of our creator. Like the serpent in the garden, nuclear power is simply part of nature, simply there as a part of the complex. In itself it is neither good nor evil, and yet as a temptation to human self-aggrandizement, it strikes *us* as evil. We wish it were not there: the knowledge that this temptation will always be in our garden, threatening to ruin it if we even once give in to its lure, makes us aware as perhaps nothing else can that our situation is a tragic one in which we are victims as well as perpetrators. We find our situation to be unfair. The cards are stacked against us, and we feel certain to fail. It is difficult to imagine a symbol more powerful than nuclear knowledge for the human dilemma as understood classically in the Christian tradition. According to this tradition, human beings are responsible for sin, for refusing to accept their place, for wanting to be like God, yet the temptation to exceed one's place is a constant, attractive lure that so invades existence that it appears inevitable that we succumb. The threat of a nuclear holocaust symbolizes the ultimate sin of which human beings are capable. That we are truly capable of such sin is manifest in the other holocaust, the Jewish one. We stand between these two holocausts, which witness to the depths of human evil and illuminate the nature of sin as such: it is the desire to be like God, with control over good and evil, life and death.

Granted that the situation we inhabit is flawed and tragic, granted that we feel victimized, is there not also, in most of us in our more honest moments, a sense of responsibility? Responsibility for what and to whom? Here we take exception to the classical view of sin, for the answer to these questions in the Augustinian-Thomistic synthesis is that we are responsible for turning away from God in pride and unbelief. The picture of the universe in which this turning-away and centering on the self occur is a hierarchical, dualistic one, in which one should order one's allegiance, the direction of one's will, toward God and away from the world since things temporal and physical are inferior to things eternal and spiritual. Sin is understood as operating against God, the highest being and source of all being, and as involving other beings only to the extent that one loves them rightly or wrongly—rightly if they are loved as means to one's own salvation, and wrongly if they are loved for their own sake. One uses but does not enjoy the things of this world; to enjoy the world is to turn away from God and find satisfaction in the world.

From the perspective of our model of God as lover of the world, it is obvious why this description of sin is lacking. Nonetheless, within a nonhierarchal, holistic ontological context, it can be interpreted with fresh power. That is, in the context of our model, sin is the turning-away not from a transcendent power but from interdependence with all other beings, including the matrix of being from whom all life comes. It is not pride or unbelief but the refusal of relationship—the refusal to be the beloved of our lover God and the refusal to be lover of all God loves. It is the retention of hierarchies, dualisms, and outcasts so as to retain the superiority of the self. It is a horizontal refusal to be part of the body of God rather than a vertical refusal to be inferior to God. Nonetheless, there is much that unites the classical view and the present revision, most especially in the notion that sin is a turning of the self that disrupts the right balance of things. In the classical view, the balance was conceived hierarchically and dualistically, whereas in our model it is understood ecologically and holistically. But in both cases it is the "inordinate desire" of the self (what the tradition has called concupiscence) that disrupts the balance. In other words, it is love gone awry: the deepest desire in all life for union with everything else that is—the love symbolized by sexual union—is now perverted into self-love. What in the nature of our being was meant to be our direction toward unity with others is given an about-face in the love of self. Concupiscence, intense desire, becomes the desire of the self for the self rather than the desire to be united with other beings. Desire gets out of hand: the passion that is attracted to others as valuable and lovable turns its direction inward, narcissistically loving the self, refusing the relationality that in our model of God as the lover of the world is the nature of things.

By refusing the balance of radical interdependence, we, the only conscious ones among the beloved—the ones responsible in special ways—disrupt the ontological order and threaten life itself. The extent of our freedom to do this and of our power to disrupt the order of things is only too evident in our oppression of others owing to gender, race, or class, and in the genocide of other peoples, the deterioration of the ecosphere, and the threat of nuclear disaster. It would be difficult to find a better illustration of Augustine's view of sin as engendering chaos in all dimensions and aspects of life than we find in our present situation. We continue to stress the flawed, tragic context in which sin occurs; nonetheless, much of what we call evil does stem from human selfishness, from the desire of the self for the self, from the refusal to direct one's passion, one's innate drive toward unity, outward toward others. What results is estrangement and alienation, the wounding of the body of God, the fragmenting of relationships, the refusal of interdependence. Hierarchies, dualisms, and outcasts become the norm: the inclusive vision of fulfillment for all is perverted beyond all recognition.

But is God, then, not in some sense responsible for the horrendous evil that has already occurred in evolutionary and in human history, and for that which lies ahead, including the possible extinction of life? In a monist ontology, one has to give a qualified yes to the question: since there is no evil power comparable to God, God is in some sense responsible for the worst that happens in the cosmos. But qualifications are crucial. First, the universe is, as an evolutionary phenomenon, so immense and complex, with so many constituent phenomena interrelating in so many ways, that evil is a relative concept. What is evil to some species, what diminishes or destroys them, is good to other species, for it brings them satisfaction and fulfillment. This is a modern version of what has been called the Augustinian theodicy, in which the aesthetic panorama of the whole justifies the sacrifice of some of the parts. God is the artist of the universe and alone can see the beauty of the whole. The Augustinian theodicy is implicit in God's answer to Job: "Where were you when I laid the foundation of the earth?" (Job 38:4a). This rhetorical answer introduces a list of the wonders of the divine artistry, of which Job is but a puny part. To defend in this way God's part in the world's evil may be intellectually and aesthetically satisfying, but it is a cold, unfeeling defense, which makes one feel that God is not involved and does not care about the suffering of her creation. Nonetheless, when translated into an evolutionary context this explanation of evil underscores the unfathomable complexity of the cosmic whole in which good for some will inevitably mean evil for others. It also cautions us against special pleading for oneself or one's kind—as for instance, in thanking God that one has escaped a disaster that befell others.

The second qualification of God's responsibility for evil recognizes human freedom. We are responsible for a great deal of the evil, but says the Irenaean theodicy, the experience of evil is educational. God in this theodicy is not the artist but the educator who is slowly forming us through many trials to enter into fuller fellowship with him. We are the children being trained for a greater future through the evils that befall us. The price is high, that is, the inevitable misuse of our freedom, but the alternative is to be puppets on a string, pets in a cage, creatures with no freedom. God's caring involvement with us is more obvious here than in the Augustinian theodicy, for God can be seen to identify with the pains of growth. This model of theodicy also has clear evolutionary overtones, allowing for change and transformation. Its tendency, however, is toward an easy optimism and sense of progress which neither contemporary evolutionary theory nor contemporary events—witness our two holocausts—support.

Therefore, although acknowledging the value of both the artist and the educator versions of theodicy—that, indeed, the complexity of the whole and the reality of human freedom qualify God's responsibility for evil—the lover model of theodicy offers something more. God as lover suffers with those who suffer. God was not in the Nazi death camps, but they are in God. God as lover is totally opposed to such monstrous treatment of the beloved and has no part in it (apart from having created the world in which it occurred and the creatures with free will who perpetrated it). When such events occur, God participates in the pain of the beloved as only a lover can. God as lover takes the suffering into her own being; God feels the pain in his own body in an immediate and total way. God as lover cannot be aloof like the artist nor identify at a distance like the educator but will be totally, passionately involved in the agony of the evil that befalls the beloved. God's involvement with the world in its struggles with evil will embody passion as both deep feeling and suffering. Does such identification, such caring, justify the evil? No, and any theodicy that attempts a justification succeeds only to the extent that it sacrifices the persuasive ambivalence and the grounding in experienced reality of the classical Christian view of sin and evil. But the model of God as lover offers something perhaps more important than a defense of God: it offers the presence of God to the suffering beloved. We do not suffer alone. Does suffering, then, characterize the presence of God as lover of the world? Is salvation achieved merely through God's suffering with us? Such sharing is the passive side of passion and is the last, not the first, stance toward sin and evil. The first stance is one of resistance, active efforts to heal, make whole, mend the body that has been torn by hierarchies, dualisms, and outcasts. The understanding of salvation in the model of God as lover differs in significant ways from the reigning classical model of Jesus Christ, who by his substitutionary, sacrificial death makes amends for our sins, the benefits of which amends we receive through the preached word of forgiveness and the sacraments. Our understanding of salvation will differ in terms of *who* brings it about, *what* its nature is, and *how* it is received.

In the classical view Jesus acts alone. What occurs, the atoning act, takes place for all time and for all people in one individual who represents and includes all other individuals. Just as all sinned in Adam, all are saved in Christ—so the reasoning goes. But this kind of thinking makes little sense in our day. The kind of solidarity that is ingredient in an ecological, evolutionary perspective is not the kind found in substantialist Greek thinking. There the idea is that we share a human "substance" and hence can participate ontologically in an atonement wrought by one divine individual two thousand years ago. The kind of solidarity ingredient in the model of God as lover set in a holistic context is different: it is the solidarity of the body of God which in different ways and in different times can manifest God's love. In other words, who does the work of salvation is spread out, and it is work that must be done again and again. Salvation is not a once-for-all objective service that someone else does for us. Rather, it is the ongoing healing of the divided body of our world which we, with God, work at together. This, as I have already suggested, does not preclude special, paradigmatic manifestations of God's love: Jesus of Nazareth is certainly such a manifestation for Christians. But the kind of solidarity implicit in the model of God as lover in an ecological, evolutionary context does not allow the work of one individual to be effective for all space and time. We must all be involved in the work of salvation, and it must be ongoing.

In the model of God as lover, what that work is differs also from what it is on the classical view. The several versions of the classical view share a common presupposition: that atonement is made for sins. The stress is on sins, individually committed against God, for which some sort of amendment must be made before reconciliation can occur between God and human beings. We have already said that the classical view is individualistic and anthropocentric; we now add that it sees salvation as basically a negative event, with the focus on what has gone wrong. Salvation in the model of God as lover is not individualistic, anthropocentric, or negative; rather, it is holistic, inclusive, and positive, for the heart of salvation in this view is the making manifest of God's great love for the world. God as lover values the world and all its creatures so passionately and totally that God enters into the beloved, becoming one with them. From time to time we *see* God in these beloved ones, working and suffering to overcome the divisions and heal the wounds of selfish sinfulness and tragic evil. The work of salvation is first of all the illumination that all of us are loved by God with the greatest love we can imagine—the love that loves us not in spite of who we are but because of who we are. The work of salvation is, in this model, the address not to a sinner but to the beloved; it assumes that the beloved is not evil but is loving wrongly, loving the self rather than God in the body of the world. It assumes that the first work toward making the body whole again is the revelation we could not imagine on our own: we are loved, loved deeply and passionately, by the power whose love pulses through the universe. What this knowledge does is what the announcement of the lover to the beloved at its best always does: it calls forth a response in kind. The beloved, feeling valuable, wants to return the love, wants to be at one with the lover.

The beloved in our model, we recall, is not this or that individual human being but the world: different phenomena in the world will have different ways of responding to the love of God. Our way is twofold: we are aware, through the illumination of God's great love for us, of a redirection of our love away from self and toward others in the beloved world, and we feel energized to work to overcome alienation, to heal wounds, to include the outcasts. One sees this twofold pattern of awareness of the depths of divine love, and active participation in love's inclusive, healing work, in the destabilizing inclusive, nonhierarchical life and death of Jesus of Nazareth. And one sees it as well in the lives and the deaths of others.

We may be inclined to ask, Is this enough? Is not the classical, objective understanding of redemption from sin and evil more satisfying? Does not the classical view with its assertion that God took the sins of the world upon himself once and for all, did battle with the powers of evil and won, make a stronger claim? Yes, that view may be more satisfying and make a stronger claim, but it is simply irrelevant to an understanding of sin and evil in an ecological, nuclear age. It is also part of an outmoded mythology. The sins we must deal with are not the sort that can be atoned for and forgotten; they are daily, present refusals, by all of us some of the time and some of us all of the time, to acknowledge the radical relationality and interdependence of all God's beloved with one another. Likewise, the evil we must deal with, epitomized in our systemic structures of oppression due to race, class, and gender, as well as the deterioration of the ecosphere and the monstrous escalation of nuclear weaponry, will not disappear through God's having "conquered" it in battle. We live with sin and evil that derive principally (though not totally) from ourselves and that are directed against others of our own kind of being as well as of other kinds. What is needed then is renovation on two fronts: on the springs of our own action, and on the devastation that our misdirected action has brought about. In other words, we need to become disciples of Jesus of Nazareth, become lovers of the world and healers of its wounds.

We come finally to how salvation is received or made effective. In the classical view, focused on an atoning event for human beings which occurred two thousand years ago, salvation is available through the preached word and the sacraments. In the preached word, individuals hear that their sins have been forgiven through Christ's death and resurrection, and in the sacraments, the forgiving word takes visible shape in the symbolic acts of baptism and the eucharist. For an understanding of the salvation that must be the present work of all the beloved working with the lover to overcome the painful estrangements in the body, the classical view of how salvation is made effective is not, however, persuasive.

In our model of God as lover, salvation is not something received so much as it is something performed: it is not something that happens to us so much as something we participate in. The lover loves the beloved, and wants and expects a response. In this model of salvation, it is not sufficient to be loved; it is necessary also to love. This implies a very close relationship between soteriology and ethics: that we are made whole only as we participate in the process of making whole. We participate, then, in our own salvation. This would, perhaps, be a heresy from the perspective of classical atonement theories, where it would mean that individuals helped to save themselves, but in the context of the model of God as lover of the world, it means that we are loved and saved only as we love and work to save the world. Salvation, as always, is a "matter of life and death," but now it is the life and death of the whole body of the world that is at stake, rather than the eternal life of some individuals after death. What is needed on this view of salvation is not the forgiveness of sins so that the elect may achieve their reward, but a *metanoia*—a conversion or change of sensibility, a new orientation at the deepest level of our being—from one concerned with our own salvation apart from the world to one directed toward the well-being, the health, of the whole body of the world. Salvation, then, is not a "second work" of God; it belongs intrinsically to the "first work," creation. Salvation is a deepening of creation: it says to all, even to the last and the least, not only, "It is good that you exist!" but also, "You are valuable beyond all knowing, all imagining." The saviors of the world are lovers of the world.

THE ETHIC OF GOD AS FRIEND: COMPANIONSHIP

One of the traditional images for the Christian church is as the "body of Christ." But . . . we have spoken of the world, the cosmos, as God's body, finding that this metaphor brought out the inclusive character of God's presence both to all human beings and to all forms of life. Thus, when we turn to the specific community and the mode of existence intrinsic to it that are identified with Jesus of Nazareth, the limitations of the image of the church as the body of Christ must be acknowledged. The community of Jesus' followers is not the body of God, it is not the universal community implicitly embracing all, but it is rather one way that this body, our world, is cared for and loved. This particular way is characterized by a vision of destabilizing, nonhierarchical, inclusive fulfillment, epitomized in the shared meal in which hospitality is extended to all outsiders. This is a specific vision of salvation, the characteristic notes of which suggest that an appropriate way to speak of those united by this vision is as a "community of friends" or, more precisely, a "fellowship of the friends of Jesus."[7] Such a community is obviously modeled not on the elitist, separatist view of friendship, as suggested by the church as the "communion of saints" but on the solidarity view, as epitomized in Jesus' table fellowship. To be friends of Jesus, in this sense, means to stand with him and with all others united by and committed to the common vision embodied in the shared meal extended to the outsider. It means choosing, freely and out of a sense of joy, to be friends of the world one likes and wishes to see fulfilled. It means being willing, as an adult, to join in mutual responsibility with God and others for the well-being of this world. It means being to it as a mother and father, a lover, and a friend. It means welcoming different others and many others into the community, for such a friendship is not limited to the like-minded few: it invites and needs all who share the vision.

What creates this friendship is the common vision: in this model of fellowship, God and human beings are both friends of the world. In an ecological, nuclear era, salvation must mean this; hence, the friendship is not between two—God and individual human beings—but between all those who are united by love for the world. As with the models of God as mother and lover, so with the model of friend, what appear to be individualistic images for the relationship between God and the world become universalized when the world, and not specific human beings, is seen as the focus of divine love.

Let us now look more specifically at two ways in which this fellowship of the friends of Jesus, this companionship of those who share meals with all, is especially pertinent as a mode of existence in an ecological, nuclear time. The first is in respect of what we shall call fear of others; the second, care for others. As to the first: One way to characterize the mentality promoting the escalation of nuclear weapons is as extreme xenophobia, a fear of the stranger, the other, the outsider. That such fear is deep within all of us, human and nonhuman, is well illustrated by animal territorial patterns and by our national boundaries. If friendly feelings are intrinsic to human beings, unfriendly ones certainly are as well. Many in fact believe that unfriendly feelings are more intrinsic, since a case can be made that evolutionary survival depends not on cooperation but on superiority of various kinds. Whatever may be the case with this hotly debated issue, it is difficult to think of a more precise symbol for xenophobia than a nuclear holocaust. In such an occurrence, all others would be extinguished, including, ironically, the like-minded who feared the others. It is suicidal xenophobia: such fear of the stranger that one wills the end of all existence, including one's own. The seriousness of xenophobia in our time can scarcely be overstated: the fact that we live in a global village and must accept that fact if we are to survive does not, unfortunately, mean that we will accept it or even that we know how to accept it in significant ways. It is not the task of a heuristic theology to deal with the complex technical, economic, political, and social dimensions of reducing xenophobia, but it is its task to offer contrary models. The inclusive character of the Christian vision, epitomized in the shared meal with the outcast and stranger—the image of the church as the community of friends—is a powerful countermodel to xenophobia. It focuses on exclusion as the heart of the problem, insisting that what we fear most and apparently are willing to kill and die for, namely, the outsider, is not necessarily the enemy but is rather only the stranger. What Greek culture recognized in the reversal of host and guest (that we all are potential strangers) and what Christian culture claims in befriending the stranger (that God is also present in such occurrences) suggest that the willingness to risk such encounters is central to overcoming xenophobia. Openness to the different, the unexpected, the strange, an openness that identifies with the outsider as embodying a condition common to all and that is receptive to possible value in such encounters, can be seen as the negative side of our model to counter xenophobia. It merely suggests that strangers need not be enemies, that in a sense we are all strangers, and that when we risk encounters with strangers, surprising things can happen. In its negative work, the model raises the question whether exclusion is necessary or beneficial.

The positive side of the model of the community of friends concerns care for others. In an ecological, nuclear age, the decline of xenophobia is not sufficient; in addition, a new kind of community needs to be built, and the work of heuristic theology in this task is at the level of helping to form the sensibility necessary for the task. The sensibility is an inclusive one, and the term "companionship," which embraces many levels of friendly fellowship, including advocacy and partnership, is a good one for the range of care for others needed in the new kind of community. The shared meal of friends with outsiders of the Christian community is one form of an inclusive sensibility, but an inclusive sensibility is by no means solely the possession of Christians. Many cultures, especially those modeled on an organic image, have a version of it. An interesting case is found in the notion of civic friendship in Greek political life. According to Aristotle, there is political bonding that is mutual well-wishing and well-doing by and for all citizens. There is reciprocal benefit in such civic bonding, to be sure, but it emerges out of warmth and attachment and not just from a sense of cold justice. In fact, in Aristotle's view, if friendship is present among citizens, the claims of justice become greater, for citizens who live in mutual well-wishing are not satisfied with a notion of justice as mere fairness and legality but insist on much more for a truly just society. Thus, friendship has been called the "soul of socialism," giving the inside to justice, and justice has been seen as the outside of friendship, insuring that neither special interests nor preferential treatment dominates.[8] In a truly socialized society the assumption is that citizens should conduct themselves toward one another not just in terms of rectitude but also in terms of friendship. One can see in civic friendship expansion of the host-guest bond: "The city which forgets how to care for the stranger has forgotten how to care for itself."[9]

Our model of the church as a community of friends united by a common vision of fulfillment for all can also be seen as the product of an inclusive sensibility. Beginning with the image of a shared meal open to outsiders, it expands to include the entire cosmos in its circle of care. What is evident in both the Greek and Christian instances is a deprivatization of friendship: what is usually seen as a personal relationship between two (or a few) is politicized and becomes a model for public policy. Although some would prefer to keep friendship as a private and indeed romantic relationship, unconcerned and uninvolved with public matters, the qualities that we have found to be present in solidarity friendship are far too important to be relegated to the fringes of life. Of all human loves, philia is the most free, the most reciprocal, the most adult, the most joyful, the most inclusive. Its range, from best friend to partner, as well as the depths we uncovered through an analysis of its paradoxes, reveals it to be eminently suited to participate in the formation of a new sensibility for the conduct of our public life and not just for our private pleasure. Thus, when we speak of the kind of care for the world that our model suggests, we extend the model (as we did with the mother model, in elaborating the idea of universal parenthood, and with the lover model, in elaborating the idea of fellow feeling) and suggest that to befriend the world is to be its companion—its advocate and partner. In the solidarity view of friendship that we have promoted, private versus public is not a relevant division, for hospitality to the stranger, though ostensibly a private event, is in both its Greek and Christian forms implicitly and intrinsically public. For, once the door has been opened to the other, the different, the stranger one does not know, it has been opened to the world. All can become companions together, sharing the bread of life with one another in an atmosphere of both justice and concern. Both justice and friendship, both advocacy and partnership, then, are aspects of companionship. To participate in the ongoing, sustaining work of God as friend of the world means, as the word "sustain" suggests, to support the world, to be its companion, both as advocate for its needs and as partner in its joys and sufferings. What we are suggesting, therefore, is that the notion of companion of the world, modeled on God as the sustaining friend of the world, comprises being with the world in two ways: as an advocate fighting for just treatment for the world's many forms of life, and as a partner identifying with all the others. Both aspects of this public model of a "companionable sensibility" are extensions of hospitality to the stranger: they represent the just provision of necessities, epitomized in the shared meal, in an atmosphere of fellowship and concern.

Is such a sensibility possible as our public stance toward others? Or is it simple naïve sentimentality to suggest something other than the xenophobic sensibility that fuels nuclear escalation and that not only denies to others what is justly theirs but does so "in cold blood"? A companionable sensibility is certainly needed in our time: one that accentuates neither dependence nor independence but interdependence. A companionable sensibility stresses, as no other model can, the reciprocity of all life, the mutual give-and-take, that is central to an ecological, evolutionary perspective. Is this sensibility an utter absurdity? It does not seem that it should be. One need not be a Christian or an adherent of any religion to be converted to a companionable sensibility. As we have seen, the awareness of divine oppression (or absence) as well as of divine presence can be the occasion for the development of a companionable attitude toward others. And there are innumerable ways that advocacy of and partnership with strangers and outsiders can take place; again, Christians have no corner on that market. What they do have, however, is a very powerful model of God as friend to sustain them as they go about the work of sustaining the world. In the model of the church we have sketched, God is present as our friend in all our companionable encounters with the world. For the Christian community, companionship is not necessary because of divine oppression; rather, it is possible because of divine presence. The model of God as friend says that we are not our own, but also that we are not on our own: as friends of the Friend of the world, we do not belong to ourselves nor are we left to ourselves.

It is in this context of God as present with us as we work together to feed, heal, and liberate the world that prayer becomes both natural and necessary. We ask God, as one would a friend, to be present in the joy of our shared meals and in the sufferings of the strangers; to give us courage and stamina for the work we do together; to forgive us for lack of fidelity to the common vision and lack of trust in divine trustfulness. Finally, we ask God the friend to support, forgive, and comfort us as we struggle together to save our beleaguered planet, our beautiful earth, our blue and green marble in a universe of silent rock and fire. Just as betrayal is the sin of friendship in which one hands over the friend to the enemy, so intercessory prayer is the rite of friendship in which one hands over the friend to God.[10] When we pray for our friend the earth, for whose future we fear, we hand it over not to the enemy but to the Friend who is freely, joyfully, and permanently bonded to this, our beloved world. The model of God as friend defies despair.

Notes

1. Gordon Kaufman, *Theology for a Nuclear Age* (Philadelphia: Westminster, 1985), 42.

2. Schubert Ogden, "The Reality of God," in *Process Theology: Basic Writings,* ed. Ewart H. Cousins (New York: Newman, 1977), 129.

3. Paul Tillich, *Systematic Theology,* vol. 3 (Chicago: University of Chicago Press, 1963), 293–94.

4. C. S. Lewis, *The Four Loves* (New York: Harcourt Brace & Co., 1960), 176.

5. This phrase comes from Josef Pieper's book *About Love,* trans. Richard and Clara Winston (Chicago: Franciscan Herald, 1974), 22.

6. Paul Tillich, *Love, Power, and Justice: Ontological Analyses and Ethical Applications* (New York: Oxford University Press, 1954), 25.

7. See Jürgen Moltmann, "Open Friendship," in *The Passion for Life: The Messianic Lifestyle,* ed. M. Douglas Meeks (Philadelphia: Fortress Press, 1977), 60.

8. Ibid., 53.

9. Robert Meagher's introduction to *Albert Camus: The Essential Writings* (New York: Harper & Row, 1979), 22.

10. William F. May makes this point in his essay "The Sin against the Friend: Betrayal," *Cross Currents* 17 (1967): 169.

5

A Meditation on Exodus 33:23b

The metaphor of the world as God's body that McFague introduces in Models of God *forms the core for her fourth book,* The Body of God *(1993). Here once again the God-world relationship is key to her argument, and she analyzes the four major models for this connection: the deistic, the monarchical, the agential, and, most importantly, the organic. However, the organic model that she introduces here differs from the classic model, which she regards as too spiritualized and androcentric. Her organic, or ecological, model instead is built from the common creation story emerging from the sciences. It radicalizes both unity and difference—a panentheistic understanding based in a model of God "as the spirit that is the source, the life of breath of all reality." She continues, "Everything that is is in God and God is in all things and yet God is not identical with the universe, for the universe is dependent on God in a way that God is not dependent on the universe" (149). But first, she offers this brief biblical meditation, grounded in the sort of biblical hermeneutic suggested in her earlier work, underscoring God's embodiment and radical immanence and transcendence.*

Source: 1993:131–36

> "And you shall see my back; but my face shall not be seen"

When Moses in an audacious moment asks of God, "Show me your glory," God replies that "no one can see me and live," but he does allow Moses a glimpse of the divine body—not the face but the back (Exod. 33:20-23). The passage is a wonderful mix of the outrageous (God has a *backside?!*) and the awesome (the display of divine glory too dazzling for human eyes). The passage unites guts and glory, flesh and spirit, the human and the divine, and all those other apparent dualisms with a reckless flamboyance that points to something at the heart of the Hebrew and Christian traditions: God is not afraid of the flesh. We intend to take this incarnationalism seriously and see what it does, could, mean in terms of the picture of reality from postmodern science. Were we to imagine "the Word made flesh" as not limited to Jesus of Nazareth but as the body of the universe, all bodies, might we not have a homey but awesome metaphor for both divine nearness *and* divine glory? Like Moses, when we ask, "Show me your glory," we might see the humble bodies of our own planet as visible signs of the invisible grandeur. Not the face, not the depths of divine radiance, but enough, more than enough. We might begin to see (for the first time, perhaps) the marvels at our feet and at our fingertips: the intricate splendor of an Alpine forget-me-not or a child's hand. We might begin to realize the extraordinariness of the ordinary. We would begin to delight in creation, not as the work of an external deity, but as a sacrament of the living God. We would see creation as bodies alive with the breath of God. We might realize what this tradition has told us, although often shied away from embracing unreservedly: we live and move and have our being *in* God. We might see ourselves and everything else as the living body of God.

We would, then, have an entire planet that reflects the glory, the very being—although not the face—of God. We would have a concrete panorama for meditation on divine glory and transcendence: wherever we looked, whether at the sky with its billions of galaxies (only a few visible to us) or the earth (every square inch of which is alive with millions of creatures) or into the eyes of another human being, we would have an image of divine grandeur. The more we meditated on these bits of the divine body, the more intricate, different, and special each would become. Such meditation is a suitable way for limited, physical creatures with lively imaginations such as ourselves to contemplate the divine being. It is enriching for it does not occur only at one place but everywhere and not just in one form but in an infinite myriad of forms. It is neither otherworldly nor abstract, but is a this-worldly, concrete form of contemplating divine magnificence. It is a way for limited, physical beings like ourselves to meditate on divine transcendence in an immanent way. And it is based on the assumption, central to the Christian tradition, that God not only is not afraid of the flesh but loves it, *becomes* it.

If we are allowed, indeed, invited as Moses was to see God's glory in the divine back, then we experience not only awe as we meditate on the wonders of our planet but also compassion for all bodies in pain. If God is available to us in bodies, then bodies become special. The metaphor of the world as God's body knits together the awe we feel for the magnificent intricacy and splendor of all the diverse kinds of bodies *and* the pain we feel for a suffering human or animal body. We cannot in good conscience marvel with aesthetic delight at the one and not identify with the pain of the other: bodies are beautiful and vulnerable. If God is physical, then the aesthetic and the ethical unite: praising God in and through the beauty of bodies entails caring for the most basic needs of all bodies on the planet. If God is physical, then the divine becomes part of the everyday, part of the pain and pleasure of bodily existence.

We begin to see a new way of imagining and expressing divine transcendence and immanence. It is not a model of transcendence in which God is king and the world is the realm of a distant, external ruler who has all power and expects unquestioned obedience from his subjects, human beings.[1] Nor is it a model of immanence in which God the king once entered the world by becoming a servant in the form of one human being. Rather, it is a radicalization of both divine transcendence and immanence. The model of the universe as God's body radicalizes transcendence for *all* of the entire fifteen-billion-year history and the billions of galaxies is the creation, the outward being, of the One who is the source and breath of all existence. In the universe as a whole as well as in each and every bit and fragment of it, God's transcendence is embodied. The important word here is "embodied": the transcendence of God is not available to us except as embodied. We do not see God's face, but only the back. But we *do* see the back.

The world (universe) as God's body is also, then, a radicalization of divine immanence, for God is not present to us in just one place (Jesus of Nazareth, although also and especially, paradigmatically there),[2] but in and through all bodies, the bodies of the sun and moon, trees and rivers, animals, and people. The scandal of the gospel is that the Word became flesh; the radicalization of incarnation sees Jesus not as a surd, an enigma, but as a paradigm or culmination of the divine way of enfleshment.

We are suggesting, then, that the model of the universe as God's body is a way of expressing both radical transcendence *and* immanence, but in a fashion that limits our perception and knowledge to the back of God. In other words, we are dealing here with a model or metaphor, not a description: the universe as God's body is a rich, suggestive way to radicalize the glory, the awesomeness, the beyond-all-imagining power and mystery of God in a way that at the same time radicalizes the nearness, the availability, the physicality of divine immanence. In this one image of the world as God's body, we are invited to see the creator *in* the creation, the source of all existence in and through what is bodied forth from that source. And yet, as we contemplate divine transcendence immanently in the bodies of all things and creatures, we know what we see is the back, not the face, of God. The very recognition and acceptance of that limit gives us permission, as the Hebrew psalmists also felt, to revel in the many embodiments divine transcendence takes: the clouds and winds, thunder and water, deer and young lambs, midwives and mothers, kings and shepherds. Everything can be a metaphor for God, because no *one* thing is God. The body of God is neither the human body nor any other body; rather, all bodies are reflections of God, all bodies are the backside of divine glory. Radicalizing the incarnation, therefore, by using the model of the universe as God's body is neither idolatry nor pantheism: the world, creation, is not identified or confused with God. Yet it is the place where God is present to us. Christianity's most distinctive belief is that divine reality is always mediated through the world, a belief traditionally expressed in the Chalcedonian formula that Christ was "fully God, fully man." For our time when we understand human existence in continuity with all other forms of life and hence must think of our relation to God in an ecological context, that mediation is appropriately radicalized and expanded to include the entire cosmos. In both instances, the Word is made flesh, God is available to us only through the mediation of embodiment. We are offered not the face of God but the back. God is neither enclosed in nor exhausted by the body shown to us, but it is a body that is given.

It is enough and it is a body. "It is enough" acknowledges that for those who are persuaded to live within this model, it provides guidance and significance to life, a way of being in the world. Those who wager on this construct believe it tells them something about the way things are; in other words, that it gives them intimations of how God and the world are related. That intimation is suggested by the metaphor of body. "It is a body" suggests content, substance, for what it means to live within this particular construct. It places a premium on the physical, the lowly, the mundane, the specific, the vulnerable, the visible, the other, the needy, for all these words describe aspects of bodies of various kinds. No body, no material form, is absolute, eternal, general, abstract, otherworldly, self-sufficient, invincible, or invisible. Bodies in the universe, in all their differences, share some characteristics that suggest a focus, an area of concern, for those who would live within the construct of the body of God. At one level our model—the universe as God's body—moves us in the direction of contemplating the glory and grandeur of divine creation, an aesthetic awe at unending galactic wonders, while at another level it moves us in the direction of compassionate identification with and service to the fragile, suffering, oppressed bodies that surround us. The model embraces both the guts and the glory, both the mud and the mystery—or, more precisely, suggests that the peculiar form of divine glory available to us, if we live within this model, is *only* through the guts, the mud. Incarnationalism, radicalized, means that we do not, ever, at least in this life, see God face to face, but only through the mediation of the bodies we pay attention to, listen to, and learn to love and care for.

Notes

1. For an analysis of the monarchical model, see McFague 1987, ch. 3.
2. See McFague 1993, ch. 6, "The Shape of the Body: The Christic Paradigm."

PART II

Theology and Spirituality: Metaphorical, Ecological, and Kenotic Approaches

6

Metaphorical Theology

Part 1 of this book examined parables, metaphors, and models as key elements of theological discourse, closing with some key examples of specific models that might revitalize Christian thought. In part 2, the focus shifts to consider more how these elements "fund theology," as McFague puts it below. This section from chapter 1 of Metaphorical Theology *reintroduces many of the ideas and definitions introduced in part 1, but here it becomes more clear how they work together to form the metaphorical theological approach that marks her overall theological project henceforth.*

Source: 1982:14–29

If modernity were the only criterion, our task would be relatively easy. But such is never the case in theology. Christian theology is always an interpretation of the "gospel" in a particular time and place. So the other task of equal importance is to show that a metaphorical *theology* is indigenous to Christianity, not just in the sense that it is permitted but is called for. And this I believe is the case. The heart of the gospel in the New Testament is widely accepted to be the "kingdom of God"; what the kingdom is or means is never expressed but indirectly suggested by the parables of the kingdom. The parables are by no means the only form in the New Testament that deals with the kingdom and we must be cautious lest we make an idol of them. However, as the dominant genre of Jesus' teaching on the kingdom, they suggest some central, albeit indirect, clues to its reality. As a form of religious language, the parables of the New Testament are very different from symbolic, sacramental language. They do not assume a believing or religious perspective on the part of the listeners to whom they are addressed; they do not assume continuity between our world and a transcendent one; they do not see similarity, connection, and harmony between our ways and the valleys of God. On the contrary, they are a secular form of language, telling stories of ordinary people involved in mundane family, business, and social matters; they assume a nonbelieving or secular attitude on the part of their audience; they stress the discontinuity between our ways and the ways of the kingdom; they focus on the dissimilarity, incongruity, and tension between the assumptions and expectations of their characters and another set of assumptions and expectations identified with the kingdom. In other words, they are a form peculiarly suited to what I have called the Protestant sensibility.

They are so suited because they are metaphors, not symbols. They are metaphorical statements about religious matters, about what both transcends and affects us at the deepest level of our existence. What is it about a religious metaphorical statement which makes it more powerful than a symbolical statement? The answer to this question centers on the nature of metaphor and especially of metaphorical statements. To many people "metaphor" is merely a poetic ornament for illustrating an idea or adding rhetorical color to abstract or flat language. It appears to have little to do with ordinary language until one realizes that most ordinary language is composed of "dead metaphors," some obvious, such as "the arm of the chair," and others less obvious, such as "tradition," meaning, "to hand over or hand down." Most simply, a metaphor is seeing one thing *as* something else, pretending "this" is "that" because we do not know how to think or talk about "this," so we use "that" as a way of saying something about it. Thinking metaphorically means spotting a thread of similarity between two dissimilar objects, events, or whatever, one of which is better known than the other, and using the better-known one as a way of speaking about the lesser known.

Poets use metaphor all the time because they are constantly speaking about the great unknowns—mortality, love, fear, joy, guilt, hope, and so on. Religious language is deeply metaphorical for the same reason and it is therefore no surprise that Jesus' most characteristic form of teaching, the parables, should be extended metaphors. Less obvious, but of paramount importance, is the fact that metaphorical thinking constitutes the basis of human thought and language. From the time we are infants we construct our world through metaphor; that is, just as young children learn the meaning of the color red by finding the thread of similarity through many dissimilar objects (red ball, red apple, red cheeks), so we constantly ask when we do not know how to think about something, "What is it like?" Far from being an esoteric or ornamental rhetorical device super-imposed on ordinary language, metaphor *is* ordinary language. It is the *way* we think. We often make distinctions between ordinary and poetic language, assuming that the first is direct and the second indirect, but actually both are indirect, for we always think by indirection. The difference between the two kinds of language is only that we have grown accustomed to the indirections of ordinary language; they have become conventional. Likewise, conceptual or abstract language is metaphorical in the sense that the ability to generalize depends upon seeing similarity within dissimilarity; a concept is an abstraction of the similar from a sea of dissimilars. Thus, Darwin's theory of the survival of the fittest is a high-level metaphorical exercise of recognizing a similar pattern amid an otherwise incredibly diverse set of phenomena.

The primary answer to the question of why religious metaphorical statements are so powerful is that they are in continuity with the way we think ordinarily. We are not usually conscious of the metaphorical character of our thought, of seeing "this" in terms of "that," of finding the thread of similarity amid dissimilars, but it is the only way a child's world can be constructed or our worlds expanded and transformed. Of course, there are important differences between ordinary and religious metaphorical statements which we shall fully note, but the first thing is to insist on their continuity. Symbolic statements, on the other hand, are not so much a way of knowing and speaking as they are sedimentation and solidification of metaphor. For in symbolical or sacramental thought, one does not think of "this" or "that," but "this" *as a part of* "that." The tension of metaphor is absorbed by the harmony of symbol.

Another way to discern the distinction between metaphorical and sacramental thinking is to say that in metaphorical statements we always make judgments. That is, we make assertions; we say "I am thinking about 'this' in terms of 'that'." The only times we do not think this way is when we have already accepted a particular way of thinking of something. When we already know something, that is, when we have accepted a perspective on something, then we see and think about it "directly," or so it seems. Actually, it is not the case that anything can be known or thought of directly or literally; rather, we have simply acquired a way of looking at it which is acceptable to us. Even as simple a statement as "this is a chair" means only that I have made a judgment that I will think about this object *as* a chair because there is sufficient similarity between this object and other objects that I have called "chairs" in the past that I believe my assertion is justified. The example may appear ridiculous but it was chosen because it illustrates metaphorical thinking at its most common, continuous, and instantaneous level. It is the same *kind of thinking as the assertion "Jesus is the savior," inasmuch as here again one is making a decision to think of one thing in terms of another; in both cases, a judgment is involved that similarity is present. The differences between the two statements are vast and important, such as the degree of existential involvement and the much greater ignorance of the subject matter, as well as the novelty of the assertion in the second statement. The point to stress, however, is that human thought is of a piece, it is indirect, and it involves judgments.*

We have remarked that metaphor finds the vein of similarity in the midst of dissimilars, while symbol rests on similarity already present and assumed. But the difference is even more marked: metaphor not only lives in the region of dissimilarity, but also in the region of the unconventional and surprising. Both humor and the grotesque are distinctly metaphorical.[1] Humor is the recognition of a *very unlikely* similarity among dissimilars and we laugh because we are surprised to discover that such unlikes are indeed alike in at least one respect. A great many jokes take the form, "How is a _____ like a _____?" Likewise, the grotesque forces us to look at radical incongruity, at what is outside, does not fit, is strange and disturbing. Both are extreme metaphorical forms, which point up a crucial characteristic of metaphor: good metaphors shock, they bring unlikes together, they upset conventions, they involve tension, and they are implicitly revolutionary. The parables of Jesus are typically metaphorical in this regard, for they bring together dissimilars (lost coins, wayward children, buried treasure, and tardy laborers with the kingdom of God); they shock and disturb; they upset conventions and expectations and in so doing have revolutionary potential. In this regard, one could characterize symbolic, sacramental thinking as priestly and metaphorical thinking as prophetic. The first assumes an order and unity already present waiting to be realized; the second projects, tentatively, a possible transformed order and unity yet to be realized.[2]

Perhaps the most striking evidence of the revolutionary character of the New Testament parables is the redefinition they give to conventional understandings of the monarchical, hierarchical metaphors of "kingdom" and "rule." God's "kingdom," we discover from the parables, is not like any worldly reign; in fact, its essence is its opposition to the power of the mighty over the lowly, the rich over the poor, and the righteous over the unrighteous. It is a *new* rule, which is defined by the extraordinary reversal of expectations in the parables as well as in the life and death of Jesus.

The characteristics of metaphorical thinking we have suggested—ordinariness, incongruity, indirection, skepticism, judgment, unconventionality, surprise, and transformation or revolution—especially as they are realized in Jesus' parables, have persuaded many people [such as biblical scholars Leander Keck and John Donahue] to think of Jesus as a parable of God. That is to say, the life and death of Jesus of Nazareth can be understood as itself a "parable" of God; in order to understand the ways of God with us—something unfamiliar and unknown to us, about which we do not know how to think or talk—we look at that life as a metaphor of God. What we see through that "grid" or "screen" is at one level an ordinary, secular story of a human being, but also a story shot through with surprise, unconventionality, and incongruities which not only upset our conventional expectations (for instance, of what a "savior" is and who gets "saved"), but also involve a judgment on our part—"Surely this man is the Christ." In contrast to incarnational Christology, however, parabolic Christology does not involve an assumption of continuity or identity between the human and the divine; it is not a "Jesusolatry," a form of idolatry. It is, I believe, a Christology for the Protestant sensibility and the modem mentality.

All the foregoing comments on metaphor, parable, and Jesus as a parable require considerable elaboration. Perhaps, however, these brief introductory remarks are sufficient for us to attempt to advance a case for a metaphorical theology. If metaphor is the way by which we understand as well as enlarge our world and change it—that is, if the only way we have of dealing with the unfamiliar and new is in terms of the familiar and the old, thinking of "this" as "that" although we know the new thing is both like *and* unlike the old—if all this is the case, then it is no surprise that Jesus taught in parables or that many see him as a parable of God. For he introduced a new, strange way of being in the world, a way that could be grasped only through the indirection of stories of familiar life which both "were and were not" the kingdom. And he himself was in the world in a new, strange way, which was in many respects an ordinary life, but one which also, as with the parables, called the mores and conventions of ordinary life into radical question.

A metaphorical theology, then, starts with the parables of Jesus and with Jesus as a parable of God. This starting place does not involve a belief in the Bible as authoritative in an absolute or closed sense; it does not involve acceptance of a canon or the Bible as "the Word of God." In fact, such a perspective reverses the direction of authority suitable both to Scripture and to the Protestant sensibility. For what we have in the New Testament are confessions of faith by people who, on the basis of their experience of the way their lives were changed by Jesus' gospel and by Jesus, *gave* authority to him and to the writings about him. The New Testament writings are foundational; they are classics; they are a beginning. But if we take seriously the parables of Jesus and Jesus as a parable of God as our starting point and model, then we cannot say that the Bible is absolute or authoritative in any sense except the way that a "classic" text is authoritative: it continues to speak to us. What must always be kept in mind is that the parables as metaphors and the life of Jesus as a metaphor of God provide characteristics for theology: a theology guided by them is open-ended, tentative, indirect, tensive, iconoclastic, transformative. Some of these characteristics appear "negative," in the sense that they qualify any attempts at idolatry, whether this be the idolatry of the Bible, of tradition, of orthodoxy, or of the church. In such a theology *no* finite thought, product, or creature can be identified with God and this includes Jesus of Nazareth, who as parable of God both "is and is not" God. Against all forms of literalistic realism and idolatry, a metaphorical theology insists that it is not only in keeping with the Protestant sensibility to be open, tentative, and iconoclastic but that these are the characteristics of Jesus' parables and of Jesus' own way of being in the world.

On the other hand, metaphorical theology is not just a modern version of the *via negativa* or an exercise in iconoclasm. It not only says "is not" but "is," not only no but yes. If the parables of Jesus and Jesus himself as a parable of God are genuine metaphors, then they give license for language about life with God; they point to a real, an assumed similarity between the metaphors and that to which they refer. The many parables of the kingdom tell us something about the rule of God, of what it means to live in the world according to God's way. Jesus as a parable of God tells us actually and concretely (though, of course, indirectly) about God's relationship to us. In other words, a metaphorical theology is "positive" as well as "negative," giving license for speech about God as well as indicating the limits of such speech. Such a theology, as is true of all theologies, must be concerned not only with *how* we speak of God but *what we* say of God. On the question of how we speak of God, a metaphorical theology is firmly opposed to literalism and idolatry of all kinds; on the question of what we say about God, metaphorical theology again turns to the parables and to Jesus as a parable for beginning, foundational clues.

The parables of the New Testament are united by a number of characteristics, of which one of the most outstanding is their concern with *relationships* of various kinds. What is important in the parables is not *who* the characters are (a static notion) but what *they do* (a dynamic one). The plot is always the heart of a parable, what a character or several characters decide in matters having to do with their *relationships with each other.* Whether one thinks of the parable of the Prodigal Son, the Good Samaritan, the Unjust Steward, or the Great Supper, it is relationships and decisions about them that are critical.[3] Just as the central Old Testament religious language is relational—focused on the covenant between God and Israel; so the central New Testament language is relational—focused on persons and their way of being in the world in community. Likewise, if we look at Jesus as a parable of God, we have no alternative but to recognize personal, relational language as the most appropriate language about God. Whatever more one may wish to say about him, he was a person relating to other persons in loving service and transforming power.

I have emphasized the word "person" for two reasons. First, as we were made *in the image of God* (Gen. 3:27), so we now, with the model of Jesus, have further support for imagining God in *our* image, the image of persons. This means that personal, relational images are central in a metaphorical theology—images of God as father, mother, lover, friend, savior, ruler, governor, servant, companion, comrade, liberator, and so on. The Judeo-Christian tradition has always been personalistic and relational in its religious languages. This need not be seen as crude anthropomorphism but as foundational language, the dominant model, of God-talk. Such language, however, is not the only appropriate religious language: no one model can ever be adequate. We find—both in Scripture and in our tradition—naturalistic, impersonal images balancing the relational, personal ones: God as rock, fortress, running stream, power, sun, thunder, First Cause, and so on. The Judeo-Christian tradition has had a decidedly personalistic rather than naturalistic tendency, with appalling consequences for the exploitation of the natural environment. This tradition is personalistic, however, not in an individualistic but in a relational sense, and it is therefore appropriate and required that a revolutionary hermeneutic of this tradition broaden relationship to its widest dimensions, including the entire natural world. In any case, a metaphorical theology will insist that *many* metaphors and models are necessary, that a piling up of images is essential, both to avoid idolatry and to attempt to express the richness and variety of the divine-human relationship.

The second reason for stressing the word "person" is to underscore, in as strong and definitive a way as possible, that it is not patriarchal language which is licensed by Jesus as parable of God. The Christian tradition, and the Jewish as well, have been and still are deeply patriarchal. We will be giving substantial time to this issue, for the profound penetration of the patriarchal model not only in theology but also in the structures of Western culture makes it a critical one for any metaphorical theology to consider. What is stressed in the parables and in Jesus' own life focuses on persons and their relationships; therefore, the dominance of the patriarchal model in the Christian tradition must be seen as a perversion in its hegemony of the field of religious models and its exclusion of other personal, relational models. The dominance of the patriarchal model is idolatrous in its assumption of privileged appropriateness. To put the issue in its simplest form, God's name is not "father" although many Christians use "God" and "father" interchangeably as if "father" were a literal description of God.

A metaphorical theology, then, will emphasize personal, relational categories in its language about God but not necessarily as the tradition has interpreted these categories. On the contrary, if one looks to the parables and

Jesus as a parable to gain some preliminary understanding of what "person" means and what "relationship" means, both applied to us and to God, one finds not a baptizing of conventional hierarchies of relationships, whether these be of class, race, sex, or whatever, but a radical transformation of our expectations. For instance, if we are to say "God is father" it is both true *and* untrue, and even where true, it is different from conventional views of patriarchal fatherhood. If we are to call ourselves "children" in relationship to God, this is a limited and in some respects false image. There are personal, relational models which have been suppressed in the Christian tradition because of their social and political consequences; they are, however, as appropriate as the fatherhood model and are necessary both to qualify it and to include the images of personal, relational life of large numbers of people whose experiences have been excluded from traditional Christian language. To mention but two examples in passing, "mother" and "liberator" are metaphors of profound personal relationships with vast potential as models for God. They arise out of the depths of human relational existence and are licensed by the parabolic dimension of the New Testament, not in a literal way (the words do not appear), but in the sense that the characteristics we associate with "mother" and "liberator" fit with (and, of course, also do not fit with) the surprising rule of God as we have it in the parables and the parable of Jesus.

But a metaphorical theology cannot stop with metaphors, with the parables and the life and death of Jesus as extended metaphors of God's rule. Metaphor, parables, and Jesus as parable *fund* theology, but are not theology. If we wish to be precise, we must make a distinction between primary and secondary religious language, between metaphorical and conceptual language. But it is impossible to keep the distinction clear because most primary religious language is implicitly conceptual and most secondary theological language is latently imagistic. The parables of Jesus cry out for interpretation—not for *one* interpretation, but nonetheless for answers to the question, "What does this parable mean?" The richness of imagistic language means that it will always spawn many interpretations. Likewise, the biblical story of Jesus' life and death, an extended metaphor itself and packed with many supporting metaphors (Jesus as Messiah, as Son of man, as Suffering Servant, and so on), is not just a story but is already highly interpreted. What the story *means* is the perspective from which it is told and not something tacked on to pure, unadulterated images. Or if we think of Paul's letters, we see a mixture of images and concepts, the images moving in the direction of concepts in the sense that, for instance, when Paul tells us we are buried with Christ so that we might rise with him, he also tells us what this means (baptism, or the newness of the Christian life). Or if one considers the Nicene Creed, one sees a mixture of imagistic and conceptual language: the phrase "God of God, Light of Light, Very God of Very God, Begotten not made, Being of one substance with the Father" and so on was deemed necessary to interpret the imagistic language "one Lord Jesus Christ" and "Son of God." Whether the interpretations are good ones, are appropriate, or are still meaningful to us is beside the point. What is critical at the moment is that *some* interpretation is necessary; imagistic language does not just tolerate interpretation but *demands* it.

Thus, metaphorical theology does not stop with metaphors but must deal with the entire gamut of religious/theological language. Robert Funk has noted that it is a tortuous route between Jesus' parables and systematic theology.[4] Indeed it is, but that route must be traversed, for to stop at the level of images, of metaphor, of story is inevitably to give over either to baptizing certain images (usually biblical ones) as alone appropriate or to finding religious images sterile and meaningless. In other words, in terms of the twin issues of idolatry and irrelevance in religious language, *moving beyond* metaphors is necessary both to avoid literalizing them and to attempt significant interpretations of them for our time. It is impossible just to tell "the simple story of Jesus" and it was not told that way in the first place, for the many "stories" of Jesus in the New Testament are each told within several layers of interpretation.

In the continuum of religious language from primary, imagistic to secondary, conceptual, a form emerges that is a mixed type: *the model*. The simplest way to define a model is as a dominant metaphor, a metaphor with staying power. Metaphors are usually the work of an individual, a flash of insight, which is often passing. But some metaphors gain wide appeal and become major ways of structuring and ordering experience. Thus, T. S. Eliot's "Wasteland" or W. H. Auden's "Age of Anxiety" became perspectives from which modern culture was perceived. There are many kinds of models—scale models, picture models, analogue and theoretical models, as well as root-metaphors which are similar to models but of wider range. For our preliminary purposes, however, the main point is that models are a further step along the route from metaphorical to conceptual language. They are similar to metaphors in that they are images, which retain the tension of the "is and is not" and, like religious and poetic metaphors, they have emotional appeal insofar as they suggest ways of understanding our being in the world. The example we have used before, "God the father," comes readily to mind: it is a metaphor, which has become a model. As a model it not only retains characteristics of metaphor but also reaches toward qualities of conceptual thought. It suggests a comprehensive, ordering structure with impressive interpretive potential. As a rich model with many associated commonplaces as well as a host of supporting metaphors, an entire theology can be worked out from this model. Thus, if God is understood on the model of "father," human beings are understood as "children," sin is rebellion against the "father," redemption is sacrifice by the "elder son" on behalf of the "brothers and sisters" for the guilt against the "father" and so on.

Models, as is true of metaphors but in an organic, consistent, and comprehensive manner, give us a way of thinking about the unknown in terms of the known. As Max Black says, a model gives us a "grid," "screen," or "filter" that helps us to organize our thoughts about a less familiar subject by means of seeing it in terms of a more familiar one. He gives the example of seeing a military battle in terms of a chess game. The chess model will help to understand tactics and the movement of armies; as he shrewdly notes, however, it also "screens out" certain other aspects of battle—for instance, we will not think of blood and death if we use only the chess analogy.[5] Models are necessary, then, for they give us something to think about when we do not know what to think, a way of talking when we do not know how to talk. But they are also dangerous, for they exclude other ways of thinking and talking, and in so doing they can easily become literalized, that is, identified as *the* one and only way of understanding a subject. This danger is more prevalent with models than with metaphors because models have a wider range and are more permanent; they tend to object to competition in ways that metaphors do not. In many Old Testament psalms the psalmist will pile up metaphors for God in a riotous melee, mixing "rock" "lover," "fortress," "midwife," "fresh water," "judge," "helper," "thunder," and so on in a desperate attempt to express the richness of God's being. But models do not welcome such profusion; even in the case of models of the same *type* (for instance, "God the mother" along with "God the father") there is often great resistance. This is due, in part, to the literalization of models and it is probably the single greatest risk in their use.

It should be evident by now, however, that in all matters except the most conventional (where widely accepted perspectives or models are already operating), thinking by metaphor and hence by models is not optional but necessary. And this is true in the sciences as well as in the humanities. It is sometimes supposed that science deals with its subject matter directly, empirically; science is "factual" whereas poetry and religion are "spiritual, emotional, or imaginative." Unlike them, science does not need the indirection of metaphor but can move inductively from empirical observations to theory and from theory to verification in the "real" world. This positivistic view of science is fortunately no longer the only force in science; rather, what one finds is that much of the most interesting and suggestive work on models is being done by scientists, especially physicists. Relatively little has been written by theologians on models in religion; however, the literature on models in science is enormous, going back a good twenty-five years. As physics comes increasingly to deal with invisibles such as subatomic particles, behaviors of entities that must be imagined rather than observed, it finds itself in a position similar to poetry and religion in that it must attempt to understand the unknown in terms of known models. Also, as more and more conclusions in physics (as well as in many of the other sciences) are expressed in mathematical formulas, models become the only way of connecting scientific knowledge both with ordinary language and with other domains of science. Finally, and most importantly, scientists need models for discovering the new; to think of the new in terms of the old, so long as one does not collapse the two, can often, through the dialectic of similarity and dissimilarity, provide a breakthrough.

There are other uses of models in science as well. But the critical point for our preliminary purpose is to note the widespread acceptance of models in science as well as in many other disciplines. One finds thinking by models in biology, computer science, education theory, political science, ethics, psychology, sociology, and so on. The self-conscious use of models in regard to both their benefits and their risks, is a common phenomenon in most fields of study. What this means, among other things, is that poetry and religion, the two fields which have always known they must think via metaphor (and as a consequence have been denied by many as dealing in knowledge—truth and meaning), now find their way of metaphor and indirection is widely accepted as necessary in all creative, constructive thought. A scientist doing a routine experiment does not need models, but a scientist devising an experiment to test a hypothesis may very well need to try out various models in order to locate what is unfamiliar about the present case. And so it is in all creative ventures. What we do not know, we must simulate through models of what we do know.

Because of the centrality of models in science and the amount of analysis available on scientific models, we will be looking carefully at some of this material for possible insights into the ways models function in theology. We will discover, for instance, that as interpretive, explanatory devices religious models share structural characteristics with scientific models; but because models in religion emerge from existential experience, they have affectional dimensions as do poetic metaphors. But a metaphorical theology cannot stop at the level of models. To be sure, considerable interpretive activity takes place at such a stage: as dominant metaphors, models manifest priorities within a religious tradition; as organizing networks of images, they are well on the way to systematic thought; as comprehensive ways of envisioning reality, they implicitly raise questions of truth and reference; as metaphors that control the ways people envision both human and divine reality, they cannot avoid the issue of criteria in the choice of certain models and the exclusion of others. A further step of interpretation, however, is called for: conceptual interpretation and criticism.

Concepts and theories arise from metaphors and models; they are an attempt to generalize at the level of abstraction concerning competing and, at times, contradictory metaphors and models. By "concept" we mean an abstract notion; by "theory" we mean a speculative, systematic statement of relationships underlying certain phenomena. A concept is an idea or thought; a theory organizes ideas into an explanatory structure. Concepts, unlike metaphors, do not create new meaning but rely on conventional, accepted meanings. Theories, unlike models, do not systematize one area in terms of another, but organize concepts into a whole. These definitions are only minimally helpful, however, for they are too neat and compartmentalized for a metaphorical theology. If our thesis holds that *all* thought is indirect, then all concepts and theories are metaphorical in the sense that they too are constructions; they are indirect attempts to interpret reality, which never can be dealt with directly. Concepts and theories, however, are at the far end of the continuum and rarely expose their metaphorical roots. These distinctions mainly show the different functions of metaphor, model, and concept or theory in the *one* task of interpreting our being in the world.

Conceptual language tends toward univocity, toward clear and concise meanings for ambiguous, multileveled, imagistic language. In this process something is lost and something is gained: richness and multivalency are sacrificed for precision and consistency. Conceptual thought attempts to find similarities among the models while models insist on dissimilarities among themselves. The relationship, however, is symbiotic. Images "feed" concepts; concepts "discipline" images. Images without concepts are blind; concepts without images are sterile. In a metaphorical theology, there is no suggestion of a hierarchy among metaphors, models, and concepts: concepts are not higher, better, or more necessary than images, or vice versa. Images are never free of the need for interpretation by concepts, their critique of competing images, or their demythologizing of literalized models. Concepts are never free of the need for funding by images, the affectional and existential richness of images, and the qualification against conceptual pretensions supplied by the plurality of images. In no sense can systematic thought be said to *explain* metaphors and models so that they become mere illustrations for concepts; rather, the task of conceptual thought is to generalize (often in philosophical language, *the* generalizing language), to criticize images, to raise questions of their meaning and truth in explicit ways.

An example of the movement from parable toward conceptual thought can be illustrated briefly by the career of "the kingdom of God." I would call "the kingdom of God" the root-metaphor of Christianity, which is supported and fed by many extended metaphors, the various parables. No *one* parable is adequate as a way of seeing the kingdom, and all the parables together undoubtedly are not either, but they are all that is provided. Many extended metaphors are necessary to give meaning to the model of the kingdom; taken together they display certain common features which are not illustrations of the kingdom so much as exemplifications of it. The process of understanding and interpreting these common features is not deductive or inductive but dialectical: "the rule of God" at this stage *is* all of the parabolic exemplifications. In the hands of Paul and his notion of "justification by faith," however, we move to a higher level of interpretation by a concept generalizing on that rule. Paul Ricoeur points out, and I believe rightly, that Paul's notion is in continuity with the foundational language of "the kingdom of God" and the underlying parables, but it is less particular, more generalized; less concrete, more abstract; less imagistic, more univocal. Ricoeur calls Paul's concept a "translation language," a semi-conceptual mode of discourse that remains under the control of the hermeneutical potential of metaphor *because* it preserves the tension of the foundational language.[6]

For another example of the relationship among metaphors, models, and concepts, one must remember that metaphors and models of God will range widely and have various degrees of dominance within a tradition: person, king, rock, mother, savior, father, fortress, lover, liberator, helper, and many more. We must ask questions of these models. Which ones are dominant? Why should certain ones be dominant? Are they consistent? Are the central models comprehensive? To whom are they significant? To whom are they meaningless or objectionable? Are they fruitful in the sense that they help us to understand our lives better, and are they commensurate with other matters we hold to be important? Do they fit with lived experience or do they have to be rationalized in order to be held? All of these questions and more fall under the heading of the critique of metaphors and models that is the task of conceptual thought.

Systematic thought also tries to organize all the dominant models in a tradition into an overarching system with a key model of its own. For instance, for Paul it was justification by grace through faith; for Augustine, the radical dependence of all that is on God; for Aquinas, the analogy of being whereby each creature participates in and glorifies God through realizing its proper finite end; for Schleiermacher, the feeling of absolute dependence; for Barth, the election of all people to salvation in the election of Jesus Christ before the foundation of the world. Each of these is a medical model, which could be called a "root-metaphor": "a root-metaphor is the most basic assumption about the nature of the world or experience that we can make when we try to give a description of it."[7] Each root-metaphor is a way of seeing "all that is" through a particular key concept. It is also thinking by models and, as is evident, even these root-metaphors are still metaphors: at the highest level of abstraction and generalization one does not escape metaphor (the exceptions are symbolic logic and higher mathematics which do not pretend to refer to reality as lived).

Therefore, we will focus on *models* because, as mediators between metaphors and concepts, they partake of the characteristics of each and are an especially fruitful type of expression to investigate for a metaphorical theology. The aim of a metaphorical theology, as we recall, is to envision ways of talking about the relationship between the divine and the human that are nonidolatrous but relevant: ways which can be said to be true without being literal; ways which are meaningful to all peoples, the traditionally excluded as well as the included. Such a theology, I believe, is appropriate to the Protestant sensibility and I have suggested clues to its character from the parables of Jesus and Jesus as parable. In this framework, moreover, models are critical because models are dominant *metaphors*:they retain the tension of metaphor—its "is and is not" quality which refuses all literalization. Models are also *dominant* metaphors: they are dominant within a tradition both because they have earned that right as "classics" that speak to people across many ages and because they have usurped that right to the false exclusion of other metaphors. Both their right and their usurpation of right must be taken into account.

The tasks of a metaphorical theology will become clear: to understand the centrality of models in religion and the particular models in the Christian tradition; to criticize literalized, exclusive models; to chart the relationships among metaphors, models, and concepts; and to investigate possibilities for transformative, revolutionary models.[8] The goal of this analysis can then be thought of as an attempt to question the *didactic* tradition of orthodoxy over the more flexible, open, *kerygmatic* point of view epitomized in the parables and Jesus as parable. What must be done in a metaphorical theology is to open up the relationships among metaphor, model, and concept for the purpose both of justifying dominant, founding metaphors as true but not literal *and* of discovering other appropriate dominant metaphors which for cultural, political, and social reasons have been suppressed.

The final task of a metaphorical theology will be a reforming, transforming one. As metaphorical, such theology can never be simply a baptizing of the tradition, for that would mean giving up the tension which is at the heart of metaphor. The classic models of the Christian tradition have been and still are hierarchical, authoritarian ones that have been absolutized. As feminist theologians have become increasingly aware, the orthodox tradition did a thorough job of plumbing the depths of one such model, the patriarchal, as a way of being articulate about God. Feminists have become conscious of the profound structural implications of this model as a form of ecclesiastical, social, political, economic, and personal oppression. The problem does not lie with the model itself of "God the father," for it is a profound metaphor and as true as any religious model available, but it has established a hegemony over the Western religious consciousness which it is the task of metaphorical theology to break. The "outsiders" to the mainline Christian tradition—women, blacks, third-world people—are questioning the hierarchical, authoritarian, patriarchal models of Western theology. If Christianity is a universal religion (and not a tribal one for white, middle-class males), such voices are legitimate and necessary. . . . As Ursula LeGuin, a fantasy and science-fiction writer, says, truth lies in the imagination.[9] This may be only half a truth, but it is the half we most often forget.

Notes

1. See Kenneth Burke, *Permanence and Change: An Anatomy of Purpose* (New York: New Republic, 1935).

2. I am indebted to F. W. Dillistone for his distinction between analogical and metaphorical thinking. Of analogy he writes: "In any organic system the single member is related to the whole according to some pattern of order and proportion; no figure of speech is more fitted to express this relation than analogy" (*Christianity and Symbolism* [London: William Collins, 1955], 152). He notes that one can move from the known to the unknown because the part participates in the whole and is similar to it. Analogical thought is positive, comprehensive, and systematic. Analogy has links with the simile, metaphor with the contrast. Metaphor focuses attention on variety and the openness of reality, and on dissimilarity rather than similarity. . . [holding] together similarity and dissimilarity in a resolution. . . . Through it the imagination performs its task. . . . Finally, Dillistone notes that while analogy tends toward petrification, metaphor moves toward renovation and that Jesus was a metaphorical thinker, disrupting the old by seeing it in a new light.

3. Not all parables are of this sort: the kingdom parables of the buried treasure, lost coin, and mustard seed are not, for instance, but as we shall see, relational language, while the dominant model for God, ought to be balanced and is balanced in the Bible by nonrelational, impersonal, naturalistic language.

4. Robert W. Funk, "The Parables: A Fragmentary Agenda," in *Jesus and Man's Hope*, 2 vols., ed. Donald G. Miller and Dikran Y. Hadidian (Pittsburgh: Pittsburgh Theological Seminary, 1971), 2:287–303.

5. See Max Black's fine chapters 3 and 13 in his *Models and Metaphors* (Ithaca: Cornell University Press, 1962).

6. Paul Ricoeur, "Biblical Hermeneutics," *Semeia* 4 (1975): 138.

7. The term "root-metaphor" is Stephen Pepper's from his book *World Hypotheses* (Berkeley: University of California Press, 1942). The quotation is from Earl R. MacCormac, *Metaphor and Myth in Science and Religion* (Durham: Duke University Press, 1976), 93.

8. I have used the term "metaphorical theology" rather than "parabolic theology" because the latter limits theological discourse to the primary level. I have tried to show that, to varying degrees, all constructive thought is implicitly or explicitly metaphorical (which is not to say that "everything is metaphor," for much philosophical as well as most scientific and ordinary language is at most mainly dead metaphor and does not function as alive metaphorical language). Hence, metaphorical theology can refer to the entire spectrum from parable to concept, though by using this term stress is put on the foundational, primary language that I believe is appropriate and necessary to theology. Moreover, by retaining the term "metaphorical," the characteristics of metaphor that I find critical to a theology in keeping with the Protestant sensibility, are constantly called to mind—tentativeness, open-endedness, secularity, projected rather than realized unity, tension, transformation, revolution, skepticism, and so on.

9. Ursula K. LeGuin, *The Language of the Night: Essays on Fantasy and Science Fiction*, ed. Susan Wood (New York: Putnam's, 1979), 159.

7

Metaphors, Models, and Concepts

This selection from Models of God *reiterates some of the ideas in the previous chapter. However, where that piece worked mostly from theoretical sources, here McFague draws more from other theologians to make the case for metaphorical theology as an appropriate constructive approach for our time. It is particularly interesting to see her briefly engage Paul Tillich and her teacher, Gordon Kaufman, here. While both are clear sources for her own thought, she demures from each of them for lacking the sort of metaphorical and imagistic richness she feels is needed for a theology that can engage the urgent ecological and nuclear crises and effectively counter idolatrous rhetoric.*

Source: 1987:31–40

Dennis Nineham, in the epilogue to *The Myth of God Incarnate*, writes that it is "at the level of the *imagination* that contemporary Christianity is most weak." He goes on to say that people

> find it hard to believe in God because they do not have available to them any lively imaginative picture of the way God and the world as they know it are related. What they need most is a story, a picture, a myth, that will capture their imagination, while meshing in with the rest of their sensibility in the way that messianic terms linked with the sensibility of first-century Jews, or Nicene symbolism with the sensibility of philosophically-minded fourth-century Greeks.[1]

An important point is made in this comment: belief is related to an imaginative and credible picture or myth of the relationship between God and the world. What our time lacks, and hence a task that theology must address, is an imaginative construal of the God-world relationship that is credible to us. I have attempted to suggest that a credible theology for our time must be characterized by a sense of our intrinsic interdependence with all forms of life, an inclusive vision that demolishes oppressive hierarchies, accepts responsibility for nurturing and fulfilling life in its many forms, and is open to change and novelty as a given of existence. But it is perhaps less clear what an imaginative construal of the God-world relationship might be. . . .

The first thing to say is that theology, as constructive and metaphorical, does not "demythologize" but "remythologizes." To envision theology as metaphorical means, at the outset, to refuse the attempt to denude religious language of its concrete, poetic, imagistic, and hence inevitably anthropomorphic, character, in the search for presumably more enlightened (and usually more abstract) terminology. It is to accept as one of theology's primary tasks remythologizing for our time: identifying and elucidating primary metaphors and models from contemporary experience which will express Christian faith for our day in powerful, illuminating ways. Theologians are not poets, but neither are they philosophers (as, in the Christian tradition, they have often become). Their place, as understood by metaphorical theology, is an anomalous one that partakes of both poetry and philosophy: they are poets insofar as they must be sensitive to the metaphors and models that are at once consonant with the Christian faith and appropriate for expressing that faith in their own time, and they are philosophers insofar as they must elucidate in a coherent, comprehensive, and systematic way the implications of these metaphors and models. Thus, to suggest, as I do, that the metaphors of mother (and father), lover, and friend, and of the world as God's body, are appropriate for remythologizing Christianity in our time means making a case for them at both the imagistic and conceptual levels. My first point, then, is that a constructive, metaphorical theology insists on a continuum and a symbiotic relationship between image and concept, between the language of prayer and liturgy and the language of theory and doctrine. There is nothing distinctive about this statement except the emphasis on the theologian's contribution to remythologizing. The theologian ought not merely interpret biblical and traditional metaphors and models but ought to remythologize, to search in contemporary life and its sensibility for images more appropriate to the expression of Christian faith in our time.

A second and more complex issue in regard to theology, as constructive and metaphorical, concerns metaphor and model. What are they, and why call theology metaphorical?[2] A metaphor is a word or phrase used *in*appropriately. It belongs properly in one context but is being used in another: the arm of the chair, war as a chess game, God the father. From Aristotle until recently, metaphor has been seen mainly as a poetic device to embellish or decorate. The idea was that in metaphor one used a word or phrase inappropriately but one need not have: whatever was being expressed could be said directly without the metaphor. Increasingly, however, the idea of metaphor as unsubstitutable is winning acceptance: what a metaphor expresses cannot be said directly or apart from it, for if it could be, one would have said it directly. Here, metaphor is a strategy of desperation, not decoration; it is an attempt to say something about the unfamiliar in terms of the familiar, an attempt to speak about what we do not know in terms of what we do know. Not all metaphors fit this definition, for many are so enmeshed in conventional language (the arm of the chair) that we do not notice them and some have become so familiar that we do not recognize them as attempting to express the unfamiliar (God the father). But a fresh metaphor, such as in the remark that war is a chess game, immediately sparks our imaginations to think of war, a very complex phenomenon, as viewed through a concrete grid or screen, the game of chess.[3] Needless to say, war is not a chess game; hence, a description of war in terms of chess is a partial, relative, inadequate account that, in illuminating certain aspects of war (such as strategizing), filters out other aspects (such as violence and death).

Metaphor always has the character of "is" and "is not": an assertion is made but as a likely account rather than a definition. That is, to say, "'God is mother,' is not to define God as mother, not to assert identity between the terms "God" and "mother," but to suggest that we consider what we do not know how to talk about—relating to God—through the metaphor of mother. The assumption here is that all talk of God is indirect: no words or phrases refer directly to God, for God-language can refer only through the detour of a description that properly belongs elsewhere. To speak of God as mother is to invite us to consider some qualities associated with mothering as one partial but perhaps illuminating way of speaking of certain aspects of God's relationship to us. It also assumes, however, that many other metaphors may qualify as partial but illuminating grids or screens for this purpose. The point that metaphor underscores is that in certain matters there can be no direct description. It used to be that poetry and religion were thought to be distinctive in their reliance on metaphor, but more recently the use of metaphors and models in the natural and social sciences has widened the scope of metaphorical thinking considerably.

The differences between a metaphor and a model can for our purpose be simply stated: a model is a metaphor with "staying power."[4] A model is a metaphor that has gained sufficient stability and scope so as to present a pattern for relatively comprehensive and coherent explanation. The metaphor of God the father is an excellent example of this. In becoming a model, it has permitted an understanding of many things. If God is seen as father, human beings become children, sin can be understood as rebellious behavior, and redemption can be thought of as a restoration to the status of favored offspring. As the creeds of the church amply illustrate, models approach the status of concepts: Father, Son, and Holy Spirit are models of the divine life that inform the tradition's most central concept, the trinity.

It should be evident that a theology that describes itself as metaphorical is a theology "at risk." Jacques Derrida, in defining metaphor, writes, "If metaphor, which is *mimesis* trying its chance, *mimesis* at risk, may always fail to attain truth, this is because it has to reckon with a definite absence."[5] As Derrida puts it, metaphor lies somewhere between "nonsense" and "truth," and a theology based on metaphor will be open to the charge that it is closer to the first than the second. This, I believe, is a risk that theology in our time must be willing to run. Theology has usually had a high stake in truth, so high that it has refused all play of the imagination: through credal control and the formulations of orthodoxy, it has refused all attempts at new metaphors "trying their chance." But a metaphorical theology is necessarily a heuristic venture: it insists that new metaphors and models be given a chance, be tried out as likely accounts of the God-world relationship, be allowed to make a case for themselves. A metaphorical theology is, therefore, destabilizing: since no language about God is adequate and all of it is improper, new metaphors are not necessarily less inadequate or improper than old ones. All are in the same situation and no authority—not scriptural status, liturgical longevity, nor ecclesiastical fiat—can decree that some types of language, or some images, refer literally to God while others do not. None do. Hence, the criteria for preferring some to others must be other than authority, however defined. . . . [A]t this point I am emphasizing that metaphorical theology encourages nontraditional, unconventional, novel ways of expressing the relationship between God and the world not because such ways are necessarily better than received ways but because they cannot be ruled out as *not* better unless tried. Since metaphors are imaginative leaps across a distance—the best metaphors always giving both a shock and a shock of recognition—a metaphorical theology will dare to take risks as well, for the recognition does not come without the shock. A metaphor that has lost its shock (its "is not" quality) loses as well its recognition possibilities (its "is" quality), for the metaphor is no longer "heard": it is taken to be a definition, not a likely account. Thus, a metaphorical theology is open to change, willing to risk the disorientation of new "truths," as well as the possibility that the leap across the abyss will be unsuccessful.

The course I am recommending for theology is not that of theology as "hermeneutics" or of theology as "construction." This is the third point to make about theology as metaphorical construction. I have claimed that it remythologizes in the sense that the theologian as poet-philosopher attempts to identify primary metaphors and models from contemporary experience and elucidate their conceptual implications in order to express Christian faith for our day in powerful, persuasive ways. I have further claimed that, as metaphorical, such theology is always dealing with improper language, language that refers only through a detour, and hence that since it can always miss the mark, there can be no sacred, authoritative, or proper metaphors and models (nor concepts associated with them). I now wish to add a third characteristic of metaphorical theology by suggesting that it is best described as neither hermeneutics nor construction but heuristics. The *Shorter Oxford English Dictionary* defines "heuristic" adjectivally as "serving to find out" and, when employed as a noun related to learning, as "a system of education under which pupils are trained to find out for themselves." Thus heuristic theology will be one that experiments and tests, that thinks in an as-if fashion, that imagines possibilities that are novel, that dares to think differently. It will not accept on the basis of authority but will acknowledge only what it finds convincing and persuasive; it will not, however, be fantasy or mere play but will assume that there is something to find out and that if some imagined possibilities fail, others may succeed. The mention of failure and success, and of the persuasive and the convincing, indicates that although I wish to distinguish heuristic theology from both hermeneutical and constructive theology, it bears similarities to both.

If the characteristic mark of hermeneutical theology is its interpretive stance, especially in regard to texts—both the classic text of the Judeo-Christian tradition (the Hebrew Scriptures and the New Testament) and the exemplary theologies that build on the classic text—then heuristic theology is also interpretive, for it claims that its successful unconventional metaphors are not only in continuity with the paradigmatic events and their significance expressed in this classic text but are also appropriate expressions of these matters for the present time. Heuristic theology, though not bound to the images and concepts in Scripture, is constrained to show that its proposed models are an appropriate, persuasive expression of Christian faith for our time. Making this case involves, of course, some determination of the Christian paradigm, some statement of interpretation concerning how it should be conceived in our time—and this will be forthcoming. The point I am making here, however, is that although a heuristic theology is not limited to interpreting texts—neither the classic text nor texts of the tradition—it is concerned with the same "matter" as those texts and that tradition, namely, the salvific power of God. Its claim, however, will be that that reality is not limited to its biblical or traditional metaphors, models, and concepts, though these do provide "case studies," previously successful metaphors and models that give invaluable assistance in the attempt to characterize "demonstrable continuities" within the Christian paradigm.

If, on the other hand, the distinctive mark of constructive theology is that it does not rely principally on classical sources but attempts its articulation of the concepts of God, world, and human being with the help of a variety of sources, including material from the natural, physical, and social sciences as well as from philosophy, literature, and the arts, then heuristic theology is also constructive in that it claims that a valid understanding of God and the world for a particular time is an imaginative construal built up from a variety of sources, many of them outside religious traditions. Like theology as construction, theology as heuristics supports the assertion that our concept of God is precisely that—*our concept of* God—and not God. Different theologians have expressed this in a variety of ways: Paul Tillich draws the distinction between the symbol God and God as Being-itself, and Gordon Kaufman offers the contrast of the "available" God of our constructs and the "real" God.[6] But a metaphorical, constructive theology has a distinctive emphasis: it will be more experimental, imagistic, and pluralistic than most theologies that fall into the constructive category.

To say that metaphorical theology is experimental is to emphasize its as-if quality, its heuristic quality of finding out for itself. It is a kind of theology especially well suited for times of uncertainty and change, when systematic, comprehensive construction seems inappropriate if not impossible. Many constructive theologies of the past, such as the great systems of Augustine and Thomas, give the appearance of being finished and closed, even though their creators renounced such claims, as in Thomas's famous statement that all he had written was but "straw." But the sort of constructive theology recommended here could be called "free theology,"[7] for it must be willing to play with possibilities and, as a consequence, not take itself too seriously. Though the situation it addresses, the salvific power of God for its time, is a matter of ultimate seriousness, theology's contribution is not. Or to put it more positively, theology is but one way to address that situation, a way that demands risk and novelty. Theologians are placed among many workers in the vineyard; their task is a peculiar and, I believe, limited one, with special responsibility for the language used to express the relationship between God and the world. The kind of theology I am recommending, then, focuses on the images and concepts that have been used in classical formulations of the Judeo-Christian tradition to express that relationship as well as on alternatives one might consider. This is a different view of constructive theology from what is usual within the Christian tradition and one with greater emphasis on its tentative, relative, partial, and hypothetical character.

To say that metaphorical theology is imagistic is to state the obvious, since a metaphor is a kind of image, a verbal one. But emphasizing this is important because of the bias of constructive theology toward conceptual clarity, often at the price of imagistic richness. The kind of theology, or at least *one* kind of theology, needed to address the ecological, nuclear sensibility of our time, focuses on the construction of new metaphors and models. Although it would be insufficient to rest in new images and to refuse to spell out conceptually their implications in as comprehensive a way as possible, the more critical task is to propose what Dennis Nineham calls a "lively imaginative picture" of the way God and the world as we know it are related. Metaphorical theology will chiefly focus on trying to establish the persuasive appropriateness of the metaphors for our situation, though it will, of course, also undertake the task of showing the conceptual implications and comprehensiveness of its proposed models of God and the world. The assumption here is that belief and behavior are more influenced by images than by concepts, or to phrase it in a less disjunctive way, that concepts without images are sterile. It is no coincidence that most religious traditions turn to personal and public human relationships to serve as metaphors and models of the relationship between God and the world: God as father, mother, lover, friend, king, lord, governor. These metaphors give a precision and persuasive power to the construct of God which concepts alone cannot. Because religions, including Christianity, are not incidentally imagistic but centrally and necessarily so, theology must also be an affair of the imagination.

To say that metaphorical theology is pluralistic is to make two points. First, since no metaphor or model refers properly or directly to God, many are necessary. All are inappropriate, partial, and inadequate; the most that can be said is that some aspect or aspects of the God-world relationship are illuminated by this or that model in a fashion relevant to a particular time and place. One of the classic difficulties with metaphors that become models, such as that of God the father, is that they are often reified, petrified, and expanded so as not only to exclude other models but also to pretend to the status of definitions.[8] I would insist, however, that models of God are not definitions of God but likely accounts of experiences of relating to God with the help of relationships we know and understand. We speak of relating to God as one would to a companion or lover; or a king or master; or the sun or ocean; or a rock or mountain; or a mother or sister. Obviously, we are not here defining the nature of God, nor could we do so if we used less anthropomorphic and naturalistic language. Predicates such as omniscience, infinity, omnipotence, and omnipresence do not properly apply to God either, for the meaning of all such language—knowledge, finitude, power, presence—applies properly only to our existence, not God's. All that such predicates represent is an attempt to make human qualities limitless. In other words, how language, any language, applies to God we do not know; what religious and theological language is at most is metaphorical forays attempting to express experiences of relating to God. It is like the experience of relating to a mother, or a mountain, or a king, or a comrade, or an ocean, or a liberator—or to use the more abstract language, to One who is limitlessly good, powerful, knowledgeable, and present. In other words, if one accepts that metaphors (and all language about God) are principally adverbial, having to do with how we relate to God rather than defining the nature of God, then no metaphors or models can be reified, petrified, or expanded so as to exclude all others. One can, for instance, include many possibilities: we can envision relating to God as to a father and a mother, to a healer and a liberator, to the sun and a mountain. As definitions of God, these possibilities are mutually exclusive; as models expressing experiences of relating to God, they are mutually enriching. Thus, metaphorical theology is pluralistic, welcoming many models of God.

The second way that metaphorical theology is pluralistic is that, as a partial account focused especially on the imagistic foundation of theology, it is but *one kind* of theology, not the only or proper kind. Since metaphorical theology, as I have envisioned it, is hypothetical, tentative, partial, open-ended, skeptical, and heuristic, it would be contradictory to claim that such theology is anything more than one of many needed kinds of reflective enterprises. To propose and elucidate metaphors and models of the relationship between God and the world appropriate for an ecological, nuclear age is not to reject other theological projects. Nor does a metaphorical theology, which sees itself focused principally at the level of the imagination, denounce kinds of theology that propose to reflect on Christian faith in other ways. I am not merely suggesting that theological tolerance is a good thing; rather, my own position within a metaphorical theology demands it. The kind of theology that seems essential to me in our time, one that works at the foundational level of the imagination, where the images that form our concepts are grounded, is necessarily partial and hypothetical. It can in no way claim comprehensiveness or closure; hence, it must be open to other attempts, other methods, and other routes. Metaphorical theology is necessarily tolerant or pluralistic, aware that, just as the particular metaphors and models it proposes are but relative, heuristic ones, so also the project as such, this kind of theology as a whole, is a tentative affair and can advance few solid claims in its own behalf. In this sense, it is, I believe, in the tradition of the *via negativa:* finding little to say of God with certainty, it boldly makes its case hypothetically and lets it rest.

In summary, metaphorical theology is a kind of heuristic construction that in focusing on the imaginative construal of the God-world relationship attempts to remythologize Christian faith through metaphors and models appropriate for an ecological, nuclear age.

Notes

1. John Hick, ed., *The Myth of God Incarnate* (Philadelphia: Westminster, 1977), 201–202.
2. See McFague 1982.
3. The example is from Black, *Models and Metaphors*, 41–42.
4. The role and definition of models in other fields are complex and beyond our concern here. See McFague 1983, ch. 3 and its notes for an introduction to some of this material.
5. Jacques Derrida, "White Mythology: Metaphor in the Text of Philosophy," *New Literary History* 6 (1974): 42.
6. See Paul Tillich, *Systematic Theology*, vol. 1 (Chicago: University of Chicago Press, 1963), 235ff.; and Gordon Kaufman, *God the Problem* (Cambridge: Harvard University Press, 1972), 82–115.
7. Robert P. Scharlemann uses this phrase to describe the kind of theology that constructs theological models, and he sees it as an alternative to other kinds of theology: confessional, metaphysical, biblicistic, religious thought. "It is a free theology in the sense that it can make use of any of these materials—confessional, metaphysical, biblical, religious, and secular—without being bound to them" ("Theological Models and Their Construction," *Journal of Religion* 53 [1973]: 82–83).
8. For further elucidation of this point, see McFague 1983, ch. 5.

8

Theology of Nature: Remythologizing Christian Doctrine

The introduction to chapter 5 above introduces the organic model that is at the core of The Body of God *as well as most of her subsequent books. In her earlier work, most notably* Models of God, *McFague discusses the need for remythologizing our understandings of God. Here she extends that work of remythologizing to our understandings of nature by stressing the necessity of taking seriously the common creation story emerging from the sciences—that is, the organic interrelatedness of all creation. She also draws on the renowned theologian-scientist Teilhard de Chardin, whose own project in many ways anticipates McFague's work. Key to this selection is her hearty defense of experience "that sets a priority on physical and cultural embodiment." In so doing, she reiterates her commitment to a theology that makes a difference in the world.*

Source: 1993:78–91

While the attempt to see continuity between the Christian story of redemption and the cosmic story of the evolution of the universe is one that all Christians must support, it may be that a retrospective perspective—which is very ancient—is still the best one. That is, faith seeking understanding sees traces of divine purpose, love, and care in our cosmic story, as Christians have in other ages found them in pictures of reality current in their time. We, they, also find more than traces of evil, perversion, and seeming malevolence (the present version speaks of them in terms of the brutalities of natural selection), so that the end result is not evidence of purpose leading to belief but corroboration of faith arrived at in spite of evidence to the contrary.

Lest this distinction sound like a retreat into fideism, I suggest we look at a similar stance by the biologist Stephen Jay Gould.[1] Gould's position, as I understand it, is that evolution displays no direction or purpose, no overriding push or pull toward some goal. It is not the "conventional tale of steadily increasing excellence, complexity, and diversity" that could be imaged by a ladder or a cone.[2] Rather, the appropriate model is a bush with many branches, most of which met with extinction in a way that was "utterly unpredictable and quite unrepeatable."[3] What brings about the incredible diversity (and what we consider levels) in evolution is not purpose but small and unpredictable changes operating in a contingent fashion. Adaptations are always developed for local environments; hence, cause is always local and specific, and, if a feature proves useful for later developments, that is just a happy accident for that species, as was the development of a sturdy fin in our ancestor fishes, which proved useful as a backbone later on land.[4] Gould claims that a sense of larger purpose or direction has no support. What happens happens in the details, at the local level through the interaction of innumerable factors, and hence anything that does happen might very well *not* have happened or happened otherwise. He uses the inspired example of the Jimmy Stewart movie, *It's a Wonderful Life,* to illustrate the point: small and unpredictable changes lead to vastly different results both in human development and in evolutionary history.

Many religious people find this conclusion unnerving since it appears to eliminate purpose (God) from the evolutionary process. But there is another possibility. . . : *it is indeed a wonderful life.* What has evolved (regardless of why or how it occurred) is complex, diverse, intricate beyond our wildest imaginations.

From Where We Stand: Christian Doctrine in Light of the Organic Model

We ourselves are a marvel beyond belief, not only because we did evolve but because of what and who we are—indeed, just a little lower than the angels (or perhaps just a little higher, given the present state of angelology). I am suggesting that from the point of view of both contemporary science and Christian reformulation, one valid and important place for the believer to stand is before the *present* picture of evolutionary history. We could focus on the *what* rather than the *why* or *how*: on what (who) we have become, both in our relations with other life-forms (our place in the cosmos) and our special responsibilities, rather than on how we got the way we are. The latter epistemological question has always fascinated the West, but a more practical kind of question perhaps ought to be: Who are we in the scheme of things, and what is required of us? Likewise, within this more practical framework, to say God is creator is not to focus on what God did once upon a time, either at the beginning or during the evolutionary process, but on how we can perceive ourselves and everything else in the universe as dependent upon God now, in terms of our cosmic story. What does it mean to say that God is both transcendent and immanent in relation to the world as presently conceived and imagined? How can we model this sense of unitary dependence of the universe on God as well as our proper place in the scheme of things in light of the present state of evolutionary history?

Moreover, and of utmost importance, whatever may have been the mechanisms of evolutionary history in the past, *evolution in the present and future on our planet will be inextricably involved with human powers and decisions.* Willy-nilly, whether we want it or not, the future of our planet has to a significant degree fallen into our hands. Natural selection is not the only or perhaps even the principal power on our planet now; cultural evolution, the ability to evolve into a sharing, caring human population living with other life-forms in a fashion that our planet can sustain, may be more important. And at this point, we can certainly introduce the notion of purpose, of direction. Those from the Christian tradition might well suggest that the future direction of evolution ought to be toward wider sympathetic inclusiveness with all forms of life, especially the most needy and vulnerable, understanding this direction as a contemporary reading of the paradigmatic Christian story—the destabilizing, inclusive, nonhierarchical vision of fulfillment for all of creation.[5] The various humanitarian and religious traditions will have directions, purposes, goals to suggest for the common future of our planet. The understandings of salvation from different cultural and religious communities suggest guidelines for the present and future of creation, whatever its past. None of these can be read off evolutionary history and can only be read back into it with a very light touch and with an equal—if not greater—attention to the radical contingency, deep mystery, and seeming indifference if not malevolence (from the perspective of any particular species or individual) of the process. But we can say, from where we now stand on our planet, both that it *is* a wonderful life (a diverse, rich, complex one) *and* that we have a part to play in its future.

The present essay, then, does not so much deny the value of other projects, those with traditional epistemological concerns, as it suggests that another legitimate, and limited, issue is also valid. We can emphasize that while creation spirituality is concerned with appreciating the cosmos and natural theology with understanding it, another concern is acting responsibly within it. While this essay will focus on the ethical or pragmatic concern, it will nevertheless rely on both appreciation and understanding as necessary prerequisites for appropriate action. That is, through remythologizing the doctrines of God and human beings in light of the picture of reality from contemporary science—through the use of the organic model as a way of reconceiving the relation of God and the world—the appropriate human stance vis-à-vis God and our planet will emerge. Remythologizing involves both appreciation and understanding; it is a form of embodied thought combining image and concept that calls forth both a feeling and a thinking response. It also implies an ethical response.[6] If one uses the model of the universe as God's body, if one appreciates and understands creation as organically interrelated, one would, or at least might, act differently toward it than if one used the model of creation as a work of art (one possible model from the Genesis story). The assumption that what we appreciate and how we think influences how we behave is a very complex issue and has supporters and detracters on both sides (among them the Greeks versus Paul, the former rather optimistic about the correlation and the latter bemoaning that he knows the good but does not do it). Hence, it behooves us to be modest about any remythologizing project: it is indeed but one small voice in the planetary conversation.

It might help to situate my project if we compare it to a well-known similar one, that of Pierre Teilhard de Chardin. Teilhard's impressive achievements as a scientist and a theologian are not at issue here; rather, it is that aspect of his work concerned with internalizing the new scientific story that was just emerging in his time. He was one of the first involved in the contemporary science-theology conversation. While one aspect of his work was a strong natural theology to show the convergence of evolutionary and theological purpose, another, and I believe more important, contribution was his attempt to remythologize the new creation story from a Christian perspective. What was special about his work and why in spite of continuing criticisms of it from both scientific and theological circles it continues to draw attention is that he felt deeply the need to reimagine Christian doctrine in terms of twentieth-century science and to see the new scientific story in Christian terms. His achievement was essentially poetic, not scientific or theological (if theology is equated with conceptualization). If his project is understood as a thought experiment, a likely account, to help people internalize the new sensibility from a Christian perspective—how a Christian should feel and act in the awesome spatial and temporal dimensions of this story—then both the limitations and the distinctive contributions of his project become clear. Something of this sensibility is expressed when Teilhard writes: "Blessed be you, universal matter, unmeasurable time, boundless ether, triple abyss of stars and atoms and generations: you who by overflowing and dissolving our narrow standards of measurement reveal to us the dimensions of God . . . ."[7] Every revelation of the awesomeness of the universe as pictured by twentieth-century science became for Teilhard an occasion for celebrating God's sublimity as its creator. Teilhard's distinctive contribution was his attempt to internalize the new creation story from a Christian perspective in a series of often outrageous metaphors, such as, for instance, the bread and wine of the eucharist as embodying *in nuce* the entire universe: "There is but one single mass in the world: the true Host, the total Host, is the universe which is continually being more intimately penetrated and vivified by Christ."[8] Christ and matter, Christianity and evolutionary history, are reimagined together through the metaphor of the eucharist. My point is not that Teilhard's remythologizing of the new creation story was entirely successful; rather, it is that he attempted it at all.

Hopefully, the nature of my project, both its limitations and possible contribution, is becoming clearer. It is to embody the picture of reality from postmodern science in a model that will help us internalize its new sensibility in a way not just compatible with but enriched by Christian faith (a two-way project). In a way similar to Teilhard's project, it will try to embody the new creation story metaphorically, using the contributions of both contemporary science and Christian faith, for the organic model comes from and is enriched by both science and Christianity. Unlike some versions of natural theology that operate by reason alone (finding their material in the sciences) and unlike some theologies of nature that rely on faith alone (finding their material in revelation), our theology of nature will be dialectical. Theology of nature has sometimes been understood as the opposite of natural theology, as in this statement by Jürgen Moltmann: "Every theology of nature interprets nature in the light of the self-revelation of the creative God . . . the aim of our investigation is not what nature can contribute to our knowledge of God, but what the concept of God can contribute to our knowledge of nature."[9] Our position questions that dualism, for if one is interested in thinking holistically, as beings-in-a-world, a world of which God is the creator and redeemer, then one will search for a way to express, to model, that situation which will take both contributions seriously. The mutual influence of postmodern science and Christian faith can be seen in the model of the universe (creation) as God's body. Both can contribute to an understanding of the organic model in distinctive ways; in fact, as we will try to show, the model is a rich one precisely because of the interaction of the two kinds of organic discourse, scientific and Christian. Religious traditions, including Christianity, always have used and should continue to use the images, symbols, and concepts arising out of the common contemporary cultural field to express their most deeply held beliefs. Needless to say, the use of these materials will change the faith. But to the extent that major religious models likewise influence culture, as in the case of the monarchical model's long and deep domination over the Western sensibility, Christianity's contribution to the contemporary organic model may also be important. In the model of the universe as God's body, not only does postmodern science help us understand the unity and diversity of the body in liberating ways, but divine embodiment makes sacred all embodiment: neither perspective alone is as rich as both together.

Reasons for Living within the Organic Model

We come, then, finally, to the thorny issue of the status of metaphors and models and especially the model we have chosen to work with, the universe as God's body, the organic model. Why choose this one? What criteria support it? Does it have the backing of reason, revelation, experience, tradition, or what? Is it valuable because it is useful, liberating, or rhetorically powerful? These age-old, complex questions cannot be dealt with easily or lightly, but already in this project some directions toward an answer have emerged. First, this essay is concerned with the body, embodiment. It takes as its point of departure, its site or point of view, the supposition that embodiment is basic. This is not a foundation, revelation, or inference from reason; rather, it is a wager, proposition, or experiment to investigate. I found in my own journey as a Christian, a feminist, and an amateur ecologist that the body kept emerging in different ways as an often neglected but very important reality, seemingly a basic one. Likewise, at least on one reading of postmodern science, the organic model has emerged as a central way to interpret the contemporary picture of reality. Hence, what we will say about criteria for ways of modeling the world will be heavily weighted in the direction of embodiment. Any argument for a model of reality that neglects, disparages, or negates embodiment (such as Cartesianism, Kantianism, and deconstruction, to a lesser extent) would be operating out of a fundamentally different paradigm than the one presupposed by this essay.

Second, criteria are multiple. This is necessarily the case if one is operating experimentally with a model to be investigated rather than a truth of revelation to be illustrated or a datum of science to be proven. The model of the universe as God's body obviously does not fall into either of the above categories. To take this discussion out of the stratosphere, let us ask why someone *would or might* adopt the organic model as a major way to interpret reality. (This is assuming a more or less conscious choice; millions have adopted the model unconsciously over the course of human history.) When one decides to live as if something is the case (which is what one does in adopting models, for as metaphors they are not descriptions but invitations to experimental living) there are usually many reasons for doing so, of many different sorts, and at many levels of consciousness. Life is complex, to say the least; why, then, should the credibility, persuasiveness, and power of a model by and in which to live be less so? Any one or even two reasons for living as if the world is organic, and as if we are all interrelated and interdependent—a view that has vast and potentially demanding consequences for how one conducts one's business—are surely inadequate. One would need multiple reasons, and that, I believe, is what is the case when we consciously embrace a model, in contrast to simply accepting the dominant one in our culture.

I shall suggest a few reasons that might persuade someone to adopt a model, particularly the organic one. Our supposition is that no one reason, one basis or foundation, exists for being willing to live according to the organic model, but a variety of reasons and feelings, as well as hunches and hopes, come into play. Since we are embodied beings (not merely minds deciding in an abstract and disembodied way on truth) attempting to find satisfying, helpful, rich constructs within which to live our lives, we are likely to be persuaded to adopt a model only if it speaks to many different dimensions of our personal and social lives. It has to make sense not just to our minds, but to our bodies, our feelings, our needs, and even our hopes and dreams.

A sampling of some of these reasons includes our own embodied and cultural experience; the testimony of significant communities to which we belong; the view of reality current in our time; and the usefulness of a perspective, model, or construct for humane living. These four reasons are certainly not exhaustive; they are only meant to suggest a few important factors that might contribute to adopting this model. Let us look at each of them.

"Experience" is a word so fraught with misunderstanding, bad press, and dissension that introducing it without at least two chapters of qualifications and critiques by Kantians, Hegelians, deconstructionists, feminists and womanists, as well as Whiteheadians and empiricists, may be the height of folly. But the term will not disappear in spite of its slippery philosophical status, mainly because in its most basic sense experience simply means the act of living, which all creatures undergo. The controversy emerges when the question arises as to what we experience. From the perspective of our issue—what might persuade someone to adopt a model, especially the organic one?—I would make two points.

First, at the most basic level, experience is embodied; we are bodies that experience. Of course there is no such thing as "disembodied experience," and yet, curiously, the body is often forgotten. Those who think and write about the status of experience often seem to neglect this primordial level that connects our sophisticated mental probings into and in response to our environment with the amoeba's tentative reaching out and recoiling. Experience is *felt* experience, the experience of bodies at the most elemental level. Experience begins with feelings of hot and cold, hunger and satiety, comfort and pain, the most basic ways in which all creatures live in their environments. We live here also and this basic level connects us in a web of universal experience making possible an ever-widening inclusive sympathy for the pains and pleasures of creatures like and unlike ourselves. While some would insulate us from our citizenship in this community of nature, separating off our experience as linguistic and hence qualitatively unlike that of other animals, embodied experience links the cries of a hungry child and a wounded animal, the exhilaration we feel at the sight of a magnificent sunset and the soothing touch of a hand on a painful sore. Through our bodies, in their agonies and ecstasies that lie behind and beyond all linguistic expression, we are bound into a network of relations with our natural environment and experience ourselves as bodies with other bodies. Whatever else experience means, it includes bodily experience as a primordial reality, uniting us in ever-widening concentric circles with the entire planet in all its diverse, rich forms of embodiment.

Second, and of equal importance, experience is always embodied for human beings not only in relation to the natural world but also culturally, economically, sexually, socially, and so on. It is radically concrete: the sites of experience are particular forms of privilege or oppression as the various liberation movements have persuasively argued. Sites of experience are neither general nor neutral; they are highly specific and marked by various forms of power or lack of power. Embodiment for human beings is certainly a physical reality as we have underscored, but it is also a construction of culture, and even the physical dimension is a highly constructed reality.[10] Even physical reality is experienced differently depending on one's cultural, economic, racial, and gender situation. There is no experience-in-general nor any body-in-general, yet there is experience and there is body, both constructed and both particular. That we are embodied (all differently and constructed variously) and that we respond from our own experience (all differently contextualized) influence us as we reflect on adopting constructs within which to live our lives.

If the view of experience that sets a priority on physical and cultural embodiment is persuasive, then serious consideration of the organic model might follow. The view of experience suggested here supports adopting a model of reality that privileges the needs of bodies as well as their physical and cultural differences. Moreover, this view implies that an appropriate religious experience might be a natural affection for other creatures as manifestations or sacraments of the divine as well as a natural longing for union with God through these others.

A second reason for adopting a particular construct or model is that it carries the testimony of the religious community in which one stands. Other significant communities also influence one's decision, but religious communities in the past have functioned as primary interpretive traditions, and for many still do. Some people, of course, accept the doctrines of a religious community as absolute, believing that they have been revealed from on high, but there is also a reason to take seriously a historical, cultural tradition because it has molded one's society and one's own being. For most Westerners the important traditions are Jewish and Christian. They have given the West its identity for good and for bad, and many still find them personally nourishing. Others believe that with radical revision, they can be prophetic means of liberating the oppressed. The point is that these traditions matter and rather than abandoning them for alternatives (such as Buddhism or Goddess religions, for instance), one might judge a construct or model in light of an interpretation of one's own formative tradition. To take Christianity as an example, one interpretation of this tradition finds it to be a highly organic one, although ambivalently so, tending to stress the symbolic character of embodiment imagery rather than the physical base of the imagery. Nonetheless, it is a tradition that is open to a reconstruction of its organic model along lines more compatible with an ecological sensibility.

Another reason (one we have stressed repeatedly) for adopting a model is that it is compatible with the view of reality current in one's time. The organic model is one of the major ways that postmodern science is being interpreted. It has considerable scientific backing. While, as we have stressed, major scientific theories are constructs in a way not unlike other significant construals of reality, including religious ones, nonetheless, scientific models have both a universality and a persuasiveness at least to most Westerners that few if any other constructs can claim. If one wants to live as a whole person in the world as understood in one's time, one needs to attend seriously to the picture of reality that is assumed at that time to be the way things are. Moreover, if that picture (as in the case of the organic model) is a highly attractive one, one that not only does the usual things that major models must do, such as give a comprehensive, coherent interpretation of relevant data, but is also illuminating, rich, and thought-provoking, then one has even more reason to consider adoption.

Finally, and of primary importance, one adopts a model because it helps to make things better. One has the hunch and the hope that it is good for human and other forms of life. In spite of evidence to the contrary, one dreams of a new age when all beings shall live together in peace and justice. Some models seem to help us both to envision and to work toward that hope more than others. To believe that a perspective or construct is meaningful and true because it is useful in the conduct of life is as old and honored a tradition as the view that one should accept it because it corresponds with an ideal, eternal reality. The first tradition is Aristotelian, privileging a pragmatic, practical, concrete view of truth, while the second is Platonic, insisting on an idealistic, abstract, speculative view. The first says that truth is concerned with the good life for the members of a community that they must define and work for, while the second claims that there is an ideal reality external to the world that is the standard against which all human understanding is judged. Each has its merits. The Platonic tradition has the particular value of providing an ideal (a utopia, the kingdom of God) as a prophetic critique against all actual societies as well as a goal toward which to strive. The Aristotelian tradition, with its emphasis on practical reason, conversation in regard to the common good among the citizens of the *polis* (now the cosmos), and present, worldly goals of well-being for all members of a community, is gaining ground. It has always been attractive to the American pragmatic mind, but it also lies behind socialism, contemporary feminism, and many liberation movements. As the catchphrase expresses it, we must not only understand the world but change it. Knowledge is not just a speculative matter but has a practical end: to make things better.

And this is certainly the case with models we adopt to understand the worlds within which we live. Is it, for instance, better to live as if the world is a machine with all parts externally related, each independently serving a specific function, and the whole maintained through outside forces driving the parts, or is it better to live as if the world is an organism with all parts internally related and interdependent, with each part also independent in its own concrete particularity, and the whole maintained through powers inherent in the various parts? In assessing a model for adoption, we do (or should) base our judgment on many factors, among them, our own concrete, embodied experience; the insights and beliefs of the communities commanding our deepest allegiance; the picture of reality current in our time; and *also* whether the model will help us live so that human beings and other creatures can thrive and reach some level of fulfillment. To say a model for living is meaningful and true because it is useful in this sense is not a lesser view of the matter. It assumes that our function as human beings on this planet is not mainly to think correct thoughts that correspond to some eternal set of verities, but to live appropriately and responsibly. Our reason, understood as a practical faculty, can assist us in this task. This assumption for many of us, myself included, extends as well to faith in God, which is not so much correct thoughts about God (ones that correspond to God's being), but appropriate, responsible action to help a planet, created and loved by God, be an adequate home for all its many creatures. We are, in other words, called to a way of life, not to a set of beliefs, to a practical, mundane task involving our total embodied selves and oriented toward the fulfillment of (among other things) the basic, bodily needs of all creatures in the planetary community. We are not called to a speculative, abstract journey of enlightenment of our inner selves, which is basically indifferent to embodiment, our own and that of other beings.

In summary, I have suggested a few criteria (embodied experience, interpretive communities, the current picture of reality, and usefulness) that might be persuasive reasons for adopting a major model, especially the organic one. Taking all this into account, we still need to press the question of the status of a major construct such as the organic one. Is it a useful fiction? a given natural reality? a revealed absolute? a partial but inadequate truth? By promoting it as a worldview within which to live are we being utilitarians, empiricists, revelationists, or critical realists, to use some of the traditional epistemological positions? From the above discussion on reasons one might give for adopting a particular construct, it is evident that none of these positions is adequate alone, although we should include aspects of each of them in our answer. The reasons for adopting a construct are plural and multidimensional; the status of the adopted construct is the same. For example, the organic model is useful, based in reality (as currently understood), has connections with beliefs in some religious communities, and offers one important but only partial construct. Together these reasons might satisfy an interrogator, although she might still ask, "But is reality *really* organic, does it have the characteristics of an organism that you have spelled out?" As a metaphor or model of reality, the answer must always be a no and yes: no, of course it does not have these characteristics, since embodiment is a way of talking about reality (which can also be spoken of in many other ways); but yes, for the reasons given above, reality appears to be relatively patient in regard to accepting this construct or grid through which it is seen. If we always and only have constructs with which to interpret reality, then necessarily we have to answer the question in more or less terms—is reality more patient, open to, tolerant of this model or that one? The answer lies, I believe, in reasons such as the ones we have given for being persuaded to adopt a model. The answer, then, is finally a belief or a wager that reality is like this more than it is like that. And if enough of us were so to live, reality would *become* more like we believe. That is not a vicious circle, but a hope against hope. We can create reality—in fact, we do all the time with the constructs we embrace unknowingly. We can also create reality knowingly—and humanely—by living within models that we wager are true as well as good for human beings and other forms of life.

Notes

1. See, for instance, Stephen Jay Gould, *The Flamingo's Smile: Reflections in Natural* History (New York: Norton, 1987); idem, *The Mismeasure of Man* (New York: Norton, 1981); idem, *Wonderful Life: The Burgess Shale and the Nature of History* (New York: Norton, 1989).

2. Gould, *Wonderful Life*, 25.

3. Ibid., 14.

4. Gould, *Flamingo's Smile*, 409–10.

5. See McFague 1993, ch. 6; also McFague 1987, ch. 2.

6. See McFague 1987, ch. 2; also McFague 1982.

7. As quoted in *The Oxford Book of Prayer*, ed. George Appleton (Oxford: Oxford University Press, 1988), 57.

8. Pierre Teilhard de Chardin, "Pantheism and Christianity," *Christianity and Evolution* (London: Collins, 1971), 73–74.

9. Jürgen Moltmann, *God in Creation: A New Theology of Creation and the Spirit of God*, trans. Margaret Kohl (London: SCM, 1985), 53.

10. See McFague 1993, ch. 1, "A Meditation on the Body."

9

Consider the Lilies of the Field

In the preface to Super, Natural Christians *(1998), McFague describes the book as "the last in a series of four books on religious language" (2). In retrospect, however, this volume holds a less defined place in her oeuvre than what she suggests there; one might just as easily see her first four books as the series on religious language and* Super, Natural Christians *as her turn to focusing especially on ecology, which continues then in her next three books. Perhaps it is best seen as a sort of side trip on the journey she has been taking readers in her publishing project. It does not especially extend the line of thought begun in* The Body of God, *though it does seem to assume the organic model introduced there (while not engaging it or the concept of panentheism directly). In some ways, it is an extended meditation on how we might live holistically within that organic model, as she states in the book's thesis: "Christian practice, loving God and neighbor as subjects, as worthy of our love in and for themselves should be extended to nature" (1). As such, it is more a work of spirituality or ethics. Nevertheless, this chapter does introduce some important ideas for her project: (a) the arrogant eye over against the loving eye; and (b) the need to shift to a subject-subjects model for regarding one another and nature.*

Source: 1998·16–44

Should Christians love nature? Most have not over the last two thousand years and many today still don't. In some circles, loving nature is pagan or what Goddess worshipers do. Of course, Christians should respect nature, use it carefully, and even protect it, but isn't loving it a bit extreme? *Should* we love nature? My answer is a resounding Yes. Christians should because the Christian God is embodied. That is what the incarnation claims. God does not despise physical reality but loves it and has become one with it. The Christian tradition is full of body language: the Word made flesh, the bread and wine that become the body and blood of Christ, the body of the church. Physical reality, earthly reality—bodies and nature—are central to an incarnational theology.

Paying Attention

But *how* should we love nature? That is the more difficult and interesting question. Most people love nature in a general way and some even in a religious way. Most of us get a high from spectacular sunsets and cute panda bears; many of us have religious feelings in a cathedral of the pines. We all like to fuse with nature, enjoy oceanic feelings of oneness with it. But that is, of course, just another use of nature, a higher use than eating it or using it for recreational purposes, but a use nonetheless. Some Christians have loved nature—loved it as a way to God. The sacramental tradition, most evident in Roman Catholicism, Eastern Orthodoxy, and Anglicanism and including the wonderful voices of Augustine, Hildegard of Bingen, and Gerard Manley Hopkins, has told us, in Hopkins's words, that "the world is charged with the grandeur of God." The sacramental tradition assumes that God is present with us not only in the hearing of the Word and in the Eucharist but also in each and every being in creation. This tradition has helped to preserve and develop an appreciation for nature in a religion that, for the most part, has been indifferent to the natural world as well as justly accused of contributing to its deterioration and destruction. The sacramental tradition should be acknowledged as contributing to a sense of the world as valuable—indeed, as holy—because it is a symbol of the divine and can help us reach God.

The natural world is here, then, a stepping-stone in our pilgrimage to God—a means to an end. Its value does not lie primarily in itself: other life-forms and other natural entities do not have intrinsic value. Rather, they are valuable as pathways connecting human beings to God, as ways we can express our relationship with God. Everything in the world can become a symbol for the divine-human relationship, as Augustine so eloquently says: "But what is it I love when I love You? Not the beauty of any bodily thing.... Yet in a sense I do love light and melody and fragrance and food and embrace when I love my God—the light and the voice and the fragrance and the food and embrace in the soul..."[1]

But I would like to suggest a different way that Christians should love nature—a way in keeping with the earthly, bodily theology suggested by the tradition's incarnationalism, a way that allows us to love the natural world for its intrinsic worth, to love it, in all its differences and detail, in itself, for itself. Francis of Assisi epitomizes this sensibility in his praise of the sun, moon, earth, and water as his brothers and sisters ... Emily Dickinson suggested this way of loving nature when she wrote to a friend that the only commandment that she never broke was to "consider the lilies of the field"—not to use them to decorate her yard or pick them for her table (or even for the altar), but just *consider* them.[2] How Christians should love nature is by obeying a simple but very difficult axiom: *pay attention to it.*

But how can we learn to pay attention to something other than ourselves? What does it mean to really pay attention? Iris Murdoch, the British novelist, gives a clue when she says, "It is a *task* to come to see the world as it is." We will bracket for the moment the thorny hermeneutical issue implicit in the phrase "the world as it is" . . . , focusing now on the "me" versus "other" issue—the problem of attending to another, any other. Murdoch's suggestion is that paying attention is difficult and contrary to how we usually see the world, which is, as she says, in terms of our "fat relentless ego."[3] She gives a personal example: "I am looking out of my window in an anxious and resentful state of mind, brooding perhaps on some damage done to my prestige. Then suddenly I observe a kestrel. In a moment everything is altered. There is nothing but kestrel. And when I return to thinking of the other matter it seems less important."[4] There is a natural and proper part of us, she adds, that takes "a self-forgetful pleasure in the sheer, alien pointless independent existence of animals, birds, stones, and trees."[5] The message is that we pay attention to difference, that we really learn to see what is different from ourselves. That is not easy. We can acknowledge a thing in its difference if it is important to us or useful to us, but realizing that something other than oneself is real, in itself, for itself, is difficult. To acknowledge another being as different—perhaps even indifferent to me, as for instance a hovering kestrel—is, for most of us, a feat of the imagination.

One of the greatest contributions of contemporary feminism is its celebration of difference. To date this has been limited principally to differences among human beings—recognizing that there is no universal human being nor even any essential woman. As a recent book on liberation theologies comments, "People only look alike when you cannot be bothered to look at them closely."[6] But how does one learn to celebrate difference, differences among people and differences among life-forms? How can we know and accept real differences? The first step, we have suggested, is by paying attention. Art often helps us to do so. Art stops, freezes, and frames bits of reality and, by so doing, helps us to pay attention, as for instance in this haiku by a Japanese poet:

An old silent pond

Into the pond a frog jumps.
Splash! Silence again.

The poet has put a frame around this moment. As novelist Frederick Buechner comments on this haiku, "What the frame does is enable us to see not just something about the moment but the moment itself in all its ineffable ordinariness and particularity. The chances are that if we had been passing when the frog jumped, we wouldn't have noticed a thing or, noticing it, wouldn't have given it a second thought."[7] Art frames fragments of our world: paintings, poetry, novels, sculpture, dance, music help us to look at colors, sounds, bodies, events, characters—whatever—with full attention. Something is lifted out of the world and put into a frame so that we can, perhaps for the first time, *see* it. Most of the time we do not see: we pass a tree, an early spring crocus, the face of another human being, and we do not marvel at these wonders, because we do not see their specialness, their individuality, their difference. As Joseph Wood Krutch reminds us: "It is not easy to live in that continuous awareness of things which alone is true living . . . the faculty of wonder tires easily . . ."[8]

Simone Weil deepens the meaning of paying attention with her comment that "absolute attention is prayer." She does not say that prayer is absolute attention, but that absolute attention is prayer. By paying attention to something she says, we are, in fact praying. May Sarton, poet and essayist, comments on this phrase from Weil: "When you think about it, we almost never pay absolute attention. The minute we do, something happens. We see whatever we're looking at with such attention, and something else is given—a sort of revelation. I looked at the heart of a daffodil in this way the other day—deep down. It was a pale yellow one, but deep down, at the center, it was emerald green—like a green light. It was amazing."[9] By paying attention to some fragment, some piece of matter in the world, we are in fact praying. Is this what Alice Walker means when she writes in *The Color Purple*, "I think it pisses God off if you walk by the color purple in a field somewhere and don't notice it"?[10] Is this what an incarnational theology, an earthly, bodily theology, implies? Perhaps it is. We are asking the question, how should a Christian love nature?

The answer emerging is that we must pay attention—detailed, careful, concrete attention—to the world that lies around us but is not us. We must do this *because we cannot love what we do not know*. This profound truism is contained in the phrase we have all uttered at sometime: "If they really knew me, they wouldn't love me," implying that only love based on real knowledge is valuable. We must, as Murdoch says, try to see "the world as it is" in order to love it. To *really* love nature (and not just ourselves in nature or nature as useful to us—even its use as a pathway to God), we must pay attention *to it.* Love and knowledge go together; we can't have the one without the other.

Two Ways of Seeing the World

I would like to suggest that a branch of science, nature writing, can help us learn to pay attention. The kind of paying attention that one sees in good nature writing suggests a paradigm for us. Nature writing is not scientific writing that hides behind pseudo-objectivity; rather, it combines acute, careful observation with a kind of loving empathy for and delight in its object. In fact, as we shall see, it is more like the interaction of two subjects than the usual dualism of a subject observing an object. Nature writer Edward Abbey describes it as "sympathy for the object under study, and more than sympathy, love. A love based on prolonged contact and interaction. . . . Observation informed by sympathy, love, intuition."[11] The best nature writing has this sense of personal testimony and detail, what Murdoch calls engagement with the "unutterable particularity" of the natural world.[12] In the writings of Annie Dillard, Gretel Ehrlich, Barry Lopez, Aldo Leopold, and Alice Walker, we see this sense of personal call opening the self to the surprise and delight of deeper and deeper engagement with concrete detail, the particularities and differences that comprise the natural world. It is a way of seeing, a kind of paying attention, that thrives on differences and detail. It is also an interactive kind of knowing—the knower must be open to the known, be sympathetic to, and engaged by the known. It is a knowing that is infused with loving, a love that wants to know more.

Let me illustrate this kind of nature writing by contrasting two very different ways of seeing the world. The first example is Annie Dillard's description of a goldfish named Ellery. The detail in this passage—Dillard's paying attention to the particularities of Ellery calls forth in her, and in me, a sense of wonder and affection.

> This Ellery cost me twenty-five cents. He is a deep red-orange, darker than most goldfish. He steers short distances mainly with his slender red lateral fins; they seem to provide impetus for going backward, up, or down. It took me a few days to discover his ventral fins; they are completely transparent and all but invisible—dream fins. He also has a short anal fin, and a tail that is deeply notched and perfectly transparent at the two tapered tips. He can extend his

mouth, so it looks like a length of pipe; he can shift the angle of his eyes in his head so he can look before and behind himself, instead of simply out to his side. His belly, what there is of it, is white ventrally, and a patch of this white extends up his sides—the variegated Ellery. When he opens his gill slits he shows a thin crescent of silver where the flap overlapped—as though all his brightness were sunburn.

For this creature, as I said, I paid twenty-five cents. I had never bought an animal before. It was very simple; I went to a store in Roanoke called "Wet Pets"; I handed the man a quarter, and he handed me a knotted plastic bag bouncing with water in which a green plant floated and the goldfish swam. This fish, two bits' worth, has a coiled gut, a spine radiating fine bones, and a brain. Just before I sprinkle his food flakes into his bowl, I rap three times on the bowl's edge; now he is conditioned, and swims to the surface when I rap. And, he has a heart.[13]

Every time I read this passage I am unnerved by the juxtaposition of twenty-five cents with the elaborateness, cleverness, and sheer glory of this tiny bit of matter named Ellery. I am learning both by reading nature writing like this as well as from my own experience that the closer attention I pay to whatever piece of the world is before me the more amazed I am by it. It is not that I "see God in it" in any direct or even general way; rather, it is the specialness, the difference, the intricacy, the "unutterable particularity" of each creature, event, or aspect of nature that calls forth wonder and delight—a knowing that calls forth love and a love that wants to know more. "Amazing revelations" come through the earth, not above it or in spite of it. An incarnational theology encourages us to dare to love nature—all the different bodies, both human and those of other lifeforms, on our earth—to find them valuable and wonderful in themselves, for themselves. That is what an incarnational view assures us: it is all right to love nature; in fact, we should. We pray to God through knowing and thereby being able to love all the wild and wonderful diversity of creatures. The prayer is simple: "*Vive les différences.* Long live the differences."

A very different way of seeing the world is epitomized in the now-famous whole-earth picture of our planet from the NASA files—the photograph of the earth as a blue and white marble floating in black empty space, lonely and vulnerable. Unlike the subject-subjects kind of knowing in nature writing, it can be seen as an example of subject-object knowing. As one commentator notes, "This distancing, disengaged, abstract, and literalizing epistemology is quintessentially embodied in the whole Earth image. . . . From a distance of tens of thousands of miles away, transcendent, serene, and unaffected, we survey the whole Earth at once."[14] Since the whole-earth image is for many people *the* ecological icon, this comment may seem strange. And it did initially to me as well, for I use it in my book *The Body of God* to raise consciousness about the fragility of our planet. But there is a somber underside to this bright, aesthetically pleasing image: it eliminates all detail, not only the smells and sounds and tastes of earth (the blood, sex, feces, sweat, and decay that make up the life of the planet) but also all the signs of deterioration, rape, and pillage that have resulted in holes in the ozone, topsoil erosion, and clear-cut forests. The view from space is of a clean, sterile, beautiful—and manageable—planet, rather than the going-to-pieces one we actually inhabit. The whole-earth view simplifies and objectifies the earth: it is the outsider's view, the spectator view, as in astronaut Russell Schweichert's description of it as "a blue and white Christmas ornament." The earth is a plaything, a beach ball, a yo-yo, a lollipop. This objectifying view underlies computer games in which the earth is destroyed on the screen but instantly restored by the reset button. We can do what we want with this earth, for in the astronaut's view, there are other possibilities, other planets, as we read on the *Star Trek* bumper sticker: "Beam me up, Scotty, this planet sucks." This view from space is also, ironically, claimed to be the "God's eye view": as we are, so God is also distant and disengaged from the earth, finding it pleasing only if all the mud and guts, all the blood and sweat, all the billions of creatures, from creepy-crawly ones to two-legged ones, are invisible. "The whole Earth poster decorating the wall of a Manhattan apartment is no substitute for a true belonging to place."[15] Indeed, it is not.

The Arrogant Eye vs. the Loving Eye

Seeing Ellery and seeing the earth from space: behind these two very different ways of seeing, of paying attention, lie two different ways of knowing: what one commentator calls "the loving eye" versus "the arrogant eye."[16] We want now to reflect in some depth on the differences between these two ways of seeing. We are suggesting that a certain kind of paying attention, a certain kind of knowing, is how Christians ought to love nature. Let us now analyze this claim.

But we are immediately drawn up short: we are trying, as Murdoch says, to see the world as it is so that we can love it rightly. But how, what, *is* it? How can we "see the world as it is"? There is no "natural" view of nature. We know there is no innocent eye, that what we see is determined in large measure by where we stand. The importance of social location for interpreting the world is by now a platitude, but that does not make it any less true. We see from our *Umwelten,* our self-worlds, which are personal, cultural, even genetic. As two-legged creatures of a certain height, formed by specific personal histories as well as by different gender, racial, economic, national, and cultural realities, we each see the world differently.

Hence, when we turn now to an investigation of paying attention, of a certain kind of seeing and knowing, we must remind ourselves that all seeing, all knowing, is perspectival. The specific issue with which we are concerned—how should we love nature?—will necessarily be based on perspectival knowing. The question is, which perspective, which kind of seeing, is better for nature?

There are many kinds of seeing, many kinds of knowing, but the contrast suggested between the arrogant eye and the loving eye epitomized by the whole-earth image and the description of Ellery is a fruitful one for our purposes. The terms are from feminist philosopher Marilyn Frye, who describes the arrogant eye as acquisitive, seeing everything in relation to the self—as either "for me" or "against me." It organizes everything in reference to oneself and cannot imagine "the possibility that the Other is independent, indifferent."[17] The arrogant eye simplifies in order to control, denying complexity and mystery, since it cannot control what it cannot understand. Frye illustrates the arrogant eye with the example of how it has functioned to exploit and enslave women, "breaking" and "training" them so as to serve male interests. This breaking and training can be so subtle that the oppressed eventually willingly conforms to the wishes of the oppressor—as in the pimp-prostitute relationship—or, more commonly, the way the standardized visual images of women's bodies in the media induce women into extreme diets and even anorexia in order to conform to the arrogant male gaze. The arrogant eye is also the patriarchal eye, which, of course, is not limited to the male perceptual standpoint. All of us in the Western world share this gaze, especially as we move the object of the eye's focus from women to nature. Like women, the natural world has been the object of the arrogant eye: we have broken and trained other life-forms—domestic, farm, and zoo animals—to do our will and have perceived the forests, air and water, plants and oceans as existing solely for our benefit. The natural world with its life-forms has not been seen as having its health and integrity in itself, for itself, but rather in and for us. We can scarcely imagine what it would mean for nature to be considered Other in the sense of being independent of and indifferent to human interests and desires. We Westerners all perceive with the arrogant eye. If you doubt this, answer the following question: How important would creation be if we were not part of it? Can we honestly say, "It is good!" and mean it? Don't we always implicitly believe that it would be considerably less good without us, in fact, perhaps not much good? We never ask of another human being, "What are you good for?" but we often ask that question of other life-forms and entities in nature. The assumed answer is, in one form or another, "good for me and other human beings."

The loving eye, on the other hand, acknowledges complexity, mystery, and difference. It recognizes that boundaries exist between the self and the other, that the interests of other persons (and the natural world) are not identical with one's own, that knowing another takes time and attention. In Frye's words, "It is the eye of one who knows that to know the seen, one must consult something other than one's own interests and fears and imagination. One must look at the thing. One must look and listen and check and question. . . . It knows the complexity of the other as something which will forever present new things to be known. The science of the loving eye would favor The Complexity Theory of Truth and presuppose The Endless Interestingness of the Universe."[18]

The loving eye is not the opposite of the arrogant eye: it does not substitute self-denial, romantic fusion, and subservience for distance, objectification, and exploitation. Rather it suggests something novel in Western ways of knowing: acknowledgment of and respect for the other as *subject*. Rather than the classic relationship between knower and known as subject versus object, the model here is two subjects: what I see is another subject (like me in some ways). What I know is another being with its own integrity and interests—and this model is extended to the natural world and its life-forms. In other words, rather than the standard paradigm for knowledge being subject-object (with myself as subject and all others, including other human beings, as objects), we are suggesting two subjects. Feminist philosopher Lorraine Code puts it this way: "It is surely no more preposterous to argue that people should try to know physical objects in the nuanced way that they know their friends than it is to argue that they should try to know people in the unsubtle way that they claim to know physical objects."[19] This seemingly slight perceptual shift can have enormous implications. It means that the route to knowledge is slow, open, full of surprises, interactive and reciprocal, as well as attentive to detail and difference. And it will be embodied. The disembodied, distant, transcendent, simplifying, objectifying, quick and easy arrogant eye becomes the embodied, lowly, immanent, complexifying, subjectifying, proximate, and "make-do" loving eye. The pure mind's eye becomes the messy body's eye, and those lowly senses (the so-called female ones of taste, touch, and smell) are allowed back into the knowledge game.

In the West, however, knowledge has been associated almost exclusively with sight and since Plato sight has been associated with the mind (as in "the eye of the mind").[20] This kind of vision discovers truth by recognizing likenesses—universals—and by dissociating itself from the messiness, complexity, and teeming differences of the body and the earth. This view of sight connects truth with what transcends the earth: we can see the more universal and hence "truer" truth the further we are from the bodily. For this kind of truth, we need the God's eye view, the angelic view: we must objectify in order to simplify, we must distance ourselves in order to see the big picture. Recall the whole-earth image: we can see the whole object only from a great distance; and it is then easy to say high-sounding things about the earth, for instance, that it is a beautiful Christmas ornament. Of course, such statements have little to do with the actual mind-boggling unknown or little-known mud-and-guts complexity of the planet's life-systems, let alone the baffling mystery of even one of its life-forms, from an earthworm to a human being.

A very different kind of vision from the so-called God's eye view is suggested by the phrase "locking eyes." Imagine shifting your vision from the picture of the whole earth to the eyes of another person—not to look at him or her, but into their eyes. Sight is not necessarily the eye of the mind; it can also be the eye of the body—in fact, it rightly and properly is. When we lock eyes something happens: we become two subjects, not subject and object. Locking eyes is perhaps the ultimate subject-subject experience: it is what lovers do and what nursing mothers do with their babies. A version of it can happen with other animals, especially the eerie experience of locking eyes with a lowland gorilla or chimpanzee at a zoo. It is possible even with a tree or plant. It all depends on whether we can "see without staring."[21] The loving eye, paying attention to another (another person, animal, tree, plant, whatever) is not staring; it is, in Martin Buber's suggestive phrase, relating to the other more like a Thou than an It. There is nothing sentimental or weak-minded about this: it is simply a refusal to assume that subjectivity is my sole prerogative. Iris Murdoch puts it bluntly, "Love is the extremely difficult realization that something other than oneself is real. Love . . . is the discovery of reality."[22] The loving eye is not the sentimental, mushy, soft eye; rather, it is the realistic, tough, no-nonsense eye, acknowledging what is so difficult for us to recognize: that reality is made up of *others*. Love, then, is no big deal or a specific virtue reserved for Christians; it is simply facing facts. It is, in a nice twist, being "objective."

But as we all know, this is not what objectivity usually means. In fact, just the opposite. It has been reserved for the mind's eye, the distant eye, the arrogant eye, the eye that can objectify the world. This eye lies behind the Western scientific understanding of objectivity. From the time of René Descartes on, science has advanced on the assumption that what is known is passive and inert, laid out before the subject so it can be reduced to its smallest parts, studied exhaustively, and thereby known. As Hans Jonas puts it, "I see without the object's doing anything. . . . I have nothing to do but to look and the object is not affected by that . . . and I am not affected. . . . The gain is the concept of objectivity."[23] Feminists and others have criticized this view of objectivity, seeing it as a mask for Western male privilege as well as for technological exploitation of women and nature.

THE SUBJECT-SUBJECTS MODEL

What is the alternative? There may well be more than one, but an intriguing possibility is the suggestion from feminists, ecologists, process philosophers, phenomenologists, and others that we pattern our knowledge, all knowledge, on a subject-to-subjects model, and more specifically, on friendship. This will involve the eye—the loving eye—but also the other senses, for it moves the eye from the mind (and the heavens) to the body (and the earth). It will result in an embodied kind of knowledge of other subjects who, like ourselves, occupy specific bodies in specific locations on this messy, muddy, wonderful, complex, mysterious earth. But appreciation for the particular and concrete is not the way I began my acquaintance with the natural world. I am going to become autobiographical now, using my own experience with nature to illustrate how I've come to believe a Christian should love nature: as subject to subject, on the analogy of friendship. My love for nature began when I was fourteen years old, hiking in the White Mountains in Vermont. I was not captive to the Western Platonic-Cartesian-scientific subject-object dualism (of which I was blissfully unaware) that I and other feminists have criticized. Just the opposite: I wallowed in oceanic feelings of oneness-with-it-all. I fused with nature: lying on mountaintops covered with billowing clouds, I sank into Wagnerian religious raptures. The New England transcendental poets were my favorites—I could sense Ralph Waldo Emerson's "oversoul" enveloping me as I relaxed into the arms of Mother Nature. I was one with nature. As a critic of deep ecology (a sensibility close to mine at that time) writes: "The correct metaphor for such fusion is of a lonely but megalomaniacal pond sucking up all the water of the world and becoming itself the ocean."[24] Indeed, I was not relating to nature as subject to subject but as the one and only Subject: I was the whole, the only one.

Gradually, over the years, I changed. I became "Elleryfied," interested in detail, in difference. I learned the names of some birds and wildflowers—a study that encourages paying attention to what is other than oneself. In fact, you can't identify a bird or a flower unless you pay close attention to detail. Such a simple desire as wanting to know the names of things is an opening to other attitudes toward the natural world. One day while hiking, I recall coming across a bi-footed, tri-colored violet, a rare and extraordinarily beautiful, tiny flower. It was all alone by the side of the trail. I had never seen one before. I squatted down to look at it closely and for a few minutes it was my whole world. I was transfixed by its beauty, its specialness, its fragility, and by the sense of privilege I felt to be looking at it. I was, I believe, seeing it as a subject; that is, I was relating to it with a recognition of its own intrinsic value quite apart from me. I was surprised and delighted by it and felt respect for it as well as a desire to care for it (in fact, I thought of putting some rocks around it to protect it from a careless hiker's boot, but decided this was too controlling). The violet was not a subject in the way you or I or one of the higher mammals is, but I could recognize its otherness and yet at the same time feel a connection with it. It was not simply an object to me. Rather, it had its own very special being, which surprised and delighted me even as I appreciated and felt empathy and concern for it. Which analogy is more appropriate for describing this experience—a subject viewing an object or a subject trying to know another subject?

Lorraine Code calls the subject-subjects analogy an ecological model of knowing because it assumes that we always know *in* relationships: we are not solitary individuals who choose to be in relationship with others, but we *are* in relationships, from before our birth until after our death.[25] Hence, the language of relationship—respect, reciprocity, interest in the particular, listening, openness, paying attention, care, concern—all this sort of language becomes relevant to how we know others. The way we come to know another, for instance a friend, becomes a model for ecological knowledge: it is a practical knowledge with the goal of responding to the other in terms of their own well-being. We want to know them better so we can empathize with and care for them more appropriately. It is a more-or-less knowledge, based on hints and nuances, open to surprises and changes, and infinitely more complex than knowing an object. Feminists have come to realize that knowing other women, especially across racial lines, involves this sort of thing—recognizing that the other must be taken as a subject in all her own irreducible particularity and difference. Knowledge of an African American woman by a white woman, for instance, is proximate and always open to revision, because it is a practical knowledge, concerned first of all not with a theory about the other but with her concrete well-being.

To sum up: we have been asking how a Christian should love nature and have suggested that practicing the loving eye, that is, recognizing the reality of things apart from the self and appreciating them in their specialness and distinctiveness, is a critical first step. It is opposed to the arrogant eye, the objectifying, manipulative, and disengaged kind of knowledge that supposes that I am the only subject and the rest of reality merely an object for me or against me. We have suggested further that a helpful way to think about knowledge with the loving eye is in terms of a subject knowing another subject, especially on the analogy of friendship.

There are several things to note about this model. First of all, it is not the reverse of the subject-object model, but a *different* model. The subject-object model assumes a hierarchical dualism of one over another. It is the basic pattern for a number of other common hierarchical dualisms: male/female, whites/people of color, rich/poor, heterosexual/homosexual, West/East, North/South—and humans/nature. One solution proposed for this problematic pattern is to reverse it (female/male or nature/humans), but the difficulty here is that the domination intrinsic to this way of thinking continues. The arrogant eye remains; it simply becomes someone else's. The model we are suggesting is a different one, not the old one reversed. It is a relational model derived from the evolutionary, ecological picture of reality, a picture that underscores both radical unity *and* radical individuality. It suggests a different basic sensibility for *all* our knowing and doing and a different *kind* of knowing and doing, whether with other people or other life-forms. It is a different posture and presence in the world, in all aspects of the world. It says: "I am a subject and live in a world of many other different subjects." The second thing to note about this model is that what I know is *many* subjects. The model is not subject-subject, replacing the singular object with a singular subject, but subject-subjects. The other is a multitude, a myriad of subjects. If the other were one subject, we could know all subjects by knowing just one—all others would be forms or reflections of the one basic or universal subject. Presumably this would be the human subject with all other subjects simply variations of it. But just as feminists have insisted that there is no essential human being, no one type which can stand for all, so also we must insist that there is no one, essential subject that I know. In the subject-subjects model, I know a *world* of subjects, different subjects.

The third thing to note, then, is the *differences* among subjects. We have praised difference as our planet's glory (the heart of the daffodil, the color purple, the uniqueness of each human face), but difference also means that we will not respond to all subjects in the same way. The AIDS virus, just like a wood tick, is a subject in its own world. This does not mean, however, that when it attacks my body I should honor it or allow it to have its way. I should fight it (if "natural" can ever be used literally, it would be of such a response). The subject-subjects model could, however, in this case, help me see that the virus is not against me; as a subject, it is simply "doing its thing" in its own world. The model would help me to avoid seeing it as punishment: the world is not organized around me, for my benefit *or* my punishment. In an unbelievably complex world of billions of subjects, the sole criterion cannot be what is "good for me." In this instance, then, the model would operate to neutralize demonizing fantasies. Chickens being raised for human consumption in inhumane conditions present a different level of subject, and my response would be different. In the subject-subjects model I might decide that the cruelty involved in commercial chicken farming is such that I will not eat chicken. Another possible response is to eat only free-range chickens or to work for legislation to improve the conditions under which chickens are raised. Vegetarianism is also an option, but not the only one (Native American traditions that have related to animals as subjects have also condoned hunting and meat eating).

Care or Rights?

What is beginning to emerge from the subject-subjects model is a clue for an environmental ethic of care. At the present time, a lively debate among environmentalists concerns a "rights" versus a "care" ethic. A rights ethic seeks to extend the rights accorded to human beings since the Enlightenment—the right to "life, liberty, and the pursuit of happiness"—to all animals and even forests, oceans, and other elements of the ecosystem. A rights ethic functions on the model of the solitary human individual (originally the landed, white, Western male); it details what one such person owes to another similar one. This ethic is beset with a number of problems when applied to the natural world. . . . Does the lamb or the wolf have the right to survive—does the wolf have the right to eat the lamb for dinner, or does the lamb have the right to protection against the wolf's needs? Can such an ethic address the complex issue of biodiversity or only the more simple one of individual animal rights? Is it an appropriate and helpful one for the natural world, given its human, individualistic base?

A care ethic, on the other hand, is based on the model of subjects in relationship, although the subjects are not necessarily all human ones and the burden of ethical responsibility can fall unequally. The language of care—interest, concern, respect, nurture, paying attention, empathy, relationality—seems more appropriate for human interaction with the natural world, for engendering helpful attitudes toward the environment, than does the rights language. As with friends, we come to know and love the natural world with an open and inquiring mind, trying to discern what will be best for its health and well-being. Often there is no easy answer, for it is seldom so clean a matter as one creature's rights over against another's.

A case in point: logging companies engaged in clear-cutting old-growth forests replant the areas with a monoculture—a single species of fast-growing tree—claiming they are restoring what they have removed. Thus, they have presumably respected the right of the forest to survive. However, these monoculture forests are not only vulnerable to fire and blight, but they lack the rich, complex diverse insect, bird, and mammal life as well as underbrush and underground root systems of a natural forest with its many different kinds of trees. In fact, they are not forests at all, but plantations of single-species trees. The appropriate ethic in this instance is not one of rights but of care—paying attention to what truly constitutes forests and then providing the conditions to maintain and restore them; for instance, selective tree cutting for intact forests and reseeding for biodiversity in clear-cut areas.

But is all of this *Christian?* What makes the subject-subjects model a Christian option? Is it commensurate with the radical, destabilizing, inclusive love of Jesus? It appears to be, for Jesus is reputed to have made the classic subject-subjects statement when he said, "Love your enemies." Treat the person who is against you, perhaps even out to kill you, as a subject, as someone deserving respect and care, as the Good Samaritan treated his enemy in need. The subject-subjects model is countercultural: it is opposed to the religion of Economism, to utilitarian thinking, to seeing the world as for me or against me. So is Christianity. Christianity is distinctly opposed to the subject-object way of thinking, to the arrogant eye. If Jesus could say, "Love your enemies," surely he would find the much milder statement, "Love nature," perfectly acceptable. If enemies are to be shown respect and care, should not other life-forms also, as well as the habitats that support them? Loving nature this way, not with mushy feeling or charity, but with respect for its otherness, its Thouness, and with a desire to care for it, will not be easy. But loving other humans, especially enemies, is not either. Christianity is not an easy religion. As countercultural, it will make outrageous demands, like "Love your enemies" and "Love nature."

Map or Hike?

So what does all this come to? How should we relate to the natural world? More like to another subject than to an object, and to a subject, many subjects, who are very different from ourselves. This is extremely difficult. We can learn how difficult by looking at the analogy of how feminists came to realize that there is no such thing as *woman*, but only *women*. Early in the feminist movement, white, North American, middle-class women glibly used the phrase "as a woman"; later, they came to recognize that "as a woman" was a mask for their own particular, racial, sexual orientation, or class version of what it means to be a woman. To understand what very different women in various other social locations experience, white North American, middle-class women would have to become, as Maria Lugones puts it, "world-travelers," or as Elizabeth Spelman suggests, "apprentices."[26] In other words, they would have to give up the center, admit ignorance, pack their bags, and go on a journey, a journey that would require them to listen and pay attention to others. It is not enough to imagine how women in very different circumstances might experience their lives; rather, one must learn about the lives of these different subjects much as a traveler learns her way around in a foreign country or as an apprentice studies with an expert craftsperson. Might we need to do something similar with nature—that is, to consider ourselves travelers in the world of nature we do not know, apprentices who need to listen to the others in that world?

An example might help. Anne Sellar, a British feminist who spent six months teaching at an Indian university, hoped to instill feminist theory into the minds of her women students.[27] Instead, she learned from them about their lives, for their notions of family, feminism, and patriarchy were radically different from hers—not to mention the importance of dowries and of instructing village women about infant diarrhea. Nothing was more important to these women than family; and feminism was a bad word, symbolizing all they disliked about Western civilization—individualism, sexual promiscuity, and loss of femininity. Sellar became a world-traveler and an apprentice: she said she went to India with a map—a theory of how to teach the women about feminism—but ended up taking a hike, learning by paying attention to the lay of the land, ready for discoveries around the next bend in the trail, realizing that she was in an unknown place without a map, one that would require the full engagement of all her senses and skills.

Map or hike? Which metaphor is the better one for our relationship with the natural world? We have depended heavily on the map metaphor, for we believe we *know* what nature is. As Thomas Berry says, nature has become resource, recreation, or retreat for human beings: it supplies our needs, gives us a place to play, and refreshes us spiritually. But what if we saw it more like a different subject, one vastly different from ourselves with infinite particular entities and strange, wonderful life-forms? What if we saw nature as "a world of difference"?[28] Then we might realize that we have to take a hike (with out a map), become world-travelers, become apprentices to nature.

In other words, imagination is thin compared to the perception of other persons and real things. What we imagine a person or entity in nature to be cannot begin to compare with the depth, richness, detail, and complexity of the simplest object—even the heart of a daffodil, let alone another person. Looking at the world with full attention—any bit of it—should stun us, leaving us amazed and wanting to know more. We come to value the world and want it to prosper through local, particular knowledge, for the world as it is is more amazing, more interesting, than any theory or image about it. If we practiced this sort of attention we might come to say with Annie Dillard, "My God what a world. There is no accounting for one second of it."[29]

To return to the autobiographical and to conclude: I have found that the route to some of these insights is through paying attention to the particular, to what is, as it were, in one's own path—as, for instance, a bi-footed, tri-colored violet. Anything will do, as Ellery, the twenty-five-cent goldfish, illustrates. In fact, the smaller the better in some respects. A little city park is probably a better place for one's lessons than the Grand Canyon. I took my last sabbatical in Vancouver, British Columbia, and every morning walked in a small city park—Jericho Park, an area of a few acres beside the bay. I came to know it very well. It has a duck pond and small wooded section. It also has lots of rabbits (probably unwanted released Easter bunnies), several kinds of ducks, many species of birds (including red-winged blackbirds), blue and purple lupines in the summer as well as blackberries, and even an occasional Great Blue Heron, raccoon, and red-necked pheasant. I always felt interest and even some excitement when I started out, because the sky and clouds varied every day, and I never knew what animals I might see. I came to love this small plot of land: its familiarity and its daily concrete, particular delights combined to make me feel at home there. My knowledge of the park was certainly not a mind's eye experience; rather, it was a body's eye one—my eyes reveled in the scurrying of a rabbit only a few feet away, the glory of a field of fuchsia sweet peas, the sight of a heron resting on one leg. And knowledge of this park involved my other senses as well—the smell of the salt water, the sound of bird calls, the touch of a flower's petal. These are the embodied senses, the ones that remind us that we are involved and open in our knowing: we cannot touch without being touched, or hear without listening to what comes to us. The initiative is not just ours. As I walked in this little park, soaking up its sounds and smells and sights, I came to know it—and love it—more or less as I would a friend.

But why bother with such unimportant, autobiographical, personal stories? What possible relevance can such idiosyncratic and seemingly minor incidents have for the well-being of a planet that is falling to pieces? Isn't this sort of caring for a small bit of the earth just sentimentality? Shouldn't Christians love nature in terms of the global picture—be concerned about the ozone layer, the rainforests, the greenhouse effect? Shouldn't we love the "whole earth" rather than Jericho Park? Yes, surely, but there is a connection here; in fact, a critical one. No one, I believe, loves the whole earth except as she or he loves a particular bit of it. It is more likely, I suspect, that loving Ellery or Jericho Park—appreciating, respecting, and caring for them—will move one to care for the whole earth, than admiring the NASA image will generate the energy and concern to save Ellery and Jericho Park.

Here are a few thoughts along these lines from some wise people. From Alice Walker:

> Helped are those who find the courage to do at least one small thing each day to help the existence of another—plant, animal, river, human being. They shall be joined by a multitude of the timid.[30]

From the Veda:
> O God, scatterer of ignorance and darkness,
>   grant me your strength.
> May all beings regard me with the eye of a friend,
>   and I all beings!
> With the eye of a friend may each single being regard
>   all others.[31]

And from Rabbi Abraham Heschel:

> Just to be is a blessing.
> Just to live is holy.[32]

Notes

1. *The Confessions of St. Augustine*, bks. 1–10, trans. F. J. Sheed (New York: Sheed and Ward, 1942), 10.6.

2. Letter to Mrs. Joseph Sweetser, 1884, *Letters of Emily Dickinson*, ed. Mabel Loomis Todd (New York: World, 1951), 349.

3. Iris Murdoch, *The Sovereignty of the Good* (London: Routledge and Kegan Paul, 1970), 91, 52.

4. Ibid., 84.

5. Ibid., 85.

6. *Lift Every Voice: Constructing Christian Theologies from the Underside*, ed. Susan Brooks Thistlethwaite and Mary Potter Engel (San Francisco: Harper & Row, 1990), 51.

7. Frederick Buechner, *Listening to Your Life* (San Francisco: Harper & Row, 1992), 53.

8. As quoted in Douglas Burton-Christie, "'A Feeling for the Natural World': Spirituality and Contemporary Nature Writing," *Continuum* 2 (2 & 3, n.d.): 176.

9. May Sarton, *Endgame: A Journal of the Seventy-Ninth Year* (New York: W. W. Norton, 1992), 336-37.

10. Alice Walker, *The Color Purple* (New York: Washington Square, 1978), 178.

11. As quoted by Burton-Christie, "'A Feeling for the Natural World,'" 175-76.

12. Iris Murdoch, "The Sublime and the Good," *Chicago Review* 13 (Autumn 1959): 52.

13. Annie Dillard, *Pilgrim at Tinker Creek: A Mystical Excursion into the Natural World* (New York: Bantam, 1975), 126.

14. Yaakov Jerome Garb, "Perspective or Escape? Ecofeminist Musings on Contemporary Earth Imagery," in *Reweaving the World: The Emergence of Ecofeminism*, ed. Irene Diamond and Gloria Feman Orenstein (San Francisco: Sierra Club Books, 1990), 267-68. I am indebted to Garb for the analysis in the following paragraph.

15. Yaakov Jerome Garb, "The Use and Misuse of the Whole Earth Image," *Whole Earth Review* 45 (March 1985): 20.

16. Marilyn Frye, "In and Out of Harm's Way: Arrogance and Love," *The Politics of Reality: Essays in Feminist Theory* (Trumansburg, NY: Crossing, 1983), 53-83.

17. Ibid., 67.

18. Ibid., 75, 76.

19. Lorraine Code, *What Can She Know? Feminist Theory and the Construction of Knowledge* (Ithaca: Cornell University Press, 1991), 165.

20. The following analysis is indebted to Evelyn Fox Keller and Christine R. Grontkowski, "The Mind's Eye," in *Discovering Reality: Feminist Perspectives on Epistemology, Metaphysics, Methodology, and Philosophy of Science*, ed. Sandra Harding and Merrill B. Hintikka (Dordrecht, Holland: D. Reidel, 1983), 207-24.

21. Garb, "Perspective or Escape," 276.

22. Murdoch, "The Sublime and the Good," 51.

23. As quoted in Keller and Grontkowski, "The Mind's Eye," 219.

24. Jim Cheney, "Eco-Feminism and Deep Ecology," *Environmental Ethics* 9 (Summer 1987): 124.

25. Code, *What Can She Know?*, 273.

26. See, for instance, Maria Lugones, "Playfulness, 'World-Travelling,' and Loving Perception," *Hypatia* 2 (Summer 1987): 3-19; and Maria C. Lugones and Elizabeth V. Spelman, "Have We Got a Theory for You! Feminist Theory, Cultural Imperialism, and the Demand for The Woman's Voice," *Women's Studies International Forum* 6 (1983): 573-81; Elizabeth V. Spelman, *The Inessential Woman: Problems of Exclusion in Feminist Thought* (Boston: Beacon, 1988), 181-82.

27. Anne Sellar, "Should the Feminist Philosopher Stay at Home?" in *Knowing the Difference: Feminist Perspectives in Epistemology*, ed. Kathleen Lennon and Margaret Whitford (New York: Routledge, 1994).

28. This phrase is used by Evelyn Fox Keller, *Reflections on Gender and Science* (New Haven: Yale University Press, 1985), 165.

29. Dillard, *Pilgrim at Tinker Creek*, 269.

30. Alice Walker, *The Temple of My Familiar* (New York: Pocket, 1989), 289.

31. Quoted in *Earth Prayers from around the World*, ed. Elizabeth Roberts and Elias Amidon (San Francisco: HarperSanFrancisco, 1991), 267.

32. Ibid., 365.

10

The Ecological Model and Christian Spirituality

This selection, from the final chapter of Super, Natural Christians, *deepens and expands upon some of the ideas introduced in the previous chapter, above. It explains how the organic, ecological model translates into a Christian praxis and spirituality of nature. Offering a "community-of-care" ethic, it suggests some initial ways in which our love of nature and ecological concern might be enacted among Christians and in the church (though, overall, the book, like most of her work before this, presses the reader more to new thinking rather than new action). The closing section on "horizontal Christian sacramentalism" anticipates the call to a sacramental Christology she issues in her next book,* Life Abundant.

Source: 1998:164–75

Extending Christian Love to Nature

A Christian nature spirituality is Christian praxis extended to nature. It is treating the natural world in the same way we treat, or should treat, God and other people—as subjects, not objects. But, we have to admit, we seldom act this way. Only the saints seem able to do it: recall Francis of Assisi who let things be what they are—wind is wind, death is death—and *as they were* he both loved them and saw them as signs of God. Francis's way was "to commune with all things, respecting and reverencing their differences and distinctions."[1] What is often shocking to contemporary Christians about Francis is that he treated *nature* this way, as subject. Christians have always tried to treat other people as subjects; the subject-subjects model has been *the* model of how we ought to relate to God and to other people. God is the ultimate Subject whom we are to love with our whole heart, mind, and soul simply because God *is* God. We should not fuse with God (the Christian suspicion of mysticism) nor objectify God (the Christian insistence that God is to be loved for God's sake alone, and not out of self-interest). Likewise, we are to love our (human) neighbors "as we love ourselves," in other words, as subjects who have interests, wishes, and needs that are their own. We are to love them disinterestedly, for their own sakes, not for ours.

One of the main contributions of the ecological model to Christianity is the extension of its own subject-subjects thinking to nature. For most contemporary Christians, the line stops with human beings. Post-Enlightenment Christians have bought into the subject-object arrogant eye when it comes to nature. What the ecological model offers to Christianity is a way of extending its *own most basic affirmation* on how others should be treated—as subjects—to nature. If Christians were to embrace the ecological model, they would not be doing something radical or discontinuous with their historical faith. On the contrary, they would simply be extending that faith to include nature. If we are to love God with our whole heart, mind, and soul, and our neighbor as ourselves, how, in continuity with that model, should we love nature? The answer is: with the loving eye, with the eye that realizes that even a wood tick or a Douglas fir is a subject—that each has a world, goals, intentions (though not conscious), and modes of flourishing that make them good in themselves and not simply good for us. Surely, this is what the Genesis verse means: "God saw everything that God had made, and indeed, it was very good" (1:31a). This is an amazing statement. God does not say that creation is good for human beings or even, more surprising, good for me, God, but just good, in fact, very good. God is saying that nature is good in itself—not good for something or someone but just plain good. It is like a parent saying to a child, "I love you just the way you are," or lovers saying to each other, "I love you because you are you." God's pronouncement here is an aesthetic one: appreciation of something outside of oneself, in itself, for itself. Even God can recognize that something exists outside of the divine self—and that, as such, it is good!

Because the Genesis material is often accused of being a foundational anti-nature text, we need to substantiate this reading. The writer of the first chapter of Genesis leaves no doubt but that the goodness of creation is its message: it is repeated seven times in the space of thirty-one verses. After the very first act of creation—of day and night—the text reads: "And God saw that the light was good." After making the earth and sea, we read again, "And God saw that it was good," and when finishing the sun and moon, we hear the same refrain. In fact, after every creation God pronounces its goodness—after creating the birds and sea monsters as well as "the cattle and creeping things and wild animals." Finally, after we human beings are made, God surveys the entire panorama and with what appears to be great pleasure and delight, exclaims, "Indeed, it was very good."

How have we missed this? Seven times it is repeated like a teacher drumming into a lazy student's head a bit of basic learning. We have not heard, "It is very good." What we have heard are two other motifs concerning nature that are also in Genesis 1: domination and stewardship. We have heard, "Fill the earth and subdue it; and have dominion . . . ," which is not mentioned seven times but only once. We have also heard, "I have given you every plant . . . you shall have them for food," suggesting that human beings ought to be good stewards of nature (but note that other creatures are also given the plants—"to . . . everything that has the breath of life, I have given every green plant for food").

Certainly, a conservation ethic of sustainability—an ethic of preserving and sharing the earth's bounty for all its creatures—is implicit in Genesis. And the domination theme is there also. But these three attitudes toward nature—appreciation, stewardship, and domination—are graded, with appreciation ("it is good") being the primary one. It is repeated over and over, literally pounded into our heads. Stewardship is also important in the text: it is the necessary daily practice so that the basics of life, such as food, can be shared by all. But domination, which has been the primary attitude of the West toward nature, takes up less than one verse of the thirty-one verses in the chapter. This is scant justification for treating the oceans as burial grounds for toxic waste, the forests as so many board feet, domestic animals as simply food to be eaten or material for medical experiments, and wild animals as expendable if human beings need the land.

We simply didn't get the point. The message of Genesis is not domination but appreciation. We who the text says are made in God's image ought to reflect God's attitude toward nature: appreciation. This attitude is in line with how we are supposed to relate to God and neighbor. God is the ultimate Subject: we love God (or should) because God is God and deserves our adoration. We love our neighbor (or should) because we see human beings as ends in themselves, as valuable just because they *are*. A human being is good, period. Genesis 1 is saying that we should extend the way we relate to God and neighbor *to nature:* nature is good, period. So, for Christians to relate to nature as subject is merely to extend its own relational model—loving God and neighbor—to all of creation.

This extension, however, has not been our practice; we do need help here. . . . How can we apply the ecological model to nature, and how can we develop the loving eye that respects nature as subject? There are many stories in the Bible on how to practice the loving eye toward God and other people; in fact, that is what much of both the Hebrew Scriptures and the New Testament are about. But apart from some sections in the Hebrew Scriptures (with a smattering in the New Testament), there are few biblical guides for Christians on how to practice love toward nature. Nor does traditional Christian theology or ethics help much; Francis stands out in part due to his singular concern with nature. Hence, we have turned to the ecological model and its loving eye to help educate the Christian's eye in order to develop what Christians, especially Protestants, have not had since the Middle Ages—a *nature* spirituality, sensitivity toward the natural world.

For most of its history, Christianity has preached the Good News to people, often forgetting that the redeemer of human beings is also the creator of *everything* that is. The health and well-being of the natural world have usually been a minor concern in Christian teaching and preaching. We have suggested that it is an oversight, a lack, a fault in Christian faith and that Christianity should extend its own version of the subject-subjects model—loving God for God's sake and loving other people as oneself—to nature. By doing so it would be true to its own innermost dynamic, which is not subject-object but subject-subjects. By doing so it would also intersect with the ecological model that is emerging in postmodern understandings of reality. In sum, our thesis and main question are very simple: What justification is there for limiting the subject-subjects model to human beings, drawing a line in the sand at our own species, with all other species and the rest of nature outside the circle? On the basis of Christianity's own most basic model, seeing God and others as subjects—as valuable in themselves, for themselves, and not just as for me or against me—should we not *also* love nature this way? Since we always think in terms of models (which are always relative and inadequate), is it not better (not perfect) to think of the rest of nature more or less *like ourselves*, rather than as utterly unlike us? Is it not only better for the health of our planet, but also more *Christian*?

If we were to think this way, allow this sensibility to grow deep inside ourselves, we would develop a way of thinking about God, human beings, and nature similar to the medieval view. That is, it would be an outer-directed, functional cosmology in which we and all other natural beings and entities would have a place. It would, however, be a worldview closer to that of Francis of Assisi than to most of his contemporaries: he saw all things in God, but not as signs pointing to God or as symbols transparent to God, but each and every thing telling of the glory of God *in its own distinctiveness*. Hence, the ecological model is a prime candidate to do for twenty-first-century Christians what the Great Chain of Being, the hierarchical model of interrelated signs and symbols, did for medieval people—to relate all things to one another. Christianity is always and rightly looking for ways to remythologize its understanding of the relationship between God and the world in new thought forms. There is such an obvious and close match between the ecological model and basic Christian spirituality—understanding God and other people as subjects to whom one relates in profound and disinterested ways—that Christians would be foolish not to embrace this rich paradigm as a contemporary way to construe their faith.

Deepening the Subject-Subjects Model

But Christianity is not only the learner, the receiver, in this conversation. What does Christian faith have to offer that goes beyond the ecological model? Christianity makes several very significant contributions. First, we recall how difficult if not impossible it is for most of us to treat others as subjects, whether these others be God, other people, or nature. We use these others in both explicit and subtle ways. Using God is so common we are often not even aware of it, but from tribalism (the assumption that God fights on the side of our nation or ethnic group) to fox-hole religion (the mentality that sees God as personal rescuer in times of disaster), religious functionalism is widespread. We often do not worship God because God is God and deserves our total adoration, but because we *need* God to save our country, win a basketball game, rescue our loved ones, or help someone recover from substance abuse. Likewise, we often find it very difficult if not impossible to love other people as we do ourselves. We do not treat them as subjects, as others, as having their own goals and desires; more often, they are means to *our* ends. If we do not, seemingly cannot, treat God and other people as subjects, how will we be able to treat nature this way—that part of creation that we have not even allowed inside the subjects circle?

It is at this point that Christian faith makes one of its major contributions to the ecological model. We have noted how fragile the subject-subjects model is, how anxiety pushes us either to objectify and control others or to flip over into fusion with others in the search for self-affirmation. Being a self and relating to others as selves is difficult. In fact, one definition of sin is precisely the objectification of others, using others as a means to an end—one's self-fulfillment. The classic doctrines of justification and sanctification speak to this dilemma. Justification acknowledges that we do not and cannot live as subjects relating to other subjects, whether these be the divine Subject or other persons, but that God forgives us for our failure. It says that we are accepted as we are, that we do not have to merit or win God's acceptance; we are given it as a gift. It says that we do not have to dominate others or fuse with them in fear lest we lose ourselves, because God loves us as we are (as the subjects we are). Justification grounds us as subjects, as beings valuable *as such*. As we accept our acceptance, we are directed and encouraged, through the doctrine of sanctification, to go and do likewise: to accept others as they are, in their own subjecthood. These two doctrines together set out a tough-minded agenda: justification acknowledges the depths of human sin, while sanctification insists that once free of it we have a task to do. While Christianity is certainly not the only remedy for the anxiety of human self-awareness, it is a classic and profound one. It is realistic in its analysis of the problem and persuasive in its solution, as hundreds of years of Christian history have shown.

A second major contribution of Christian faith to the ecological model is its community of care ethic. This ethic, as we have seen, is very close to Christian spirituality—the development of sensitivity toward God, other people, and nature. It fits well with the relational, subject-subjects character of Christianity: both the community care ethic and Christian faith focus on the well-being of the entire community rather than on the rights of privileged members of it. Hence, super, natural Christians will be on the frontlines in caring for the communities of which they are a part: in working for diverse, sustainable communities where social justice and environmental integrity come together. They will join forces with others from different religious faiths and who for different reasons also want this common good. But Christianity goes further than the community care ethic in at least one important respect. It gives preference to certain subjects: the needy. Here is another way in which Christians ought to be super, natural. The Christian eye is not just a loving eye, but that eye has a particular slant—it slants toward the oppressed, the poor, the despised, the forgotten. Christians will focus, on the basis of the logic of their own faith, on healing the wounds of nature and feeding its starving creatures, even as they also focus on healing and feeding needy human beings. This will mean that Christians will center on certain kinds of environmental issues, where, for instance, the neediest human beings and the neediest parts of nature meet. The phrase "environmental racism" brings these needs together—oppressed human beings and polluted nature. Christianity insists that the ecological model give priority to the neediest among both people and nature. For example, the kind of environmental issues that Christians should be concerned with, working out of the model suggested here, will be justice toward African Americans who complain that landfills are usually placed in their neighborhoods; creation and maintenance of wilderness areas to preserve forests and promote biodiversity; access by city people, especially poor ones, to small, close-by parks; opportunities for direct contact with nature by children, especially underprivileged ones; aid to third-world communities where both people and the environment are being exploited by multinational corporations. Christians will work toward creating more communities like Curitiba and Kerala, where mostly poor people and "second-chance" nature exist together in a sustainable, shared, modest lifestyle. Christianity gives a particular slant to the loving eye, a slant that confers preference to needy people in their negative and positive dealings with nature as well as to needy nature itself. Christianity says that "nature is the new poor" or the "also poor," which, in unity with poor people, commands our special attention.

A local example of a project that might command the special attention of Christians is the maintenance and health of urban parks. Such parks bring together poor people and the new poor, nature. In 1995 several bills were introduced into the U.S. Congress to close some urban parks and turn others over to local governments or private entrepreneurs in order to save money.[2] The Director of the National Park Service fought back, claiming that urban parks offer an inexpensive recreation alternative for people who cannot afford "to drive the Lexus to Glacier" for a vacation.[3] Targeting urban parks while shielding the national parks from threat is implicitly classist and racist, for national parks are used largely by the white middle and upper classes while urban parks offer minorities and poor people rare opportunities. A warden at Golden Gate Park in San Francisco said that for some kids a trip to the park means "going for a walk on the beach for the first time."[4] White, European-descended Americans follow an old tradition for their vacations of traveling to remote wilderness areas to fish, camp, and hike. More recent immigrants from Africa, Asia, and Latin America have a different idea of how to spend their leisure time, preferring family or clan gatherings in a village square, an orchard, or a city park. A policy that supports wilderness areas but not city greenspace discriminates against poor people and certain ethnic groups. While Christians certainly need to support wilderness areas for biodiversity, another priority might be city parks, which bring nature and poor people together.

Working at the local level to integrate needy nature and needy people will form a sensibility in Christians so that we might become a force supporting sustainable communities at all levels, with special attention to the poor, both human and natural. It is very difficult to imagine what sustainable regional, national, or global communities might be. That they are necessary is self-evident, if we accept the ecological model as the one in which we live, think, and act. But we can educate ourselves in the global implications of this model as we practice it in our communities and cities. The basic pattern, whether small or large, is the same: it is a model of sustainability in which respect and care for others are primary, especially care of the neediest.

A global example of Christian care can be seen in the impending crisis of climate change. There is now consensus among weather experts that global warming has begun and that by 2050 CE we can expect a 2.5° C. increase in the worldwide temperature.[5] Since the earth's temperature during the last Ice Age was only 5° to 6° C. *cooler* than now, one can see that a 2.5° C. *increase* is substantial. The results will be devastating (desertification, scarcity of fresh water, loss of tree cover, flooding of coastal areas and islands, shortages of food, etc.). The effects will also be spread unevenly, with the southern, third-world countries experiencing the worst consequences, even though global warming is caused mainly by emissions from the burning of fossil fuels by northern, industrialized countries. What is the specific Christian response to this situation? It is, I think, twofold: a word to the oppressor and a word to the oppressed.

A Christian ethic of care condemns the arrogant eye of the oppressor. A word of repentance should be spoken to the elites of both the first and third worlds as well as a call for a radical change in their consumer lifestyle. These people are not loving the earth; rather, they are casting an arrogant eye on it, perceiving it to be theirs for the taking. They do not accept the intrinsic value either of other people or other life-forms: these others are simply "for" or "against" the one Subject, which is me and my kind. Christian witness, which demands that all God's creatures must have their basic needs met, condemns such outrageous greed.

A Christian ethic of care sides with the oppressed, in this case those creatures and aspects of earth that are experiencing the greatest deterioration. A symbol of this deterioration is a poor third-world woman of color, for she is a barometer of the health of both humanity and nature. Living as she does at the juncture of the poorest human beings and the most devastated nature, she tells us how both are faring. While the world's elites have the power to direct earth's diminishing resources to their own uses, this woman does not. In her increasing poverty, we see also the increasing poverty of nature. Christian radicalism—love for the neediest humans and devastated nature—helps to push more moderate forms of the care ethic toward greater justice for the forgotten and the voiceless. Its particular role in issues of public policy is to move the powers in control beyond "business as usual" compromises on critical issues toward decisions that show concern for the most vulnerable.

Horizontal Christian Sacramentalism

Finally, Christianity also believes nature gives us intimations of the divine. As stated early on, the sacramental use of nature is the oldest and in many ways the noblest of Christian understandings of nature. We have avoided it, however, because of its utilitarianism: nature is seen as a way to reach God. Nonetheless, as we noted with Francis of Assisi, it is possible both to appreciate things in themselves, for themselves, *and* to see them as signs of God. Most of Francis's medieval brothers and sisters saw nature as a sign of God, but they failed to acknowledge it as having intrinsic value. The main project of this book has been to take us on a journey that would help us see nature this way—as subject. But now as we consider what Christianity might offer to the model, we must add a new sacramentalism. This sacramentalism would, while "holding on hard to the huckleberries," see all things in God. However, the focus of this Christian loving eye is not vertical but horizontal; not on "God in this tree," but "*this tree in God.*" The focus of this eye is not on seeing God, but on seeing the tree (this particular tree) which, in its own way, as itself, is *also* in God. The Christian eye does not need training to see God but to see other things, especially earth others—and *then* to see them in God. The ecological model with its stress on the embodied, concrete, particularity of all things, each in its own subjectivity, helps us to do this. When the Christian eye has been so educated, it can and should then see them also as intimations of the divine.

Moreover, this new sacramentalism will give Christians a new, rich vocabulary with which to speak of God. The Christian tradition has limited God-language largely to metaphors taken from human beings: since we alone, among created beings, are made in the image of God, only we, in turn, can image God. God-talk has been mainly human talk writ large: God is imagined to be a super-person, doing things people do but on an infinite, eternal scale. Thus, God loves (as we do) but infinitely and eternally; God wills, judges, acts, sees, hears, knows, but always to the nth degree and in a perfect fashion. Language about God in the Western, Christian tradition has been accused of being anthropomorphic and anthropocentric. It is these things, but there is some justification. The reply to these accusations is: "Of course. Since all talk of God is necessarily metaphorical, shouldn't we use ourselves as metaphors with which to speak of God?" The counter-reply, however, goes like this: "Why limit talk of God to metaphors based on humanity? Does not the whole creation mirror God's being and glory? Are not other life-forms and the earth itself subjects whom God loves and cares about?" Just as feminists, early and late, from Mary Daly to Elizabeth Johnson, have pointed out the error of limiting God-talk to male imagery, so also, as we now move the line beyond ourselves to include nature, ought we not to move our God-talk as well? As Daly said over twenty years ago, "If God is male, then the male is God" and as Johnson wrote recently, "The glory of God is . . . the human being, the whole human race, every individual person, fully alive."[6] If we now accept that language about God can result in "She who is" as well as "He who is," ought it not also, on the basis of the same reasoning, include "Nature which is"? Just as the psalmists and medieval women and men did not shrink from using the natural world to speak of God, neither should we.

But we do so now taking into full account the diversity, particularity, and thickness of natural forms. They are not transparent to the divine; they are first of all themselves, and as such, in the intricacy and uniqueness of who, what, they are, they speak elliptically of God. Just as feminists have insisted that there is no universal woman who can image the divine, that God must be spoken of in images from the actual, concrete, diverse circumstances of women's lives, so also "Nature" is not a metaphor for God. The natural world is not a single entity but a marvelously rich, multidimensional, diverse, and intricate collection of life-forms and things. It is precisely this character of the natural world that presents itself to us as a new and exciting way to speak of God. (Actually, it is not new at all, but appears so to post-Enlightenment Christians, especially Protestants, who narrowed the world to themselves and God.) As Augustine noted many hundred years ago, we do not know how to speak of God, what words to use, and the words we do use are not much better than a baby's babble. One might say that in desperation we have turned to what we know best—ourselves—for material to talk about God. That tactic is understandable and it has been rewarding: we have a rich reservoir of personalistic words, concepts, and images for talking about God. But we have neglected another rich reservoir—nature—both to the detriment of God and nature. We need to speak of God in metaphors drawn from nature for at least two reasons: the richness of the divine being demands it and nature deserves it. The fullness of God cannot possibly be reflected only through human reality, and nature should be honored, as we are, by being a source for metaphors for God.

Hence, the movement of the subjects line beyond us to include nature can and should restore nature as a divine sacrament. It will, however, be closer to Francis's kind of sacramentalism than to the typical medieval view. It will be a kind of sacramentalism that focuses on the things themselves rather than on their divine message. It will be a kind of sacramentalism that is radically incarnational: God is with us here and now in and on our earth. The things of the earth do not point away from the earth to God; rather, they are themselves the "body" of God—one of the major metaphors that Christians might now use from nature to speak of God. God's body in this metaphor is not one body, but all the bodies, from subatomic to galactic ones, and all the ones in between, from robins and tigers to mountains and oceans, from mites and microbes to trees and plants, as well as, of course, ourselves. All of these millions, billions of creatures and entities, are, like us, made for the glory of God, and they deserve, as all human beings do, to be part of the language we use to speak of God.

The color purple in its purpleness and a horse named Blue in his horseness are traces of God, even as each human being in his or her uniqueness is a witness to God's creative genius. Thomas Aquinas once said that the whole creation, every tiny scrap of it (and for us this would include every galaxy and every microbe) is necessary to even begin to mirror the glory of God. But he also suggested, and the ecological model affirms it, that each bit of creation, whether in interstellar space, Tinker Creek, or Kerala, gives glory to God by *being itself*, fully and wonderfully. God is glorified not by the denial of difference, but by its flourishing and fulfillment. The incarnation of God in Christ Jesus further claims that the glory of God is revealed in the least, the most despised, the most oppressed of God's creatures. Surely, in our time, the natural world is joined in its oppression with Christ: it too is being crucified. Just as in the face of a suffering child, woman, or man, Christians see the face of Christ, so also there is a trace of that face in a clear-cut forest, an inner-city landfill, or a polluted river.

To sum up: the conversation between the ecological model and Christianity is a rich one, with important offerings from both sides. The ecological model offers Christianity a way to construe its own basic understanding of relationality between God and human beings, but extends it as well to nature; it also offers education in how to relate to other subjects with a loving eye. Christianity with its doctrines of justification and sanctification offers the ecological model a remedy for the anxious self, poised between objectification and fusion, while seeking genuine acceptance of its own and others' subjecthood. It also offers the ecological model a direction to the loving eye: toward the oppressed, both among people and nature. Finally, Christianity suggests that nature is not "just nature," but as one sees the face of Christ in the needy sister or brother, so also nature, in its own way, is a vision of God.

Notes

1. Leonardo Boff, *Saint Francis: A Model for Human Liberation*, trans. John W. Diercksmeier (New York: Crossroad, 1982), 39.
2. See Jim Woolf, "Metropolitan Mosaic," *National Parks* (January/February 1996), 41–44.
3. Ibid., 42.
4. Ibid., 44.

5. See the *Intergovernmental Panel on Climate Change: Second Assessment—Climate Change 1995*, published by the World Meteorological Organization and the United Nations Environmental Programme.

6. Elizabeth A. Johnson, *She Who Is: The Mystery of God in Feminist Theological Discourse* (New York: Crossroad, 1992), 14.

11

How Shall We Live? Christianity and Planetary Economics

In 1993, McFague published Life Abundant: Rethinking Theology and Economy for a Planet in Peril, *noting in the preface, "After completing* Super, Natural Christians, *subtitled* How We Should Love Nature, *I realized that love was not enough. I realized that we middle-class North American Christians are destroying nature, not because we do not love it, but because of the way we live: our ordinary, taken-for-granted high-consumer lifestyle. I realized that the matter of loving nature was a deep, complex, tricky question involving greed, indifference, and denial. . . . I realized that a basic deficiency . . . was the neglect of economics. . . . There is, however, no avoiding it—and what ordinary people need to know is not its technical side but the assumptions and results of consumer-oriented economic theory" (xi–xii). This selection, excerpted from* A New Climate for Theology *(2008), summarizes significant points from* Life Abundant *(esp. chs. 4 and 5). In addition to explaining the economic ideas that entered McFague's theological thought then, it provides a rationale for Christians to embrace the ecological economic model she introduces, particularly in light of the urgent dilemma posed by global climate change.*

Source: 2008:81–97

> *It is notable that none of the world's religions has as its maxim: "Blessed are the greedy."*
>
> —SALLIE MCFAGUE

We have looked at who we are and decided that an ecological anthropology is necessary for our contemporary context of global warming. It is also commensurate with Christian faith. We have looked at who God is and suggested that the model of the world as God's body might be a persuasive contemporary and Christian expression for the God-world relationship in our time. We have, then, sketched out a picture, a way of imagining both ourselves and God within the context of radical environmental threat.

It is time now to look at how we should live. If we are interdependent with all other creatures as well as radically dependent on God, the source of reality and goodness—who is transcendentally immanent in the world and expects us to be partners in earthly flourishing—then what should we do? Can we continue living in a way that consumes the world's resources and undermines its most basic systems, as global warming is warning us we are doing? Must we not see *the essential connection between economics and ecology*: between the insatiable consumer society and the wreckage it creates at all levels—resource depletion and greenhouse gases, as well as a growing split between the poor and the wealthy?

Religion and Economics

It is notable that none of the world's major religions has as its maxim: "Blessed are the greedy." Given the many differences among religions in doctrines and practice, it is remarkable to find such widespread agreement at the level of economics. Often, however, people do not consider that religion has anything to do with economics; in fact, in most societies many do not want religion to intrude into economics. It is preferable, they say, for religion to attend to "religious matters" and to leave economics to the economists.

But most religions know better. They know that economics is about human well-being, about who eats and who does not, who has clothes and shelter and who does not, who has the basics for a decent life and who does not. Economics is about life and death, as well as the quality of life. It is also about the life and death not just of human beings but of the planet itself and all its life-forms. Economics is not just about money; rather, it is about sharing scarce resources among all who need them. Economics is a justice issue, so why would religions not be concerned with it?

In many religions, the concern for justice has been focused on human beings—and this is certainly the case with Christianity, at least for the last few centuries. But recently, the issues of well-being and justice have been extended to embrace the entire planet: the well-being of people and the well-being of the planet are increasingly seen to be inextricably related. Climate change makes this case with stunning clarity. In Christianity, there is a return to the cosmological context for interpreting the faith, rather than the narrow psychological focus prevalent since the Protestant Reformation. In fact, many current Christian theologies incorporate all three of the classical interpretive contexts: the cosmological, the political, and the personal. These theologies claim that Christian faith embraces the *world*—all of creation and not just we human beings who make up less than 1 percent of it. The redeemer is also the creator: all of creation, including dying nature as well as oppressed people, is within God's "economy," God's "household."

As we have noted, it is no coincidence that the Greek word for house, *oikos*, is the source of our words *economics, ecology,* and *ecumenicity*. The three belong together: in order for the whole household of the planet to flourish, the earth's resources must be distributed justly among all its inhabitants, human and earth others, on a sustainable basis. This involves economics, for the distribution of scarce resources among needy users is the essence of economics. That economics and ecology are interconnected can be seen negatively in our consumer culture, which sets no limits on human consumption of resources—except monetary ones. Human beings, especially well-off ones, are permitted to consume all they can afford: no other criterion is applied. A market economy in a time of rising ecological destruction has no means of assuring that the third term—*ecumenicity*—will be included. Good "home economics" insists that the whole household must be fed now and in the future. As the effects of global warming accelerate, we see clearly that the economics being practiced globally is not contributing to a just, sustainable planet. What we need, instead, is an *ecological economics*.

But an economic paradigm based on ecological health is certainly not the dominant one in global society today. Nor is it the one that most Christians seem to be embracing. To be sure, Christians do not openly support the maxim "Blessed are the greedy"; nonetheless, that is the way most of us live. Why? Quite simply, because we are members of a society, now a worldwide one, that accepts, almost without question, an economic theory that supports insatiable greed on the part of individuals, regardless of its consequences to other people or to the planet. This assumption lies behind present-day market capitalism, and since the death of communism and the decline of socialism, it has been accepted by most ordinary people as a description of the ways things are and must be. It is "the truth." Although market capitalism is "a description of the way things are" in our society, it is not a description of the way things must be—or should be. Market capitalism is an economic *model*, not a description.[1] Market capitalism is a type of economics that allocates scarce resources not in regard to the needs of the planet's inhabitants nor with an eye to its sustainability, but rather on the basis of individuals' successful competition for them. Its criterion is who can pay. It is an economic theory that makes a case for the way scarce resources might be distributed, not how they must be.

This realization—that economics is not a hard science but an ideology with an assumed anthropology and a goal for the planet (summarized by greed and growth)—is the first step in seeing things otherwise. Ecological economics—economics for the well-being of the whole household of planet Earth—is also a model with an anthropological and planetary ideology. It claims that human beings, while greedy to be sure, are even more *needy*: we depend on the health of all the other parts of the planet for our very existence—clean water, breathable air, arable land, thriving plants, and so on. It claims that market capitalism denies one huge fact: unless the limited resources of the planet are distributed justly among all life-forms so they can flourish, there will be no sustainable future for even the greediest of us. Global warming is unmasking the presumed "objectivity" of market capitalism, for we see now that this model of economics is biased not in favor of the well-being of the whole planet, but in favor of a segment of the human population for its short-term gratification. Global warming is the stark evidence of the disaster that awaits us unless we shift swiftly and deeply to another form of economics.

Christianity and Economics

But why should Christians be concerned with models of economics? Is ecological economics "Christian"? No, but it is an emerging economic model that is gaining the support of a wide range of nongovernmental organizations (NGOs), protest movements, and people who believe an alternative economics is necessary. Its motto is "A different world is possible," and its basic tenets are concerned with fair labor laws and environmental health. Lynn White's oft-quoted 1967 essay lays the blame for environmental deterioration at the feet of religion, specifically Christianity.[2] If Christianity was capable of doing such immense damage, then surely the restoration of nature also must lie, at least in part, with Christianity. I believe it does, but also with other world religions as well as with education, government, and science. The environmental crisis we face—and which is epitomized by climate change—is a planetary agenda, involving all people, all areas of expertise, and all religions.

This is the case because the environmental crisis is not a "problem" that any specialization can solve, as climate change is increasingly demonstrating. Rather, it is about how we—all of us human beings and other creatures—can live justly and sustainably on our planet. Climate change is telling us that we must live differently. We need to pay attention to the "house rules" that will enable us to live as we ought. These house roles include attitudes as well as technologies, behaviors, and science. They are what the *oikos*, the house we all share, demands that we think and do so that there will be enough for everyone. The house rules are concerned with the management of the resources of planet Earth so that all may thrive indefinitely.

How does religion and specifically Christianity fit into this picture? It fits where all religions do: at the point of the worldview underlying the house rules. It fits at the level of the deeply held and often largely unconscious assumptions about *who we are in the scheme of things and how we should act*. While anthropology—the interpretation of human nature—is not the only concern of religions, it is a central one and, for the purposes of the ecological crisis, the one that may count the most.

I wish to make the case that Christianity, at least since the Protestant Reformation and especially since the Enlightenment, has through its individualistic view of human life supported the neoclassical economic paradigm, the current consumer culture, which is widening the gap between the rich and the poor and is a major cause of global warming. As an alternative, I suggest that Christianity should support an ecological economic model, one in which our well-being is seen as interrelated and interdependent with the well-being of all other living things and earth processes. In other words, religions, and especially Christianity in Western culture, have a central role in forming *who we think we are and what we have the right to do*. The individualistic anthropology is deep within our consumer-oriented culture and is presently supported not only by religion but also by government and contemporary economics. When these three major institutions—religion, government, and economics—present a united front, a "sacred canopy" is cast over a society, validating the behavior of its people. It is difficult to believe that science and technology alone can solve an ecological crisis supported by this triumvirate, for it legitimates human beings continuing *to feel, think, and act in ways that are basically contrary* to the just distribution of the world's resources and the sustainability of the planet itself.

Neoclassical and Ecological Economics

The two worldviews—the neoclassical economic one and the ecological economic view—are dramatically different, suggesting different anthropologies and different house rules. The first model sees human beings on the planet as similar to a corporation or syndicate, a collection of individuals drawn together to benefit its members by optimal use of natural resources. The second model sees the planet more as an organism or a community, which survives and prospers through the interdependence of all its parts, human and nonhuman. The first model rests on assumptions from the eighteenth-century view of human beings as individuals with rights and responsibilities, and of the world as a machine or a collection of individual parts, related externally to one another. The second model rests on assumptions from postmodern science in its view of human beings as the conscious and radically dependent part of the planet, and of the world as a community or an organism, internally related in all its parts. *Both are models*, interpretations, of the world and our place in it; neither one is a description. This point must be underscored, because the first model seems "natural"—indeed, "inevitable" and "true"—to most middle-class Westerners, while the second model seems novel, perhaps even utopian or fanciful. In fact, both come from assumptions of different historical periods; both are world pictures built on these assumptions and each vies for our agreement and loyalty.

I will suggest that the corporation or machine model is injurious to nature and to poor people, while the other one, the community or organic model, is healthier for the planet and all its inhabitants. In other words, we need to assess the "economy" of both models, their notions of the allocation of scarce resources to family members, in order to determine which view of the "good life" is better.

The mention of "allocation of scarce resources" brings us to the heart of the matter. The reason economics is so important, the reason it is a religious and ecological issue, is that it is not just a matter of money; rather, it is a matter of survival and flourishing. Economics is a *value* issue. In making economic decisions, the bottom line is not the only consideration. Many other values are present in decisions concerning scarce resources and the way they should be deployed: from the health of a community to its recreational opportunities; from the beauty of other life-forms to our concern for their well-being; from a desire to see our children fed and clothed to a sense of responsibility for the welfare of future generations. Climate change is intimately involved in this value issue: one of the reasons global warming is occurring is our preference to make money through excessive consumption regardless of the consequences to the planet.

Contemporary neoclassical economists, however, generally deny that economics is about values. But this denial is questionable. By neoclassical economics, we mean market capitalism as conceived by Adam Smith in the eighteenth century and, more particularly, the version of it practiced by major economies of our time. The key feature of market capitalism is the allocation of scarce resources by means of decentralized markets: allocation occurs as the result of individual market transactions, each of which is guided by self-interest. At the base of neoclassical economics is an anthropology: human beings are individuals motivated by self-interest. The value by which scarce resources are allocated, then, is the fulfillment of the self-interest of human beings. The assumption is that everyone will act to maximize his or her own interest, and by so doing all will eventually benefit—the so-called invisible hand of classical economic theory.

Neoclassical economics has *one* value: the monetary fulfillment of individuals provided they compete successfully for the resources. But what of other values? Two key ones, if we have the economics of the entire planet in mind, are the just distribution of the earth's resources to all needy users and the ability of the planet to sustain our use of its resources. However, these matters—distributive justice to the world's inhabitants and the optimal scale of the human economy within the planet's economy—are considered "externalities" by neoclassical economics. In other words, the issues of who benefits from an economic system and whether the planet can bear the system's burden are not part of neoclassical economics.

These so-called externalities are, in fact, not minor or extraneous matters. On the contrary, as climate change is illustrating, they are the heart of the matter. For example, environmental deterioration, a prime "externality," is not figured into the price of goods in market capitalism. A company may have to pay a penalty for ecological damage—as in the oil spill from the *Exxon Valdez*—but it did not have to include in the price of the oil the greenhouse gas emissions caused by its initial production. Other "externalities" include the issues of justice and sustainability, as well as recreational and aesthetic values. None of these matters counts in the price tag according to market capitalism.

In sum, the worldview of neoclassical economics is surprisingly simple and straightforward: the crucial assumption is that human beings are self-interested individuals who, acting on this basis, will create a syndicate, even a global one, capable of benefiting all eventually. Hence, as long as the economy grows, individuals in a society will sooner or later participate in prosperity. These assumptions about human beings are scarcely value-neutral. They indicate a preference for a certain view of who we are and what the goal of human effort should be: the view of human nature is individualism, and the goal is growth. Neither human poverty nor nature's deterioration has a place in this model of economics—and certainly not the issue of climate change.

When we turn to the alternative ecological economic paradigm, we see a different set of values. Are we basically greedy or needy? Probably both, but as our answers veer toward one pole or the other, we will find ourselves embracing an individualistic or a communitarian model of life. Ecological economics claims that we cannot survive (even to be greedy) unless we acknowledge our profound dependence on one another and on the earth. Human need is more basic than human greed: we *are* relational beings from the moment of our conception to our last breath. The well-being of the individual is inextricably connected to the well-being of the whole.

These two interpretations of who we are and where we fit in the world are almost mirror opposites of each other on the three critical issues of allocation of resources, distributive justice, and sustainability. Neoclassical economics begins with the unconstrained allocation of resources to competing individuals, on the assumption that if all people operate from this base, issues of distribution and sustainability will eventually work themselves out. Ecological economics begins with the viability of the whole community, on the assumption that only as it thrives now and in the future will its various members, including human beings, thrive as well. In other words, ecological economics *begins* with sustainability and distributive justice, not with the allocation of resources among competing individuals. Before all else, the community must be able to survive (sustainability), which it can do only if all members have the use of resources (distributive justice). Then, within these parameters, the allocation of scarce resources among competing users can take place.

Ecological economics does not pretend to be value-free: its preference is evident—the well-being and sustainability of the whole household, planet Earth. It recognizes the *oikos* base of ecology, economics, and ecumenicity: *economics is the management of a community's physical necessities for the benefit of all.* Here we see the tight connection between economics and ecology—and in our present situation, the connection between market economics and global warming. Climate change clearly shows that neoclassical economics is a failure in managing the planet's resources for the benefit of all. Ecological economics, on the other hand, is a human enterprise that seeks to maximize the optimal functioning of the planet's gifts and services for all users. Ecological economics, then, is first of all a vision of how human beings ought to live on planet Earth in light of the perceived reality of where and how we do in fact live. *We live in, with, and from the earth.* This story of who we are is based on postmodern science—not, as in neoclassical economics, on the eighteenth-century story of reality—a story that eliminated nature as a major player.

Neoclassical or Ecological Economics: Which Is Good for Planet Earth?

In answering this question, we are asking about the most important of the three economic issues: sustainability, with climate change as our case study. Can neoclassical economics as currently understood sustain the planet? In the neoclassical economic view, the "world" is a machine or a collection of individuals; presumably, then, when some parts give out, they can be replaced with substitutes. If, for instance, our main ecological problem is the scarcity of nonrenewable resources (oil, coal, minerals, and so forth), then human ingenuity might well fill the gaps when shortages occur.

The problem facing our planet at the beginning of the new millennium, however, is far greater than simply the loss of nonrenewable resources. In fact, that problem is of less importance than two other related ones: the rate of loss of *renewable* resources and the manner in which these losses overlap and support further deterioration. . . . [W]hen an organic-like entity, such as the earth, undergoes change, everything is affected—and the change snowballs. The big problems are the loss of water, trees, fertile soil, clean air, fisheries, and biodiversity *and* the ways the degradation of each of these renewables contributes to the deterioration of the rest. In other words, if the planet is seen more as an organism than a machine, with all parts interrelated and interdependent, then after a certain level of decay of its various members, it will, like any "body," become sick at its core, sick to the point of not functioning properly. It will not be able to sustain itself. We have already noted this phenomenon in our discussion of the "tipping point" of global temperature, an increase of such proportions that the life-sustaining systems of the planet are undermined.

This process refers to the *synergism* of planetary operation. The various parts of the planet work together both in health and in decay to create something either better or worse than the individual parts. When the various members of an ecosystem are healthy, they work together to provide innumerable "free services" that none could provide alone, services that we usually take for granted: materials production (food, fisheries, timber, genetic resources, medicines), pollination, biological control of pests and diseases, habitat and refuge, water supply and regulation, waste recycling and pollution control, educational and scientific resources, and recreation.[3] These services are essential to our survival and well-being; they can continue only if we sustain them. This list of services should be seen as a web: none of them can function alone—each of them depends on the others. These services are the "commons" that is our very lifeblood and that we hold in trust for future generations.

The most important services are not necessarily the most visible ones; for instance, in a forest it is not only the standing trees that are valuable but also the fallen ones (the "nurse logs" on which new trees grow); the habitat the forest provides for birds and insects that pollinate crops and destroy diseases; the plants that provide biodiversity for food and medicines; the forest canopy that breaks the force of winds; the roots that reduce soil erosion; the photosynthesis of plants that help stabilize the climate. The smallest providers—the insects, worms, spiders, fungi, algae, and bacteria—are critically important in creating a stable, sustainable home for humans and other creatures. If such a forest is clear-cut, everything else goes as well. Or, in a situation such as the extreme deterioration that climate change will create, *all of these services will disappear as well*. A healthy ecosystem—complex and diverse in all its features, both large and small—is resilient like a well-functioning body. A simplified, degraded nature, supporting single-species crops in ruined soil with inadequate water and violent weather events, results in a diminished environment for human beings as well. "The bottom line is that for humans to be healthy and resilient, nature must be too."[4]

An outstanding example of *negative* synergy is global warming, which undermines all of the wonderful "free services" nature gives us when it is healthy. Over the past two hundred years since the Industrial Revolution and the sharp increase of carbon dioxide emissions, we have seen a gradual unraveling of the billions of complex threads—flora and fauna, systems and processes—that work together to create the intricately patterned "cloak of life" that covers our earth. When we list the effects of global warming, we must remember more than just the most visible ones, such as desertification of grain-producing lands, scarcity of fresh water, loss of trees, flooding of coastal lands and islands, the spread of tropical diseases, torrid temperatures, and the decline of biodiversity. It is what we don't see in negative synergy that is crucial: the way that a whole healthy system is undermined as the threads that constitute the fabric unravel. We not only lose polar bears with global warming; we lose the entire Arctic climate system that supports polar bears—and so much more. Through our high-energy consumer lifestyle, we have triggered fearful, though still not fully understood, consequences for the most important and sensitive systems within which we and everything else exist. Global warming is a canary in the mine; the deterioration and death it is bringing are the signal that our lifestyle lies outside the planet's house rules.

An economic model that does not have as its first priority the sustainability of the planet cannot be good for human beings. The neoclassical economic model does not have such a priority. Hence, it is not good for us *even if we like it*—and we do like it. We are addicted to our consumer lifestyle and are only beginning to wake up to how bad it is for us and for the planet.

CHRISTIANITY AND THE ECOLOGICAL ECONOMIC MODEL

The model we need is very different. . . . [T]he ecological model claims that housemates must abide by three main rules: (1) Take only your share. (2) Clean up after yourself. (3) Keep the house in good repair for future occupants. We need to abide by these rules at personal, societal, and global levels. We don't own this house; we don't even rent it. It is loaned to us "free" for our lifetime with the proviso that we obey the above rules so that it can continue to feed, shelter, nurture, and delight others. These rules are not laws that we can circumvent or disobey; they are the conditions of our existence, and they are intrinsic to our happiness. If we were to follow these rules, we would be living within a different vision of the good life, the abundant life, than the current vision in our consumer culture that is destroying the planet.

Given these two economic worldviews—the neoclassical and the ecological—which should Christianity support? Presently, it is supporting the neoclassical economic paradigm *to the degree that it does not speak against it and side publicly with the ecological view*. Does this matter? Yes, if one accepts the assumption that worldviews matter. While there is no direct connection between believing and acting, thinking and doing, there is an implicit, deeper, and more insidious one: the worldview that persuades us it is "natural" and "inevitable" becomes the secret partner of our decisions and actions.

Moreover, a persuasive case can be made that there is an intrinsic connection between the ecological economic model and Christianity. Distributive justice and sustainability, as goals for planetary living, are pale reflections, but reflections, nonetheless, of what Jesus meant by the kingdom of God. . . . [Let us look at] the portrait of Jesus by New Testament scholar John Dominic Crossan . . . : "The open commensality and radical egalitarianism of Jesus' Kingdom of God are more terrifying than anything we have ever imagined, and even if we can never accept it, we should not explain it away as something else."[5] For Jesus, the kingdom of God was epitomized by *everyone* being invited to the table. *The kingdom is known by radical equality at the level of bodily needs*. Crossan names the parable of the feast as central to understanding what Jesus meant by the kingdom of God. This is a shocking story, trespassing society's boundaries of class, gender, status, and ethnicity—since its end result is the invitation of *all* to the feast. There are several versions (Matt 22:1-13; Luke 14:15-24; *Gos. Thom.* 64), but in each a prominent person invites other, presumably worthy, people to a banquet, only to have them refuse: one to survey a land purchase, another to try out some new oxen, a third to attend a wedding. The frustrated host then tells his servants to go out into the streets of the city and bring whomever they find to dinner: the poor, maimed, blind, lame, good, and bad (the list varies in the three versions). The shocking implication is that everyone—*anyone*—is invited. As Crossan remarks, if beggars came to your door, you might give them food or even invite them into the kitchen for a meal, but you wouldn't ask them to join the family in the dining room or invite them back on Saturday night for supper with your friends.[6] But that is exactly what happens in this story. The kingdom of God, according to this portrait of Jesus, is "more terrifying than anything we have ever imagined" because it demolishes all of our carefully constructed boundaries between the worthy and the unworthy and does so at the most physical, bodily level.

For first-century Jews, the key boundary was purity laws: one did not eat with the poor, women, the diseased, or the "unrighteous." For us in our consumer society, the critical barrier is economic laws: one is not called to sustainable and just sharing of resources with the poor, the disadvantaged, the "lazy." To do otherwise in both cultures is improper; it is not expected—in fact, it is shocking. And yet in both cases, the issue is the most basic bodily one—who is invited to share the food. In other words, the issue is who lives and who dies. In both cases, the answer is the same: everyone, regardless of status (by any criteria), is invited. This vision of God's will for the world does not specifically mention just, sustainable planetary living, but it surely is more in line with that worldview than with the worldview based on the satisfaction of individual consumer desires.

Unlike our first-century Mediterranean counterparts, North American middle-class Christians are not terrified by the unclean, but we are terrified by the poor. There are so many of them—billions! Surely we cannot be expected to share the planet's resources justly and sustainably with all of them. Climate change is making this terror very clear: it demands basic changes in our economic policies toward greater egalitarianism at all levels. It demands that we think of the "body" of the world and what it needs in order to flourish, rather than focusing on our own consumer desires. One of the principal reasons for global warming denial is the realization that "everyone is invited" to the table of household Earth—including not just needy human beings, but the air, the water, the land, and each and every creature, no matter how small and seemingly insignificant. The terror implicit in this parable lies with its radical inclusivity—nothing, no one, is left out. "The Kingdom of God . . . began at the level of the body and appeared as a shared community of healing and eating—that is to say, of spiritual and physical resources available to each and all without discrimination, or hierarchies."[7]

The body is the locus: how we treat needy bodies gives the clue to how a society is organized. It suggests that correct "table manners" are a sign of a just society, the kingdom of God. If one accepts this interpretation, the "table" becomes not primarily the priestly consecrated bread and wine of Communion celebrating Jesus' death for the sins of the world, but rather the egalitarian meals of bread and fish that one finds throughout Jesus' ministry.[8] At these events, all are invited, with no authoritarian brokering, to share in the food, whether it be meager or sumptuous. Were such an understanding of the Eucharist to infiltrate Christian churches today, it could be mind-changing—in fact, world-changing. The parable of the feast is a metaphor for Christians encountering climate change because *it focuses on the body and its needs*. It reminds us that our planet is a deteriorating body in desperate need, and only as we begin to live differently—to live by its house rules of just distribution and sustainability—will we begin to respond appropriately to the crisis.

If this is the case, then for middle-class North American Christians, it may well be that *sin* is refusing to acknowledge the link between the kingdom and the ecological economic worldview, denying it because of the consequences to our privileged lifestyle. Sustainability and the just distribution of resources are concerned with human and planetary well-being *for all*. This proposition is indeed terrifying, but it is not absurd. In fact, it is, I suggest, the responsible interpretation of the parable of the feast for twenty-first-century well-off North American Christians. It demands that we look at the behaviors and systemic structures that are causing poverty and ecological deterioration in our world and name these behaviors and structures for what they are: evil. They are the collective forms of "our sin." They are the assumptions, institutions, and laws of market capitalism (often aided by the silence of the churches) that allow people and the planet to become impoverished. Our sin is one of commission, but perhaps more damningly of omission: our greed camouflaged by indifference and denial, while at the same time we offer charity to the poor and green rhetoric to "the environment."

Next Steps: A Christian Response

To dislodge the neoclassical economic worldview and Christianity's complicity with it, we must take four steps.

The first step is to become conscious that neoclassical economics is a model, not a description, of how to allocate scarce resources. There are other ways to live, other ways to divide things up, other goals for human beings and the planet. "Economics" is always necessary, but not necessarily neoclassical economics: ecological economics is an alternative. Since the death of communism and the retreat of socialism, religious worldviews are one of the few sources left to critique the hegemony of market capitalism. Without the presence of alternative visions, a model becomes an ideology, as market capitalism has become in our time.

A second step is to suggest some visions of the good life that are not consumer dominated, visions that are just and sustainable. The good life is not necessarily the consumer life; rather, it could include the basic necessities for all, universal medical care and education, opportunities for creativity and meaningful work, time for family and friends, green spaces in cities and wilderness for other creatures. We need to ask what *really* makes people happy and which of these visions are just for the world's inhabitants and sustainable for the planet.

A third step is for well-off Christians as well as others to publicly advocate the ecological model as a more just and sustainable one for our planet—and as the model that climate change is demanding we accept. While the ecological model is not the kingdom of God, Christians have the obligation to work for systems that are at least faint approximations of the kingdom, rather than clear opponents. Specifically, this means becoming informed about the global injustices of market economies; joining with other NGOs to change the policies and practices of so-called free trade that result in impoverishment and unsustainability; and accepting the consequences for one's own lifestyle that sharing earth's resources justly and sustainably will entail. It means also acknowledging the tight connection between market economics and global warming: unlimited consumerism is a major contributor to greenhouse gases.

The fourth step is to rethink what such a different context—the ecological economic one—would mean for the basic doctrines of Christianity: God and the world, Christ and salvation, human life and discipleship. Such reconstruction is the central task of this book, but here we will close the chapter with a few brief comments summing up the picture of God and the world that has emerged so far. This picture is at the heart of *who we think we are and what we should do*. Since our interpretive context, the ecological economic model, is about the just and sustainable allocation of resources in our time of climate change, the framework for speaking of God and the world becomes worldly well-being. Dietrich Bonhoeffer called it "worldly Christianity": he said that God is neither a metaphysical abstraction nor the answer to gaps in our knowledge—God is neither in the sky nor on the fringes, but at "the center of the village," in the midst of life, both its pains and its joys.[9] This is an earthly God, an incarnate God, who cares about the flourishing of creation.

As we look at the general outline of this theology, we find that it is basically different from the theology implied by the neoclassical model. Broadly speaking, the differences can be suggested as *a movement toward the earth*: from heaven to earth; from otherworldly to this-worldly; from above to below; from a distant, external God to a near, immanent God; from time and history to space and land; from soul to body; from individualism to community; from mechanistic to organic thinking; from spiritual salvation to holistic well-being; from anthropocentrism to cosmocentrism. The ecological model means a shift *not* from God to the world, but from a distant God related externally to the world to an embodied God who is the source of the world's life and fulfillment. The neoclassical model assumes God, like a human being, is an individual, in fact, the super-individual who controls the world through laws of nature, much as a good mechanic makes a well-designed machine operate efficiently. This God is at the beginning (creation) and intervenes from time to time to influence personal and public history, but otherwise is absent from the world. The ecological model, on the contrary, claims that God is radically present in the world, as close as the breath, the joy, and the suffering of every creature. The two views of God and the world, then, are very different: in the one, God's power is evident in God's distant control of the world; in the other, God's glory is manifest in God's total self-giving to the world.

In closing, let us note that the two pictures of God and the world suggest different answers to the question we have been pursuing in this book: Who are we, and what should we do? In the first view, we are individuals responsible to a transcendent God who rewards and punishes us according to our merits and God's mercy. In the second view, we are beings-in-community living in the presence of God, who is the power and love in everything that exists. In the first, we should do what is fair to other individuals while taking care of our own well-being; in the second, we should do what is necessary to work with God to create a just and sustainable planet, for only in this way will all flourish.

A just and sustainable planet is the great work of the twenty-first century to which all religions—indeed, all areas of human endeavor—are called. The crisis of climate change is making the necessity of this common task crystal clear. It is no longer debatable. But we are neither left alone to do this work nor ignorant of what needs to be done. God is with us—closer to each and every creature than we can ask or imagine—and we have some clues on how to proceed—in the kingdom of God and its pale reflection, the ecological economic model. Thanks be to God!

Notes

1. For a fuller treatment of metaphors and models, see McFague 1987; also see McFague 2008, ch. 6.

2. Lynn White Jr., "The Historical Roots of Our Ecological Crisis," *Science* 155 (March 10, 1967): 1203–7.

3. Janet N. Abramowitz, "Valuing Nature's Services," in *State of the World 1997: A Worldwide Institute Report on Progress toward a Sustainable Society*, ed. Lester R. Brown et al. (New York: Norton, 1997).

4. Ibid., 109.

5. John Dominic Crossan, *Jesus: A Revolutionary Biography* (San Francisco: HarperSanFrancisco, 1994), 73–74.

6. Ibid., 68.

7. Ibid., 113.

8. See ibid., 79–81.

9. See letter of April 30, 1944, in Dietrich Bonhoeffer, *Letters and Papers from Prison* (London: Collins, 1960).

12

A Spirituality for the Whole Planet / Kenotic Theology

Sallie McFague's most recent book, Blessed Are the Consumers: Climate Change and the Practice of Restraint *(2013) is built around the Christian concept of kenosis—or self-emptying, commonly associated with Jesus' self-sacrifice—a idea she began to work with in* A New Climate for Theology. *Here the idea is applied especially to how we are called to live in the world in the context of climate change and global poverty. Interested in religious autobiographies from the beginning (as evidenced in ch. 1, above), McFague here uses the autobiographical writings of three "saints," John Woolman, Simone Weil, and Dorothy Day, as examples of kenotic living and spirituality. The two brief excerpts offered here both hearken back to earlier themes and introduce yet another new model for doing theology. First, she revisits what it means to love God and the world (recalling* Super, Natural Christians*) and more explicitly embraces language of spirituality, here framed in terms of kenoticism. Then, the final section on "Kenotic Theology" radicalizes the work on embodiment that she discussed at length in* The Body of God, *but is here connected to the metaphor of food revealed in the lives of her saints and the need to share resources.*

Source: 2013:18–22; 171–74

The current fascination with "spirituality" versus "religion," with spirituality seen as inner and personal, while religion is institutional and traditional, is yet another indication of the narcissism of our culture. However, a 1977 definition of *spirituality* by the Scottish Churches Council claims it is "an exploration into what is involved in becoming human," and "becoming human is "an attempt to grow in sensitivity to self, to others, to the non-human creation, and to God who is within and beyond this totality."[1]

Spirituality is not about a one-on-one relationship with God, but about growing in relationship with others, including the natural world. Spirituality is *communal*, learning about and caring for the world. And what is our world like these days? If we were to answer the question, Where are we? two main crises would surface immediately: global warming and the economic recession. Since climate changes are happening much faster than thought even a few years ago,[2] the urgency of the situation is evident. In less than two decades the Arctic Ocean will be free of ice all summer, melting permafrost and releasing methane gas, which will further accelerate global warming. Researchers fear tipping points with irreversible temperature rise, and its terrifying effects.

The economic crisis has retreated a bit since the dire days of spring 2008, but the possibility of further global economic meltdown is still with us. And there is little optimism about finding a way forward to ensure that another Great Recession does not occur. These two crises point to a dilemma deep at the heart of where we live—we are living in la-la land, a place that has no relationship to the finitude of our actual home, planet earth. We are living beyond our means, both financially and ecologically. We are consuming with an insatiable, and unsustainable, appetite.

We need to change our minds and change our behavior. Thomas Friedman, writing in the *New York Times*, puts it this way: "What if the crisis of 2008 represents something much more fundamental than a deep recession? What if it's telling us that the whole growth model we created over the last 50 years is simply unsustainable economically and ecologically and that 2008 was when we hit the wall—when Mother Nature and the market both said: 'No more.' What if we face up to the fact that unlike the U.S. government, Mother Nature doesn't do bailouts?"[3]

One way we can begin to change our minds and our behavior is through a communal spirituality. The poet Robinson Jeffers says that we should "fall in love outward"; we should fall in love with the world rather than "inward" with ourselves.[4] For some, spirituality is about the individual—how might I live serenely and happily? But what would a "communal" spirituality look like—one that was good for both the planet and all its creatures?

The religions—the wisdom traditions—might have something to teach us. They move us from individualism to community, for they are not just about "me and my well-being." Rather, they are tough-minded and objective, insisting on global kinship—that all creatures have the right to the basics of existence. How can you get more revolutionary than that? Such a revolution would involve immense changes in the lifestyle of us well-off North Americans. Some have suggested that the religions encourage people to be good "stewards" of creation, and I agree. However, most religious traditions suggest much more: most make the radical suggestion that to find your life, you must lose it, that sacrificing for others is not just for the saints but for all of us, that when the basic necessities of life are limited, they should be shared fairly. John Hick claims that the function of the main religious traditions is "the transformation of human existence from self-centeredness to Reality-centeredness."[5] And Gandhi claimed that "worship without sacrifice" was one of the seven deadly sins.[6]

CAN WE LOVE BOTH GOD AND THE WORLD?

Pierre Teilhard de Chardin said that at seven years old he had two passions—for the world and for God—and he could not imagine giving up either one. Must it be beauty versus duty, an either/or, or is there another way? What is the character of the spiritual practice for just, sustainable living? What kind of spiritual practice is called for?

Both God and the world *call* to us to "fall in love outward" (Robinson Jeffers), not inward. One is not duty and the other love; rather, both call for our *attention* and do so primarily by focusing on the world. Spirituality is not a one-on-one inner relationship with God; rather, it is meeting God in the world, in both its beauty and its pain. An incarnate God directs our attention to what God loves—the world, all its creatures, human and otherwise. We are constituted by this call outward, this call to pay attention to the beauty and pain of the world. It is "who we are" (made in the image of God who loves the world). We are not first of all selves who then respond to a call to love the world; rather, this is *who* we are—world-lovers—which always means world-bearers, for both nature and the neighbor are the "new poor" in our time.

So, it is not God *or* the world, but the world *in* God. We must love nature as it is: physical, needy, interdependent, vulnerable. If we find God in the world, then we have set the context, the place, where we meet God. This perspective militates against an individualistic, spiritual relationship between God and the soul. It unites mystical spirituality—our personal relationship to God with the world—with the needy body, which must have the basics for flourishing. Finding God in the world means as well that our use of energy becomes important, for nature and its many creatures can only live by energy. Hence, mundane things like transportation, heating and cooling systems, concrete for buildings and roads, food production (whether local or brought from afar) become the way we love God. Loving God and sharing energy are one and the same thing. This kind of spirituality leads not only to delight and joy in the beauty of the world but also to kenosis, limitation, self-restraint, ecological economics, a sense of finitude, the need to share space, as we come to realize who we are in the scheme of things.

Kenoticism and Reality

Is this religious insight of the transformation from self-centeredness to reality centeredness simply wild, crazy idealism? Is reality anything like this? The evolutionary, interdependent story of reality that we are presently learning from the sciences suggests it is. Nature is the grandest, most intricate, most complex system of give-and-take, of debt and payback, of borrowing and lending, and of sacrifice (albeit unwilling sacrifice). Everything—from one-celled organisms to mosquitoes to whales to human beings—lives within a vast system of exchange, whether they know it or not, whether they want to or not. We give and take constantly at every level of existence, simply to exist at all. Every breath we take is borrowed, and our lives depend on being able to borrow more and more breaths every moment for the rest of our lives. Nature says this is the way the system works: if we live at all, we live off each other.

A good example is an old-growth forest. When I moved to Vancouver, I was introduced to them for the first time. I did not know anything like them existed. The forests back east do not have the complexity and bizarre qualities of old-growth forests, which are a mess—literally, a mess. On first view, such a forest strikes one as a tangle, a jumble of trees standing lying down or halfway down; caves, holes, and openings; ferns, mosses, and lichens; mushrooms, rocks, and epiphytes; springtails, crustaceans, and dragonflies; water dripping, running, standing; trees on top of other trees, trees with bushes growing out of them, trees with holes and knobs and twisted limbs like pretzels. An old-growth forest is seemingly chaotic, but it works, it sustains billions of different forms of life. Its haphazard quality is part of its genius: anything that is successful, that can find a way to live, is okay. Animals and plants live with, inside of, on top of, beneath, partly inside and partly outside one another. It is often impossible to tell what is what: where does this tree begin and this other one end?

The best example of this marvelous messy muddle is the phenomenon of the "nurse log." Nurse logs are lying-down trees—some would say dead trees—that, having lived several hundred years as standing trees, have now begun a second career as homes for other trees. The body of the nurse log provides a warm, nutrient-rich birthplace for young saplings of all sorts to grow. And it is not just seeds from the nurse tree that grow on a nurse log, but anything and everything. All are welcome! The nurse log can live another several hundred years as the giver of new life from its body. Sometimes one sees ghost nurse logs: big empty holes under the roots of trees where a nurse log used to be. The new tree stretched its roots around the nurse log and still retains this odd position after the nurse log disappears. With the hole between its roots, it is a visible sign of the tree that nurtured it.

Life and death are mixed up here. What is living and what is dead? Is the nurse log dead because it is no longer standing up straight? Scarcely. Is the sapling living because it has new leaves? Yes, but barely, and only because it is living off the nurse log. It all works by symbiosis—living off one another. Nothing in an old-growth forest can go it alone; nothing could survive by itself; everything in the forest is interrelated and interdependent: all flora and fauna eat from, live from the others. The nurse log is but a clear example of what occurs everywhere in such a forest.

A Communal Spirituality

The recognition that we own nothing, that we depend utterly on other life-forms and natural processes, is the first step in our "rebirth" to a life of self-emptying love for others. The religious insight that we should move from self-centeredness to reality centeredness is not contrary to the way nature works; rather, it is an intensification of it. In fact, self-centeredness and reality centeredness are not total opposites; rather, recognizing that all life is interrelated and interdependent is the basis for a new view of the self, one that does not try to hoard everything, one that recognizes that others beside oneself truly exist and need resources in order to live. The religions say that the self is found, is "reborn," when it acknowledges ultimate nature of self-giving, by sharing space and food with others. Many call such sacrifice for others contrary to reality, but nature's brutal exchange system, in which everything is borrowed and payment exacted, is a preparation for the further, total step of self-emptying. What is distinctive about human beings is not we that we escape the economy of debt and payback, but that we can not only recognize that this is the way things work, but we can take it one step further and *give* when we see the balance sheet to be unfair to the weak, the oppressed, the needy. The debt-and-payback system is not merciful or fair or compassionate, but human beings have the capability of making it more so, of sharing when they have too much, of sacrificing for others, of limiting their wants so the needs of others can be met.

At the heart of most religions is a message, an invitation to a marvelous, messy, muddle where we must live in and with and off of one another—if we live at all. Like the plants and animals in an old-growth forest, we are interrelated and interdependent. We live or die together. Along the way we find some nurse logs, those people and places of exceptional warmth and nutrition, who give us the extra help we need. We also can become nurse logs to others. But like any forest, we can be clear-cut, made into a lifeless, sterile, straight superhighway; we, our world, can also become a desert, where few can thrive. Or we can welcome the good news that all of us, all human beings in our incredible and delightful diversity, as well as all other creatures and plants in their awesome differences, are invited to the feast table of planet earth.

In sum, we are not called to love God *or* the world. Rather, we are called to love God *in* the world. We love God *by* loving the world. We love God *through* and *with* the world. But this turns out to be a kenotic, a sacrificial love . . .

Kenotic Theology

A kenotic theology is necessarily a body theology, for kenosis is about the sharing of scarce resources among the needy. We are all needy at the most basic level of food in order to survive from one day to the next. This is certainly what the lives of our three saints tell us—the primary symbol of need at all levels of our existence is "food," whether it be Woolman's economics based on universal love, Weil's notion of "cannibalism" of others as the most basic sin, or Day's endless soup kitchens feeding hungry bodies. Our saints are not pie-in-the-sky spiritualists who see religious practice as focused on people's souls. Rather, the "pie" is concrete and physical. It is the grocery business that Woolman sold in order to keep his eye "single," in order to see his own body, as he says interpreting a dream, as mixed up with the mass of "human beings in as great misery as they could be," no longer considering himself "as a distinct or separate being."[7] Or the pie is Weil's "paralytic" prayer, in which she asks that her body "be stripped away from me, devoured by God, transformed into Christ's substance, and given for food to afflicted men whose body and soul lack every kind of nourishment."[8] Or the pie is the bread crust that Day shared with others. ("If there were six small loaves and a few fishes, we had to divide them. There was always bread.")[9]

A kenotic theology is therefore an incarnational theology, a theology that focuses unapologetically on "food," the lowliest, most basic need shared by all living beings. A kenotic theology is not a lofty theology, not a theology glorifying "God or man"; rather, it is a theology that begins with need, both God's need and ours, a need that runs all the way from the most elemental biological processes of the energy transformation to understanding the Trinity (the being of God) as one of continuous and total exchange of love. Kenosis is the process that begins and continues life, all the way from the splitting of cells to the sacrifice (and death) of some human beings for the nourishment of others, and of God's quintessential act of self-emptying both within the divine being and for the creation and salvation of the world. Thus Christianity's manner of making contact with the most basic physical, biological processes is through an inclusive, radical interpretation of its doctrine of the incarnation of God, not now merely in one human being, Jesus of Nazareth, but in the world as God's body.[10] This model attempts to express the most basic relationship of God and the world as one of shocking totality and intimacy, one that goes to the core of what it means to live and flourish. Moreover, it implies that we human beings, made "in the image of God," likewise might model our relationship with the world in a similar fashion: the world as *our* body. A thumbnail sketch of this model suggests that all flesh, all matter, is included within God (as God's "body") but that God is not limited to this body, to matter. Here, God is understood to be "more than" the body, more than the world, but intimately, radically, and inclusively identified with it. We human beings are likewise thoroughly linked with the world; in fact, to see the world as our body is one metaphor expressing what we have called the "universal self," the awareness that the self has no limits. Moreover, by focusing our understanding of the divine-world relationship at the most basic, physical, bodily level, we avoid tendencies by many religions, including Christianity, to "spiritualize" the relationship, insisting now that God is the creator par excellence and that creation is composed of bodies that must be fed.

This primary belief that God and the world are bound together in a network of physicality, vulnerability, and need sets the framework for a kenotic theology of power as love, not as control. It suggests that seeing the world as God's beloved rather than as his kingdom is the appropriate metaphor since, in this theological paradigm, God is *always* incarnate, always bound to the world as its lover, as close to it as we are to our own bodies, and concerned before all else to see that the body, God's world, flourishes. Thus a kenotic theology begins not with the doctrine of creation but with the incarnation, not with the picture of God fashioning the world like an artist from alien materials but from God's own body, as God's body. "The Word was made flesh" is first of all an empirical assertion on the basis of the life and death of Jesus of Nazareth, the judgment that Christians make about the meaning of the story of this man. Like the stories of our saints, which speak by embodiment, so also what Christians say about the basic God-world relationship is not a speculative assertion about creation but a tentative judgment that here in this story we have our best clue not only to the nature of God but to our own nature as well. Thus, as Paul puts it, we read in the "face" of Jesus the most basic relationship between God and the world. What we see in the face of Jesus Christ is knowledge of the glory of God, and this glory includes the creative light that shone out of darkness (2 Cor. 4:6). We "read back" into the creational relationship between God and the world what we see in the life and death of Jesus of Nazareth. This message is, first of all, about the God who empties the divine self into a human being both in his life of radical service to others and in his death on a cross, thus telling us that all God's relations with the world are of a kenotic character.

It is necessary to pause for a moment . . . to acknowledge how different it is from the traditional, establishment theology.[11] While there are many variations of this theology, its broad picture is of a powerful God who creates a world "from nothing," where the distinctive relationship is one of control by God and submission by human beings who are, in the most basic respects, different from God. The story starts with creation, includes a "fall" on the part of human beings, and hopefully a return to the pristine conditions of creation through the sacrifice of God's son, Jesus Christ. It is an "external" story, told "about" us rather than arising from anyone's lived experience with the divine. It is both individualistic and anthropocentric, taking as its primary focus the creation, fall, and salvation of particular human beings who are only marginally related to the rest of the world.

A kenotic theology, however, begins with the stories of people who claim to experience God as both the source of their own lives, as well as of everything else, with this experience, while mystical in the sense that it is a profound sense of personal engagement with the divine, is also prophetic, since it carries a call to love others in the same manner that God loves. It is deeply intimate (God, says Augustine, is closer to us than we are to ourselves) and yet at the same time universal in scope and focused above all on assuring the flourishing of all life at the most basic level of food. Since its primary source is personal stories that read the glory of God in the face of Jesus Christ, its central content is self-emptying for others, ranging from sharing food and healing bodies to the sacrifice of one's own body on a cross, the ultimate gift of the self so that others might have new, abundant life. No story could be more personal, intimate, bodily, or basic; no story could also be more universal, radical, or total. It has everything to do with us human beings (but it is not anthropocentric) and everything to do with power (but it is not about control). It is a countercultural story, calling on our "wild space" to imagine a different way to live in the world, one at odds with our economic, governmental, and often religious interpretations of the good life. This interpretation is best expressed in the lives of those who have attempted to live it, for it is not a set of concepts, but a journey of gradual self-emptying of the ego so that the new self, the universal self, may begin to develop at both personal and public levels. It claims that embodiment, lives as lived, is a more powerful statement than words about this way of life, since it involves a constant translation of the paradigm (the bare bones of disorientation, self-emptying, and a new direction for flourishing) from the lives and times of others to one's own life and times. What we see in the stories of Woolman, Weil, and Day—not to mention Jesus—is paradigmatic but not programmatic. A kenotic theology must be reconstructed for each new age and set of circumstances. Here . . . I am attempting to see what it might mean for the twenty-first-century twin crises of increasing poverty and increasing temperatures, creating a situation that calls for a radically different lifestyle, one of restraint, sharing, limits, sacrifice, and death.

Notes

1. Scottish Churches Council, "Working Party Report on 'Spirituality'" (Dunblane: Scottish Churches House, 1977), 3.
2. United Nations Intergovernmental Panel on Climate Change Report, 2007.
3. Thomas Friedman, "The Inflection Is Near?" *New York Times*, March 8, 2009.
4. As quoted in David Abram, *The Spell of the Sensuous: Perception and Language in a More-Than-Human World* (New York: Vintage, 1996), 271.
5. John Hick, *An Interpretation of Religion* (New Haven: Yale University Press, 1989), 300.
6. Quoted in Gary T. Gardner, *Inspiring Progress: Religions' Contribution to Sustainable Development* (Washington, DC: Worldwatch Institute, 2006), 4.
7. John Woolman, *The Journal of John Woolman and a Plea for the Poor* (New York: Corinth Books, 1961), 214.
8. Simone Weil, *First and Last Notebooks*, trans. Richard Rees (London: Oxford University Press, 1970), 244.
9. Dorothy Day, *The Long Loneliness* (New York: Curtis, 1952), 317.
10. For more thorough treatments of this model, see McFague 1987; 1993; 2001.
11. For a sketch of the traditional view, as well as alternatives, see "Who Is God? Creation and Providence," ch. 3 in McFague 2008.

PART III

Constructing Theology: God, Humans, and the World

13

The Christian Paradigm

This selection from Models of God *steps back into the world of parable and metaphor to explore how a metaphorical approach might change how we understand and practice Christian faith. The earlier exploration of Jesus' parables is here put into service to set forth a new understanding of Jesus himself and of his ministry, focused particularly on those parables, his practice of table fellowship, and the cross, as "a paradigm of God's relationship to the world." For McFague, this reinterpretation of the faith is imperative, necessitated by the ecological sensibility that emphasizes interdependence rather than the triumphalist and hierarchal understandings that have marked Christian tradition.*

Source: 1987:45–57

The material norm of Christian faith involves a specification of what distinguishes this faith. It involves risking an interpretation of what, most basically, Christian faith is about. Such interpretation is, of course, not done in general or for all time; it is always a partial, limited account of the contours of the salvific power of God in a particular time in light of the paradigmatic figure Jesus of Nazareth. To see the story of Jesus as paradigmatic means to see it as illuminative and illustrative of basic characteristics of the Christian understanding of the God-world relationship. These characteristics are not known solely from that story nor exemplified only in it, but that story is a classic instance, embodying critical dimensions of the relationship between God and the world. A metaphorical theology ... does not take the Christian constant, in either its formal or material mode, as the only source and resource for theology. The question as we approach the issue of the paradigmatic figure Jesus of Nazareth is not whether everything we need in order to do theology in our time can be generated from that figure but whether there are clues or hints here for an interpretation of salvation in our time. That is to say, are there distinguishing marks of the story of Jesus that are relevant to a holistic, nuclear age? If one understands the life and death of Jesus of Nazareth as a parable of

God's relation to the world, and if to be a Christian means to be willing to look "'God-wards" through his story, then one is constrained to say in what ways that story is significant now.[1]

This will involve understanding the story differently from in the past, but, I believe, in a way that has "demonstrable continuities" with the past. My perspective on that story is similar to that of the so-called liberation theologies. Each of these theologies, from the standpoint of race, gender, class, or another basic human distinction, claims that the Christian gospel is opposed to oppression of some by others, opposed to hierarchies and dualisms, opposed to the domination of the weak by the powerful. These theologies, however, unlike the short-lived death-of-God or play theologies, are not just another fad; like other major revisions of the Christian paradigm, they are a new way of understanding the relationship between God and the world, a new way of interpreting what salvation means. These theologies are not marginal, strange, or even particularly novel enterprises, relevant only to the groups from which they emerge. Rather, they are in the classical tradition of fundamental reformulations of Christian faith, just like the theologies of Augustine, Luther, and Schleiermacher. In the case of each of these writers, something about the writer's own experience did not fit with current understandings of Christianity: his experience presented an anomaly that could not be contained in the contemporary paradigm. A changed interpretation was imperative if the writer was to continue to identify himself as a Christian—and if Christian faith was to speak to the critical issues of the times. These theologians, however, believed they were interpreting Christianity not just for themselves or their own kind but for all. From a particular perspective came a universal claim.

These two notes of fundamental revisionist interpretation—experience and universality—are present also in the liberation theologies. The experience of being oppressed by gender, race, or poverty does not limit the theology that emerges to women, people of color, or the poor. Rather, the particular experiences of oppression serve as glasses bringing into sharper focus what one asserts the heart of the gospel truly to be for one's own time. There are important differences among the liberation theologies, but there are common notes as well, and they stand in significant contrast to some other readings of Christianity. But such theologies, and the material norm of Christianity that they suggest, should be judged in the same way and with the same criteria as other theologies. Here I am echoing Letty Russell's objection that feminist, black, and Third World theologies need to be qualified by an adjective, whereas white, male, Western theologies are called just theology. These other theologies are also just theology. As with all theology, they emerge out of a concrete, social context; they identify what they believe the central vision of Christianity to be; they offer particular insights, insights that emerge in part because of special perspectives—insights that ought to be seen as illuminating to all people, if they are indeed in continuity with the Christianity paradigm and an appropriate rendering of it for our time. The crucial difference between these new theologies and classical theology is that for the first time they are coming from women, from people of color, and from the poor.

These theologies share a common reading of the material norm of Christianity in certain respects. First, Christian faith is seen as destabilizing conventional expectations and worldly standards. At the very least, it is a disorienting perspective that upsets usual divisions and dualisms. Second, Christian faith is inclusive, reaching out to the weak, to the outsider, to the stranger, to the outcast. Third, Christian faith is antihierarchical and antitriumphalist, epitomized in the metaphor of the king who became a servant, one who suffers for and alongside the oppressed. These points are general ones (and different liberation theologies would orient them differently—toward, especially, the oppressive situation of women, people of color, or the poor); nonetheless, they constitute a significantly different rendering of Christian faith from that found in other interpretations. It is not the traditional and still-popular message that Jesus Christ, fully God and fully man, died for the sins of all humanity and was resurrected to new life, as his followers shall be also. Nor is it the more recent so-called liberal interpretation that Jesus is the power by which the individual can overcome alienation, meaninglessness, and despair. In the first case, the issue to which the gospel speaks is death from sin; hence, the good news is eternal life. In the second case, the issue to which the gospel speaks is personal, existential anguish; hence, the answer is new meaning. Liberation theologies claim (in different ways) that the issue to which the gospel speaks is the destructive, oppressive domination of some over others; hence, the answer is a new way of being in the world free of all hierarchies. If one were to identify the heart of the gospel for these theologies—their material norm—it would be the surprising invitation to all, especially to the outcast and oppressed. It is a destabilizing, inclusive, nonhierarchical vision of Christian faith, the claim that the gospel of Christianity is a new creation for all of creation—a life of freedom and fulfillment for all.

But is this vision in continuity with the Christian paradigm? Is it a revision, a reseeing of that vision, or is it a substitution for it? Can a claim be advanced that it is one credible, strong candidate for interpreting salvation in our time within the Christian paradigm, or is it a marginal or even bogus view? To answer these questions, we will first look briefly at the story of Jesus as a destabilizing, inclusive, nonhierarchical vision. Second, we will go beyond most of the liberation theologies to extend this vision to the cosmos and our responsibility for it. That is, we will look at the paradigmatic story of Jesus for clues and hints concerning the kind of metaphors most appropriate for modeling the relationship between God and the world, and hence between human beings and the world, in an ecological, nuclear era.

It is clear that the story of Jesus is a resource, but not the only source, for the material norm of the liberation theologies, that Christian faith gives a destabilizing, inclusive, nonhierarchical vision of fulfillment for all of creation. For although that vision is compatible with and illuminated by the paradigmatic story of Jesus, it is generated as much by the social, economic, political, and ecological realities of the late twentieth century. Nonetheless, if the paradigmatic story is revelatory of God's "way with the world," then it will be relevant to our world and can, without misrepresentation or distortion, be shown to be. Does this mean that each age reads into the story what it needs to, what it must, in order to make it speak to the deepest crises of its own time? Perhaps. Still, each theology—and liberation theologies are no exception—claims that its interpretation is a truer, less distorted interpretation of the story. Interpretations can and must change from age to age, and often they change substantially in order to address radically new situations; nevertheless, the theologian is constrained to return to the paradigmatic story of Jesus for validation and illumination.

What case can be made that the paradigmatic Christian story is a destabilizing, inclusive, nonhierarchical vision of fulfillment for all of creation? Can a portrait—though not necessarily the only portrait—be sketched along these lines? Nothing more than a "cartoon," in the sense of a preliminary draft, is possible here, but that is sufficient, for what we seek are the chief features or characteristics of that story, not its historical basis or subsequent interpretation. Three aspects that appear to be characteristic of the story of Jesus are his speaking in parables, his table fellowship with outcasts, and his death on a cross. Each is suggestive, and much has been made of each. The parables have been interpreted as moral imperatives; the table fellowship as a symbol of the eucharistic sacrifice; the death on the cross as God's triumph over sin, death, and the devil. But whatever the interpretations, few dispute that these three features are part of the story. A liberation theologian would interpret them differently: the parables illuminate the destabilizing aspect of the good news of Christianity; the table fellowship its inclusive character; and the death on the cross its nonhierarchical emphasis. As we look at each of these in more detail, what is being sought is not primarily validation of the story of Jesus as having these characteristics but illumination of our situation by that paradigmatic story.

The interpretation of the parables of Jesus in the last quarter century makes the case that they are a destabilizing, disorienting inversion of expectations and conventional standards. The parables, brief stories told in the secular language of Jesus' time, are extended metaphors that say something about the unfamiliar, the "kingdom of God," in terms of the familiar, a narrative of ordinary people doing ordinary things. They work, however, on a pattern of orientation, disorientation, and reorientation: the parable begins in the ordinary world with its conventional standards and expectations, but in the course of the story a radically different perspective is introduced, often by means of a surrealistic extravagance, that disorients the listener, and finally, through the interaction of the two competing viewpoints tension is created that results in a reorientation, a redescription of life in the world. A parable is, in this analysis, an assault on the accepted conventions, including the social, economic, and mythic structures that people build for their own comfort and security. A parable is a story meant to invert and subvert these structures and to suggest that the way of the kingdom is not the way of the world. In Jesus' parables we see an elder son who does not get what he deserves and a younger son who gets what he does not deserve; late workers being paid the same as those who have labored all day; a feast that is given for the poor and the outcasts when the prominent guests decline; a foreigner who comes to the aid of a Jew when his own religious leaders walk by on the other side. Throughout the parables two standards are in permanent tension with each other, and the effect of their interaction is disorientation for the listener. As John Dominic Crossan points out, not "liking" the parables is the appropriate reaction to them, for they undermine efforts at conventional security: "You have built a lovely home, myth assures us: but, whispers parable, you are right above an earthquake fault."[2]

At the very least the parables suggest that attempts at separating the "worthy" from the "unworthy," dualisms such as rich/poor, Jew/Gentile, elder/younger son, etc.—and by implication, male/female, white/colored, straight/gay, Christian/non-Christian—are without basis in the vision of existence alluded to by the phrase "the kingdom of God." What is suggested is a radically egalitarian, nondualistic way of being in the world. Liberation theologies make the case that Scripture is on the side of the poor and oppressed, but what is distinctive in the parables is not primarily a reversal that elevates the "unworthy," but a destabilization of *all* dualisms. Such destabilization is far more radical than an inversion, for it means refusing all categorizations of insider/outsider, though human beings appear naturally and deeply to desire such distinctions. But the parables, as one aspect of the portrait of our paradigmatic story, sketch a world in which such categorizations are disrupted and overturned.

Is it appropriate to extend this disruption beyond the human dualisms to those of spirit/flesh, mind/matter, soul/body, human/nonhuman, sky/earth? Flesh, matter, body, the nonhuman, and the earth are conventionally, perhaps even "naturally," considered inferior, and notably in the Christian tradition they have been so considered. But if the destabilization of the parables is to support the holistic sensibility needed in our time, then the oppression of flesh, matter, body, the nonhuman, and the earth must also be ended. If sin from the perspective of parabolic destabilization is the "natural" desire of human beings to separate themselves, in superior/inferior dualisms, from one another and from the earth, then salvation from this perspective would be an overturning of those patterns—a making whole or healing of the divisions. What is needed for a holistic sensibility to become a reality in our time is a change of consciousness in the way we see our world and ourselves in relation to the world. The destabilization of the parables is a necessary radical first step: when extended to the cosmos, it proclaims the end of the conventional, hierarchical, oppressive dualism of human/nonhuman.

What we see in Jesus' parables becomes more explicit in his table fellowship: the destabilization of the parables becomes an "enacted parable" as Jesus invites the outcasts of society to eat with him. Some scholars argue that Jesus' practice of eating with "tax collectors and sinners" was both the central feature of his ministry and its major scandal.[3] Like the parables, Jesus' table fellowship is destabilizing, but it goes further than the disruption of conventional dualisms, for as a friend of outcasts (Matt. 11:19), inviting them to eat with him, he epitomizes the scandal of inclusiveness for his time. What is proclaimed in Luke 4 as the heart of Jesus' ministry—good news to the poor, release to the captives, liberty for the oppressed—and what is manifested as well by his healings of the sick is pushed to an extreme in his invitation to the ritually unclean to eat with him. Jesus offended by inviting the outsiders to come in, to join with him not merely as needy outcasts but as his friends in joyful feasting. The central symbol of the new vision of life, the kingdom of God, is a community joined together in a festive meal where the bread that sustains life and the joy that sustains the spirit are shared with all. The radical inclusiveness of this vision is eloquently summarized by Elisabeth Schüssler Fiorenza: "'Since the reality of the *basileia* for Jesus spells not primarily holiness but wholeness, the salvation of God's *basileia* is present and experientially available whenever Jesus casts out demons (Luke 11:20), heals the sick and the ritually unclean, tells stories about the lost who are found, of the uninvited who are invited, of the last who will be first.... Not the holiness of the elect but the wholeness *of all* is the central vision of Jesus."[4]

The emphasis here is on inclusiveness: all are invited and what they are invited to is a feast, fulfillment, joy. The invitation is not to chosen individuals but to all. But unless we envision this feast as merely an allegory of a spiritual feast in another world—as solely an eschatological, mythological feast—it has implications for the holistic sensibility needed in our time. That is, the insistence of liberation theologies that salvation must be a social, political, economic reality in history, since oppression is precisely that kind of reality, means that in order for all to be invited, an ecological attitude must emerge. Without enough bread, some cannot be invited. An ecological sensibility that cares for the earth that "cares for us" must accompany a vision of social, political, economic justice if that vision is to become anything other than rhetoric. Only a sensibility that accepts our intrinsic interdependence not only with all other people but also with the earth will be able to create the conditions necessary to help bring about the fulfillment of all as salvation for our time.

An ecological sensibility is not only an aesthetic appreciation for the intrinsic value of all forms of life—an attitude of "bending toward the mountain"—though it includes such appreciation; it is also a different way of thinking, a change to thinking the way nature itself works in terms of interdependence, rationality, reciprocity. As Rosemary Radford Ruether puts it, we must "convert our minds to the earth," turn away from linear, dichotomized, dualistic thinking that gives the human desire for short-term gains predominance over the long-term well-being of the earth and its ability to support us.[5]

The aesthetic and utilitarian (in the sense of ecologically wise) attitudes are intrinsically related: we cannot be supported by an earth we do not support. Hence, political and economic liberation and the ecological, holistic sensibility are not two projects but one. The inclusiveness of the gospel—the invitation to fulfillment for all—must extend to the cosmos as well as to all peoples. The feast of joy, the invitation to share the bread and wine that symbolize both life itself and the good life, cannot be accepted unless we become caretakers of the earth. In our time, salvation must be understood to extend to all, or it will apply to none.

Nowhere is this fact more evident, of course, than in the threat of a nuclear holocaust. It stands as the ultimate challenge to accept the global village as our model of reality as we approach the twenty-first century. If political and economic liberation are intrinsically related to an ecological sensibility, so also is the acceptance of human responsibility for nuclear knowledge, for here also, and with chilling exactitude, salvation must be seen as extending to all people and to our earth: if we do not learn to live together, we will die together.

The parables, the table fellowship, and now the cross—they form a pattern in the sketch we are attempting of an interpretation of the story of Jesus for an ecological, nuclear age. The destabilization of the parables that is fleshed out in the invitation to all, especially to the "unworthy" and the outcast to share in the feast of life, is radicalized further in the cross. Here the way necessary to bring about this new mode of being is suggested. The way is radical identification with all others. In a world in which hierarchies and dualisms are fiercely defended, such identification will bring punishment, often swift and brutal punishment. The cross epitomizes the retribution that comes to those who give up controlling and triumphalist postures in order to relate to others in mutual love.

As many have noted, there are ambiguous if not contradictory interpretations of the cross in Christianity, some seeing it as the critique of triumphalism epitomized in the king who becomes a servant, and others as but the prelude to the resurrection, when the king will reign in glory, as shall his loyal subjects. The first interpretation is consonant with the parables and the table fellowship, for it continues and sharpens the distinction between two ways of being in the world, one of which is destabilizing, inclusive, and nonhierarchical and the other of which is conventional, exclusive, and triumphalist. That is to say, the first interpretation is a direct assault on the second; in fact, if one accepts it, one must criticize the second as a perversion of the gospel. If one accepts the interpretation of the parables and the table fellowship of Jesus advanced here, then a triumphalist Christology and atonement must be rejected. The mythology in which the cross and especially the resurrection have been interpreted is not only anachronistic but harmful, for the destabilizing, inclusive, nonhierarchical vision of salvation needed in a holistic, nuclear age is undermined by it. For instance, if we see Jesus as "fully God and fully man," the substitutionary sacrifice who atoned for the sins of the world two thousand years ago and who now reigns triumphant along with all who loyally accept his kingly, gracious forgiveness of their sins, we not only accept a salvation we do not need but weaken if not destroy our ability to understand and accept the salvation we do need. The triumphalist mythology makes impossible the interpretation of the way to our salvation on several points.

First, it insists that salvation rests with one individual and in one past act. In first-century Palestine and throughout many centuries of Christian history, the notion of a representative human being in whose act and existence others, even centuries removed, could participate made sense in terms of Platonic and Aristotelian philosophies. It does not any longer. Both the individualism and the remoteness of this view, from our perspective, are contrary to the idea that salvation in our time must be the task of all human beings working in concert with the loving power of God as a present and future activity. It is not what one individual did two thousand years ago that is critical but what we, with God, do now. Second, the classical mythology assumes that sin is against God—that it is traitorous or rebellious behavior against the King, Lord, or Father—whereas in the interpretation of the parables and table fellowship we have suggested, sin is against other people and the earth: it is exclusivistic, dualistic, hierarchical separation of insiders from outsiders. The classical mythology supports escapism of the worst sort; it is a misplaced religiosity that provides comfortable, personal assurance while undermining the will to work to overcome the oppression and domination of some by others—to overcome, that is, sin as it needs to be viewed in our time.

Third, the classical mythology supports metaphors and models of God contrary to those needed for imagining the God-world relationship in our time. It encourages us to think of God in triumphalist, royalist, highly individualistic, "distant" political imagery that is counterproductive to the kind of metaphors in which *we* need to think of God. In the classical imagery the king '"empties" himself, becoming a servant only for the duration of Jesus' brief ministry and the sacrifice of the cross, but his true being is as almighty King, Lord, and Father, and he returns in the resurrection to his power and glory. If, however, one sees the cross not as the King's sacrifice, in the mode of his Son, for the sins of the world, but as a paradigm of God's way with the world always, other possibilities emerge. If one sees the cross as revealing God's distinctive way of being in and with the world, one will have a significantly different understanding both of God and of the way to speak to God—and an understanding more relevant to *our* salvation. In other words, if Jesus of Nazareth as paradigmatic of God is not just a "phase" of God but is genuinely revelatory of God, then the mode of the cross, the way of radical identification with all, which will inevitably bring punishment, sometimes to the point of death, becomes a permanent reality. It becomes the way of the destabilizing, inclusive, nonhierarchical vision.

Jesus of Nazareth, then, does not "do something on our behalf" but, far more important, manifests in his own life and death that the heart of the universe is unqualified love working to befriend the needy, the outcast, the oppressed. This we never would have guessed; it can scarcely be believed; and mostly, it is not. But if one takes clues from the parables, Jesus' table fellowship, and the cross, to believe in Jesus as a paradigm of God means that or something like that. It means that God is "like Jesus" and if Jesus is not a king but a servant, then God should be spoken of in "servant" language in relation to the world.

At this point, however, metaphorical theology should step in. That is to say, although the inclusive way of the cross and the triumphalist way of resurrection were in Jesus' time powerfully and appropriately contrasted by the metaphors of servant and king, they can be no longer. The language of servitude is no longer current, acceptable, or significant for expressing the distinctive and unconventional kind of love epitomized in the cross. There are, I believe, other metaphors, such as those of mother, lover, and friend, that express dimensions of that love more fully and appropriately for our time. If one accepts that salvation in our time needs to be understood as a destabilizing, inclusive, nonhierarchical vision, these metaphors with their associations of caring, mutuality, attraction, nurturing, supporting, empathy, responsibility, service, self-sacrifice, forgiveness, and creativity are highly suggestive. They not only underscore self-sacrifice and radical self-giving to others, as does the servant metaphor, but also suggest dimensions of salvation for our time that the servant metaphor cannot: the interdependence of all life, including the life of God with the world, and reciprocity, including our responsibility to work with God for the fulfillment of all that lives. To see God's relationship to the world through the paradigm of the cross of Jesus is illuminating of salvation for our time if neither the servant nor the king is a major model but some other highly significant and very rich metaphors are investigated for their potential as expressions of the destabilizing, inclusive, nonhierarchical vision in an ecological, nuclear age. That is my thesis.

If, in other words, Jesus of Nazareth in his parables, table fellowship, and cross is a paradigm of God's relationship to the world, if he is a model or parable through which we can grasp something of God as well as discover a way to speak of God, then we have to ask how this can and should be expressed in different times and places. Metaphorical theology says it always has to be interpreted differently. We circle back, then, to an opening question of this chapter: What should we be doing for our time that would be comparable to what Paul and John did for theirs? One task is to conduct a thought experiment with new metaphors (and their accompanying concepts) that appear to have potential to express the trustworthiness and graciousness of the power of the universe for our time. The first step in this thought experiment is to attend to a fourth distinctive feature of the story of Jesus—the appearance stories—and to what the feature might suggest for a contemporary way to imagine the relationship between God and the world. How can we understand the resurrection in a way that emphasizes the destabilizing, inclusive, nonhierarchical vision of fulfillment? Is the relation of a risen king to his realm the appropriate construct? I think not . . .

Notes

1. For a treatment of Jesus of Nazareth as parable of God, see McFague 1982, ch. 2.

2. John Dominic Crossan, *The Dark Interval: Towards a Theology of Stor* (Niles, IL: Argus, 1975), 56–57.

3. See Joachim Jeremias, *New Testament Theology* (New York: Scribner, 1971), 1:115–16; Günther Bornkamm, *Jesus of Nazareth,* trans. Irene and Fraser McLuskey with James Robinson (New York: Harper & Row, 1960), 80–81; Norman Perrin, *Rediscovering the Teaching of Jesus* (New York: Harper & Row, 1967), 102, 107; Elisabeth Schüssler Fiorenza, *In Memory of Her: A Feminist Theological Construction of Christian Origins* (New York: Crossroad, 1983), 121: "The power of God's *basileia* is realized in Jesus' table community with the poor, the sinners, the tax collectors and prostitutes—with all those who 'do not belong' to the 'holy people,' who are somehow deficient in the eyes of the righteous."

4. Schüssler Fiorenza, *In Memory of Her*, 120–21.

5. Rosemary Radford Ruether, *Sexism and GodTalk: Toward a Feminist Theology* (Boston: Beacon, 1983), 89–91.

14

Sin: The Refusal to Accept Our Place

The ecological theology and embrace of the common creation story that takes center stage in The Body of God *is given perhaps its most powerful and important expression in this selection on sin. Here McFague shows how the classical Christian understanding, which privileges sin against God, is not contradicted but is deepened by this ecological perspective, as it allows us to understand sin against other humans, other creatures, and against the earth itself as tantamount to sin against God, in and through whom all creation has its being. Sin, then, is living a lie relative to those key relationships, contrary to the reality of our place in the world, misunderstanding the nature of our difference in creation. Thus McFague's concept of sin may be seen as also essential to understanding her developing anthropology*

Source: 1993:113–29

The common creation story gives us a functional, working cosmology. It gives us a way of understanding where we fit.[1] It tells us that we belong and where we belong: it is both a welcoming word celebrating our grandeur as the most developed, complex creatures on our planet to date and a cautionary word reminding us that we belong in a place, not all places, on the earth. In the words of James Gustafson, human beings are thus reminded of "their awesome possibilities and their inexorable limitations."[2] The Genesis myth no longer functions for most people as a working cosmology, as a framework providing a sense of space and place, grandeur and groundedness, possibilities and limitations, for the conduct of daily living. The Genesis myth, rich and profound as it still can be shown to be, does not strike most people as a working model or construct within which the ordinary events and details of their lives can be understood. Moreover, the creation story that does function, at least implicitly, in Western culture is one heavy with otherworldly overtones, seeing human beings as resident aliens on the earth. But the common creation story has for many people immediate credibility upon first hearing. "So this is where I, we, fit, not as a little lower than the angels but as an inspirited body among other living bodies, one with some distinctive and marvelous characteristics and some genuine limitations. I am of the earth, a product of its ancient and awesome history, and I really and truly belong here. But I am only one among millions, now billions of other human beings, who have a place, a space, on the earth. I am also a member of one species among millions, perhaps billions, of other species that need places on the earth. We are all, human beings and other species, inhabitants of the same space, planet earth, and interdependent in intricate and inexorable ways. I feel a sense of comfort, of settledness, of belonging as I consider my place in this cosmology, but also a sense of responsibility, for I know that I am a citizen of the planet. I have an expanded horizon as I reflect on my place in the common creation story: I belong not only to my immediate family or country or even my species, but to the earth and all its life-forms. I *do* belong to this whole. I know this now. The question is, can I, will I, *live* as if I did? Will I accept my proper place in the scheme of things? Will *we*, the human beings of the planet, do so?"

This little meditation has led us into the second major contribution of the common creation story to a theological anthropology: not only does it give us a functional cosmology but also a grounded or earthly notion of sin. One of the advantages of starting our reflections on human existence with our possibilities and limitations as seen in light of the common creation story is that it keeps them from being overstated or spiritualized. In this story we are not a little lower than the angels, nor the only creatures made in the image of God: our particular form of grandeur is in relation to the earth and derived from it—we are the self-conscious, responsible creatures. Likewise, in the common creation story, we are not sinners because we rebel against God or are unable to be sufficiently spiritual: our particular failing (closely related to our peculiar form of grandeur) is our unwillingness to stay in our place, to accept our proper limits so that other individuals of our species as well as other species can also have needed space. From the perspective of the common creation story, we gain a sober, realistic, mundane picture of ourselves: our grandeur is our role as responsible partners helping our planet prosper, and our sin is plain old selfishness—wanting to have everything for ourselves.

We need to press more deeply into the issue of sin, both what we can learn about it from the common creation story and how this view is both like and unlike the classical understanding of sin in the Christian tradition. We need also to reflect on what an ecological view of sin means in a number of different contexts—in relation to other human beings (us versus us), other animals (us versus them), and nature (us versus it). But before delving into these matters, we need to ask why God has been left out of the contexts to be considered. Sin in the Christian tradition has usually been, first of all, against God; it is in our reflections also, for in the model of the universe (world) as God's body, sin against any part of the body *is* against God. Our model helps us to keep theology earthly; it helps us to avoid abstraction, generalization, and spiritualization.... [A]n incarnational theology always insists that both sin and salvation are earthly matters—fleshly, concrete, particular matters having to do with disproportion and well-being *in relation to* the forms of God's presence we encounter in our daily, ordinary lives: other bodies. Sin against the many different bodies—the bodies of other people, other animals, and nature—*is* sin against God in the model of the world as God's body.

What is the relation of an ecological view of sin with the classical Christian view? It deepens rather than contradicts it. The classical view can be summarized with the phrase "living a lie," living out of proper relations with God, self, and other beings. Sin, in the Hebrew and Christian traditions, is a relational notion, having to do with the perversion of fitting, appropriate attitudes and actions in relation to other beings and the source of all being. Sin is, therefore, thinking, feeling, and acting in ways contrary to reality, contrary to the proper, right relations among the beings and entities that constitute reality. Some interpretations of sin in Judaism and Christianity, such as legalism or personalism (sin as breaking God's law or offending the divine majesty), do not, I believe, point to what is most profound in these traditions. Sin is not just breaking divine laws or blaspheming God; rather, it is living falsely, living contrary to reality, to the way things are. (And yet, breaking divine laws and blaspheming God are *symptoms* of living falsely, of failing to accept one's place as limited. The limits of law and humility before the divine glory are signs pointing to our proper, realistic place in the scheme of things.)

An autobiographical point might make the point clearer. When I was first introduced to Christian theology as a college student, I recall being deeply impressed with its view of sin—it struck a chord of authenticity in me—while I remained quite unmoved by the various traditional interpretations of redemption. The classical understanding of sin focuses on wanting to be the center of things, and I already knew deeply that longing. Augustine calls it "concupiscence," literally, insatiable sexual desire but, more broadly, wanting to have it all, whatever the all is. In other words, sin is limitless greed. As a privileged member of the world's elite, I was an easy target for this view of sin. While as a female in the American fifties I perhaps lacked an overbearing sense of my own self-worth—or sin understood as pride—yet by class and race

I fit the pattern of the voracious Western appetite for more than my share: I was an "ecological" sinner. The Augustinian interpretation, in focusing on the bloated self, the self that wants it all, the self that refuses to share, highlights the ecological dimension of sin. From this perspective, selfishness is the one-word definition of sin—at least for us first-world types.

To say that sin has an ecological dimension means that we must view beings, organisms, in relation to their environment. The environment of all beings, according to our model of the universe as God's body, is the "divine *milieu*": we live and move and have our being, along with all other beings, in God. Therefore, sin or living a lie will be living disproportionately, falsely, inappropriately within this space, refusing to accept the limitations and responsibilities of our place. Moreover, this space, place, has been further defined and qualified for Christians by the cosmic Christ, the embodied life paradigmatically expressed in the liberating, healing, inclusive ministry of Jesus of Nazareth. But in order to ground living rightly in the earth, in our mundane relations, let us step back from the divine *milieu* as our environment and consider an ecological view of sin within a more lowly environment: our relations with other human beings, other animals, and the natural world.

Us versus Us: Living a Lie in Relation to Other Human Beings

This section need not be long because the evidence of disproportionate space and place of some human beings in contrast to others—the rich and poor within nations and between nations—is everywhere and growing. If the most basic meaning of justice is fairness, then from an ecological point of view, justice means sharing the limited resources of our common space. From the perspective of the one home we all share, injustice is living a lie, living contrary to reality, pretending that all the space or the best space belongs to some so that they can live in lavish comfort and affluence, while others are denied even the barest necessities for physical existence. The disproportion here, epitomized in the billionaires versus the homeless, the standard of living of the first-world versus third-world countries, the swollen stomachs of starving people versus obesity in others, forces us to think concretely and physically about sin. The common creation story deepens the classical view of right relations in regard to members of our own species: it suggests that loving our neighbor must be grounded in mundane issues of space, turf, habitat, land. Every human being needs an environment capable of supporting its sustenance and growth. While this might at first appear to be a minimalist view, reducing human beings to the physical (animal?!) level, it is precisely the minimum that those individuals and nations bloated with self, living the life of insatiable greed, refuse to recognize. It is far easier as well as less costly to one's own lifestyle to offer spiritual rather than material goods to the poor. The ecological view of sin refuses to raise its eyes above the minimalist view, insisting that justice among human beings means first of all adequate space for basic needs. It also means, for some, staying in their own proper, limited place.

While our analysis of ecological sin will focus on the more neglected areas of our relations with other animals and nature, proper relations with our nearest and dearest kin, our own species, must be first in consideration and importance. Some environmentalists, most notably deep ecologists, claim that human beings as one species among many million, perhaps billion, are of no special importance. Their needs for space, for land, for nourishment should not take precedence over the needs of all other species. This radical egalitarianism gives the assumption of a split between ecological and justice issues a theoretical base. It is not simply that space on our planet is limited and we must share it; it is also the case, say some, that we do not deserve any special space or more space than, say, the polar bear or giant sequoia trees. Undoubtedly on some scales of reckoning, we do not deserve it, but try telling this to the parent of a starving child, and all we have done, in the minds of many, is widen the abyss separating justice and ecological issues.

The issue on which to focus when we consider justice versus ecological issues is not our species versus other species, but *some members* of our species versus other members. While it is certainly the case that the human population is too large and encroaches on the habitats of other species, lumping human beings all together as *the* ecological problem masks the profound justice issues within our population. Those to whom this essay is addressed—we well-off Westerners—need to admit that the first lie we live is in relation to others of our own kind. *The* ecological sin is the refusal of the haves to share space and land with the have-nots. It has been shown that human populations stabilize when the standard of living improves; hence, it is not only our gross numbers encroaching on other species' populations that is the problem but the disproportionate way in which space is controlled by some humans to the disadvantage of others. Over the long haul, stabilizing the human population at a sustainable level is primarily a justice issue among human beings. Thus, justice issues *within* the human species have a direct effect on environmental issues between our species and other species. Simply put, we need to do some housecleaning, as a first step. Until we rectify gross injustices among human beings, in other words, begin our ecological work at home, we will have little chance of success abroad, that is, in relation to other species and the planet as a whole.

Us versus Them: Living a Lie in Relation to Other Animals

The ecological view of sin deepens when we realize that other animals, beside human ones, must have space, and that they too have a place. The common creation story not only tells us that we are related to the physical bodies of all other animals but also gives detail and depth to this statement. While there are tens of billions of known kinds of organic molecules, only about fifty are used for the essential activities of life. Molecules are essentially identical in all plants and animals. "An oak tree and I are made of the same stuff. If you go back far enough, we have a common ancestor."[3] If some degree of intimacy is true of us and oak trees, it is astonishingly true of us and other animals. We not only *are* animals but we are genetically very similar to all other animals and only a fraction of difference away from those animals, the higher mammals, closest to us. And yet one would scarcely suspect this from the way animals are conventionally regarded as well as used in our culture. While most people now have or pretend to have a raised consciousness in regard to the needs of all human beings for the basic necessities of life, the same cannot be said for attitudes about other animals. This is not the place for a review of human use and misuse of animals as manifest in pleasure hunting, excessive meat eating, the fur trade, circuses and traditional zoos, vivisection, cosmetic animal testing, and so on. But even listing a few of our more callous practices in regard to animals illustrates our degree of insensitivity to their needs, wishes, and feelings. In fact, it is by suppressing any thought that they might have needs, wishes, or feelings, in other words, that they are *anything like us* (or we like them—the more valid evolutionary comparison) that we can continue such practices with good, or at least numbed, consciences.

What does it mean to live a lie in relation to other animals? What is ecological sin in regard to them? The common creation story helps us answer this question specifically by providing a realistic picture of who we are in relation to other animals, both our profound intimacy with them and our important differences from them. We recall that one of the special features of this story is the way both unity and diversity are understood: the interrelationship and interdependence of all living things as well as the distinctive individuality and differences among living forms. Embodied knowing, paying attention to concrete differences, is a necessary step in embodied doing, behaving appropriately toward other life-forms, each of whom has special characteristics and needs. The common creation story helps us to move into a new paradigm for responding to our fellow animals, one in which we appreciate network of our interdependence with them as well as the real differences from us. In the conventional model, the model that views them as resources or recreation, as something to serve us or amuse us, we can appreciate neither our profound closeness nor our genuine differences: they are simply "other." The new paradigm, however, presses us into a much more complex, highly nuanced relationship with other animals, one that refuses either a sentimental fusion or an absolute separation. In this paradigm we are neither "a species among species" nor "the crown of creation." Who, then, are we?

One way to answer this question is to focus on the characteristic that has usually separated us totally and irrevocably from all other animals: our intellect. We are rational, linguistic, logical beings and therefore unlike all other animals. Various studies of incipient language and reasoning powers in some higher mammals have questioned this assumption, so that few would any longer agree with Immanuel Kant's inflated view of man [sic]: "As the single being on earth that possesses understanding, he is certainly titular lord of nature, and, supposing that we regard nature as a teleological system, he is born to be its ultimate end."[4] Nonetheless, few probably agree either with philosopher Mary Midgley that mathematical rationality in human beings is not necessarily superior to practical reason in a mother elephant as she cannily maneuvers to protect her young.[5] While Kant saw a human being as a thinking thing with no relation to body, many of us still see other animals as bodily things with no mind or spirit. Our common creation story tells us that neither position is the case: we are on a continuum with them as they are with us; it is not us versus them but us *and* them, for the roots of human nature lie deep within those others we call animals.[6] Who we are, then, is in some sense who they are: whatever we are and have is based in and derived from those others. Nor is it self-evident that the characteristic we have chosen to distinguish ourselves from the other animals, namely rationality, is worthy of being elevated above all others. As Midgley comments, "Being clever is not obviously so much more important than being kind, brave, friendly, patient, and generous . . ."[7] Dualism—separating reason and feeling—is part of the impasse to thinking in a connected, relational way about animals, because we lock animals into the feeling category. Rationality, however, is not just cleverness, and intelligence includes a structure of preferences, a priority system based on feeling. The higher animals have deep, lasting preferences, and hence a type of practical reason.

We are like other animals in complex ways; we are also different from them—and they from one another—in complex ways.[8] We have simplified our relationship with other animals by focusing on one human characteristic, a kind of rationality divorced from feeling, which has allowed us to put ourselves on top, with other animals as inferior to us and radically different from us. The operating model here is the ladder, with rationality at the top and ourselves as its sole possessor. Everything that does not possess rationality is alien, including our own feelings and bodies as well as other animals, plant life, and the earth. But what if the evolutionary model were the bush rather than the ladder, a model much closer to what the common creation story tells us. A bush does not have a main trunk, a dominant direction of growth, or a top. There is no privileged place on a bush; rather, what a bush suggests is *diversity* (while at the same time interconnectedness and interdependence, since all its parts are related and all are fed by a common root system). The bush model helps us to appreciate different kinds of excellence, each of which is an end in itself. In this model other animals are not defined by their *lack* of rationality. "Is there nothing to a giraffe except being a person *manqué?*"[9] Asked positively, would a dolphin think that we could swim, a dog be impressed with our sense of smell, or a migrating bird be awed by our sense of direction?[10] We are profoundly and complexly united with other animals as well as profoundly and complexly different from them and they from each other. The more we know in detail about other species, the more this abstraction will take on reality and power. Even to learn about one other species, for instance, following the research of a naturalist who has devoted her life to studying the lowland gorillas or fruit-bats or caterpillars, will raise consciousness regarding the deep as well as subtle ways that animals resemble and differ from one another.

What such study often does is return us to a state of wonder, curiosity, and affection that we as children had for other animals. Children often possess wide powers of sympathy for injured animals, demonstrating a natural affection for members of other species that we need to develop rather than squelch. The young of different species play together in a mixed community that, unfortunately, gets rather thoroughly sorted out by adulthood. But we can make at least a partial return to this mixed community by way of a "second naïveté," a way that involves educating ourselves on our genuine, deep, and concrete forms of interrelatedness with other life-forms.[11]

The study of similarities and differences among animals (including ourselves) also presses us to refuse easy notions of egalitarianism between ourselves and other animals as a solution to our historic insensibility toward them. If equality has proven to be problematic in valuing differences among human beings, tending toward universalism or essentialism in its integration of the minority into the majority's assumptions, it is even more questionable a category to help us live appropriately with other animals. "Speciesism" is not just a prejudice against other animals that can be rectified by treating them like human beings; rather, it is the refusal to appreciate them *in their difference*, their differences from us and from each other that require, for instance, special and particular habitats, food, privacy, and whatever else each species needs to flourish.

Who are we, then, in the scheme of things in relation to other animals? What does it mean to live a lie in relation to them? The common creation story tells us that we are like and unlike them; that special forms of similarity and difference unite and divide us from them and each of them from one another. We need to develop a sensibility that appreciates some of these most central ways in which we are united and different. Living a lie in relation to them means, the common creation story tells us, lumping the other animals all together in an inferior category judged by our own superior intellect; separating ourselves from them as alien creatures with whom we have no intrinsic relationships; and, most especially, numbing ourselves to their real needs, preferences, and ability to feel pain so that we can continue to use them for our own benefit.

Refusing to live this lie will not make life easier or better for us—at least not in the short run. It will complicate it. If the resources of our planet are already strained in dealing with the needs of the human population, a large proportion of whom go hungry daily, how, why should the rights of other animals be included? Again, the issue of space is central, for increasingly, it is not hunting that is decimating other animal species, but loss of habitats due to our excessive population and the voracious lifestyle of some of us. But the common creation story tells us that space must be shared. It tells us that life on our planet evolved together and is interdependent in complex ways beyond our imagining; it deepens our understanding of who "family" is and the needs of different family members. At the very least it tells us that we cannot live alone, that for utilitarian reasons we need to live truthfully, rightly, appropriately with our kin, the other animals. But the work of naturalists—as well as the wonder and pleasure we felt as children and our own children feel for other animals—makes us ask: Do we not also *want* them as our companions? Do we not also delight in them and value them, not just for their usefulness to us, but in their differences as well? Is wonder at the sublimity of a whale or the intricacy of an ant colony a marginal, dispensable part of human existence that few of us care about? It all depends on how you define our most distinctive characteristic, as rationality or wonder?

Wonder may well be what is special about us from the perspective of the common creation story. We are the creatures who *know* that we know. Many creatures know many things; intelligence is not limited to human beings. But the ability to step back, to reflect on *that* we know and *what* we know—in other words, self-consciousness—may well be our peculiar specialty. As Annie Dillard notes, "The point is that not only does time fly and . . . we die, but that in these reckless conditions we live at all, and are vouchsafed, for the duration of certain inexplicable moments, to know it."[12] To live at all and to know it: these are the roots of wonder. I was distinctly and peculiarly human when, at age seven, I thought with terror and fascination that someday I would not "be" any longer. In that thought was contained not only consciousness of life but self-consciousness of it: it is a wonder to be alive but it is a deeper wonder to know it. Knowing that we know places special possibilities and responsibilities on us. Self-consciousness is the basis of free will, imagination, choice, or whatever one calls that dimension of human beings that makes us capable of changing ourselves and our world. The issues around this area in regard to limitations and possibilities are enormous and beyond dealing with in this essay. The point relevant to our concerns is that in relation to other animals, our ability to wonder, to step back and reflect on what we know, places us in a singular position: our place in the scheme of things may well be to exercise this ability. To be sure, the distance that self-consciousness gives us has many aspects. A technological, rational dimension, one that can be used both for the destruction and preservation of our planet and its creatures, allows us to assess the results of various kinds of knowledge. But we are more likely to put this knowledge to work on the side of the well-being of the planet if we are moved by a deeper dimension of self-consciousness. That dimension is one close to the root meaning of wonder as surprise, fascination, awe, astonishment, curiosity: we are the ones capable of being amazed by life. *It is a wonder.* The common creation story deepens that wonder in us, not only through knowing that it has occurred at all on this planet, but also by knowing the complex, diverse, intricate way it has developed, eventuating in the truly wonder-filled creatures that we are. It is indeed a "wonderful life." One of the most profound lessons we can learn from the common creation story is appreciation for life, not just our own, but that of all the other creatures in the family of life. We are the ones, the only ones on our planet, who know the story of life and the only ones who know that we know: the only ones capable of being filled with wonder, surprise, curiosity, and fascination by it. A first step, then, toward a healthy ecological sensibility may well be a return, via a second naïveté, to the wonder we as children had for the world, but a naïvete now informed by knowledge of and a sense of responsibility for our planet and its many life-forms. To know that we know places special burdens on us: it means . . . being designated as God's partners. On our planet we are the self-conscious aspect of the body of God, the part of the divine body able to work with God, the spirit who creates and redeems us, to bring about the liberation and healing of the earth and all its creatures. We know that we know: we have a choice to act on behalf of the wonderful life that we are and that surrounds us.

Us versus It: Living a Lie in Relation to Nature

John Muir, the eminent American naturalist, wrote at the end of his life: "I only went out for a walk and finally concluded to stay until sundown, for going out, I discovered, was actually going in."[13] This summarizes a life-long conversion to the earth, the realization that one *belongs* to the earth. It is not natural for most of us to believe, let alone feel, that we belong to nature, to realize that by going out we are actually going in. Susan Griffin, poet and ecofeminist, eloquently expresses our complex in-and-out relationship with nature: "We know ourselves to be made from this earth. We know this earth is made from our bodies. For we see ourselves. And we are nature. We are nature seeing nature. We are nature with a concept of nature. Nature weeping. Nature speaking of nature to nature."[14] We are the self-conscious ones who can think about, weep for, and speak of nature, but we are also one in flesh and bone with nature. It is this dual awareness of both our responsibility for nature and our profound and complex unity with it that is the heart of the appropriate, indeed necessary, sensibility that we need to develop.

The proper balance of this dual awareness in relation to nature, specifically in relation to the earth, the land, may be even more difficult than in relation to other people and other animals, for we have a clearer notion of the ways we are both united to and distinct from them than we do with such things as oceans, plants, and land. Most Westerners tend to objectify nature so totally that human beings are essentially distinct from it. But for the contemporary movement called deep ecology, bent on converting us from egocentricity to ecocentricity, human beings are essentially one with nature. We see here two extremes.[15]

Nonetheless it is instructive, given how difficult it is for most of us to identify with nature, to listen to deep ecology remembering, once again, that the planetary agenda is a conversation of many voices. The limitations of any position should not blind us to its insights. The central insight of deep ecology is, as one of its founders Aldo Leopold puts it, that we are "fellow-voyagers with other creatures in the odyssey of evolution," just "plain citizens" of the biotic community.[16] We are not special: humanism is an error of egocentricity, for we live with other species in an "ecological egalitarianism," as one among many. But deep ecology presses us to acknowledge more than egalitarianism; it wants us to *feel* our deepest, physical connections with and dependence on the earth. This is its greatest asset as well as limitation, for in identifying us ever more deeply with nature, deep ecology tends to blend us into nature, which is problematic in a number of ways.

But first let us learn how this perspective can help us identify with the earth, with the land and especially its plants, waters, and atmosphere. The value of deep ecology is that it insists we are not merely connected to nature but that all its parts, including ourselves, intermingle and interpenetrate. The Amazon rainforest is not just important to our well-being; it is, literally, our external lungs without which we will not be able to breathe. Deep ecology assumes profound organicism, a reliance on the model of body absolutely and totally. This organic model is not distinguished by diversity but rather by the fusion of its many parts. The danger of a position based on this model may already be evident, but since the value of deep ecology is not, I believe, in its conceptual adequacy but in its poetic power to make us feel unity, let us listen to a few of its most able spokespersons.

Richard Nelson, anthropologist and essayist, writes of his experience on a remote Northwest island off the Pacific coast. "There is nothing in me that is not of earth, no split instant of separateness, no particle that disunites me from the surroundings. I am no less than the earth itself. The rivers run through my veins, the winds blow in and out with my breath, the soil makes my flesh, the sun's heat smolders inside me. A sickness or injury that befalls the earth befalls me. A fouled molecule that runs through the earth runs through me. Where the earth is cleansed and nourished, its purity infuses me. The life of the earth is my life. My eyes are the earth gazing at itself."[17]

Gary Snyder, poet and deep ecologist, comments on his poem, "Song of the Taste": "All of nature is a gift-exchange, a potluck banquet, and there is no death that is not somebody's food, no life that is not somebody's death ... We all take life to live ... The shimmering food-chain, food-web, is the scary, beautiful condition of the biosphere ... Eating is truly a sacrament."[18]

The following credo by poet Robinson Jeffers is often quoted by deep ecologists: "I believe the universe is one being, all its parts are different expressions of the same energy, and they are all in communication with each other, therefore parts of an organic whole ... It seems to me that this whole alone is worthy of the deeper love."[19]

Some may, however, object to the extreme fringe as expressed in a comment such as the following: "Deep ecology . . . requires openness to the black bear, becoming truly intimate with the black bear, so that honey dribbles down your fur as you catch the bus to work."[20]

At its best deep ecology helps us to enlarge our sense of self—that is, what we include in our definition of who we are. A narrow self-definition includes only one's nearest and dearest: family and friends, or at most, one's tribe or nation. A broader self-definition takes in not only all people but some of the higher or more interesting animals (at least the poster ones, such as dolphins or snow leopards). But a cosmological self-identification acknowledges that we are part and parcel of everything on the planet, or, as Alan Watts puts it, "the world is your body."[21] Only as we are able both to think and feel this enlarged definition of self will we be able to begin to respond appropriately and responsibly to the crises facing our planet. Deep ecology makes an important contribution, for it radicalizes us into a new way of looking at the earth in which we are decentered as masters, as crown, as goal, and begin to feel empathy in an *internal* way for the sufferings of other species. As Aldo Leopold comments, "For one species to mourn the death of another is a new thing under the sun."[22] It is indeed new and requires an expanded self-identification, a sense that I care about another species in a way analogous to the way I care about those near and dear to me. I do not merely regret the loss, but I feel it and weep for it. Can we also expand this sense of self to include ecosystems and even the planet? When we read of the pollution of the oceans or the destruction of rainforests, do we feel grief for the earth itself, for that beautiful blue-green living marvel of a planet spinning alone in space?

We are a part of the whole, deep ecology insists, and we need to internalize that insight as a first step toward living truthfully, living in reality. A question, however, that rises immediately is *which* part are we? just any part? no particular part? Deep ecology is based on the classic body model of a single organism, a model made more extreme by a view of ecological unity in which living things are so profoundly interrelated and interdependent that they are, in effect, one. The result is a merging of parts, "an oceanic fusion of feeling," that denies the diversity, individuality, and complexity of life-forms that have emerged from evolutionary history, and is a weak basis for an environmental ethic. The organic model based on the common creation story does not fuse all the parts; difference and individuality are central ingredients of this picture. Ecofeminists have been especially concerned to deny fusion and insist that the "loving eye" pays attention to the independence and difference of the other.[23] It is a kind of knowing that acknowledges the others in the world "as being independent, different, perhaps even indifferent to humans. Humans *are* different from rocks in important ways, even if they are also both members of some ecological community."[24]

Unless this difference is acknowledged—including the *indifference*—and acknowledged in relation to the particularity and peculiarity of this and that species, this and that ecosystem, there is no solid basis for an environmental ethic. A statement by one deep ecologist indicates the problem with an ethic based on the fused self: "Just as we need no morals to make us breathe . . . [so] if your 'self' in the wide sense embraces another being, you need no moral exhortation to show care . . ."[25] No "oughts" are necessary, for care flows "naturally" from the expanded self. The sentimentality and danger of this view are evident: even parents and lovers, whose sense of self certainly does embrace the child or the beloved, can and do engage in outrageous acts of emotional and physical destruction toward the other. What is missing from deep ecology is a developed sense of *difference*. An environmental ethic in regard to nature—the land, ecosystems, the planet—must be based on knowledge of and appreciation for the intrinsic and particular differences of various species, biotic regions, oceanic ecosystems, and so on. We need to learn about these differences and make them central in our interaction with the environment. A sense of oneness with the planet and all its life-forms is a necessary first step, but an *informed* sensibility is the prerequisite second step. Aldo Leopold, a deep ecologist who does not fall into the fusion trap, is on the right track when he tells us that we need a land ethic, an ethic toward the land that no longer sees it "like Odysseus' slave-girls" as still property, as "still strictly economic, entailing privileges but not obligations."[26] The intrinsic value and independence of the land, not our sense of oneness with it, is the basis of living rightly in relation to it. A land ethic that aims "to preserve the integrity, stability, and beauty of the biotic community" is an example of living appropriately on the land, refusing to live the lie that we are the conquerors, the possessors, the masters of the earth.[27] A land ethic deals with the issue of space—the prime issue for an environmental anthropology—in its broadest and deepest context. *The* space, the ultimate space, as it were, that we all share, is the land, oceans, and atmosphere that comprise the planet. The complex question that faces us is how to share this space with justice and care for our own species, other species, and the ecosystems that support us all. How can we live with the others that inhabit this space appropriately and justly, realizing we have a place, but not all places, that we need space but cannot have the whole space?

Our reflection on sin in three contexts—as living a lie in relation to other human beings, other animals, and nature—has highlighted space as a central category for an ecological anthropology. In each case we have insisted that the attention to difference, even though we acknowledge and feel profound unity with these others, is central. We close these thoughts with two more that lead into the rest of the book: We *are* different in the common creation picture, for we are the self-conscious ones that can care for the others; and we *are* different in the model of the body of God as qualified by the cosmic Christ, for we are called to be the liberating, healing, sharing self-conscious ones. In other words, our specialness in the common creation story takes a particular turn in the Christian story . . .

Notes

1. The notions here of "where we fit" and "proper place" in the scheme of things are *not* meant to support, in any fashion, cultural stereotypes of subservience and quietism, as when certain ethnic groups or children are told to "know their place" or "keep their place." Rather, the concept of a limited space and a proper place for human beings vis-à-vis other species (as well as other members of our own species) carries the connotation of not taking more than one's share: the implication is of justice for all, not the subservience of some.

2. James A. Gustafson, *Ethics from a Theocentric Perspective*, vol. 1: *Theology and Ethics* (Chicago: University of Chicago Press, 1981), 96–97.

3. Carl Sagan, *Cosmos* (New York: Random House, 1980), 34.

4. As quoted by Mary Midgley, *Beast and Man: The Roots of Human Nature* (Ithaca: Cornell University Press, 1978), 219.

5. See ibid., 206ff.; also Mary Midgley, *Animals and Why They Matter* (Athens: University of Georgia Press, 1983).

6. The "roots of human nature" as well as the analysis of this concept are from Midgley, *Beast and Man*.

7. Midgley, *Beast and Man*, 255–56.

8. Ibid., 206.

9. Ibid., 358.

10. Ibid., 225ff.

11. The phrase "second naïveté" is Paul Ricoeur's and refers to the possibility of returning to the most basic roots of our being by a conscious, informed route when the intuitive acceptance found in our own youth and the youth of the human community is no longer possible for us.

12. Annie Dillard, *Pilgrim at Tinker Creek: A Mystical Excursion into the Natural World* (New York: Bantam, 1974), 81.

13. As quoted by Bill Devall and George Sessions, *Deep Ecology: Living as if Nature Mattered* (Salt Lake City: Peregrine Smith, 1985), 205.

14. Susan Griffin, *Made from This Earth: An Anthology of Writings* (New York: Harper & Row, 1982), 343.

15. This distinction is from the introduction to *Dharma Gaia: A Harvest of Essays in Buddhism and Ecology*, ed. Allan Hunt Badiner (Berkeley: Parallax, 1990), xiv.

16. As quoted by Devall and Sessions, *Deep Ecology*, 85.

17. Richard Nelson, *The Island Within* (New York: Random House, 1989), 249.

18. As quoted by Devall and Sessions, *Deep Ecology*, 13.

19. As quoted by Marti Kheel, "Ecofeminism and Deep Ecology: Reflections on Identity and Difference," in *Reweaving the World: The Emergence of Ecofeminism*, ed. Irene Diamond and Gloria Orenstein (San Francisco: Sierra Club Books, 1990), 136.

20. Warwick Fox, *Toward a Transpersonal Ecology: Developing New Foundations for Environmentalism* (Boston: Shambhala, 1990), 239.

21. As quoted in the introduction to *Nature in Asian Traditions of Thought: Essays in Environmental Philosophy*, ed. J. Baird Callicott and Robert Ames (Albany: SUNY Press, 1989), 62.

22. Aldo Leopold, *A Sand County Almanac and Sketches Here and There* (New York: Oxford University Press, 1949), 110.

23. See Marilyn Frye, "In and Out of Harm's Way: Arrogance and Love," in *The Politics of Reality* (Trumansburg, NY: Crossing, 1983), 66–72.

24. Karen J. Warren, "The Power and Promise of Ecological Feminism," *Environmental Ethics* 12 (Summer 1990): 138.

25. Arne Naess, as quoted by Fox, *Toward a Transpersonal Ecology*, 217.

26. Leopold, *A Sand County Almanac*, 203.

27. Ibid., 224–25.

15

Human Existence in the Spirit

This brief selection, and the next two chapters, are excerpted from Life Abundant *(2001), but are offered here in the reverse order from how they appeared in the original context. Presented this way, this chapter not only reiterates some of what has already been discussed but also anticipates what follows (though some readers may want to jump ahead two chapters and read backward). So, the understanding of sin—and thus of anthropology—set forth in the previous chapter is recapped here but in ways that lead to concise statements on soteriology, Christology, and (without explicitly naming it) McFague's panentheistic understanding of the God-world relationship. For McFague, salvation is located foremost in incarnation, not in the cross, which itself represents the suffering that faces those who embrace this reality. Redemption, then, comes through deification, becoming like Christ, even as God is Christ-like, which provides the moral imperative to cruciform living. These are among the ideas that the ensuing chapters discuss in greater depth.*

Source: 2001:182–86

"Christians believe the world is hidden in God."[1] This is the same as saying that human existence takes place within God's Spirit. The world does not have a separate existence for Christians. Ontologically, we live from, toward, and with God. I did not used to believe this; in fact, I fought it. I wanted the world to stand on its own; I feared that otherwise it would be sucked up into God—shades of Hegel and Barth! But believers are always mystics (even if they are not philosophical idealists). One (or, at least I) cannot believe in God as a being, no matter how infinite, eternal, ubiquitous, good, powerful, or supernatural. God is either everything or nothing, or to phrase it more carefully, God is reality (or being-itself)—if not, there would be something "beyond God" or "more than God" that would be *God*.

So, how are the world and we human beings differentiated from God? In this story, we are the body of God, we are God "spread out," we are God incarnate. We (the universe) come from God and return to God, and in the "interim" we live in the presence of God—even when we do not know or acknowledge it. We are created in the image of God (the entire universe reflects God's glory, each and every creature and thing in its particular, concrete, unique way). Creation is a panoply of mind-boggling diversity, a myriad of outrageously extravagant species and individuals who all together make up the body of God—God going out, God enfleshed, God become matter. Each creature—except us, it appears—praises God by simply being itself, by being fully alive. The whole universe, in this story, desires to grow back into God: the beloved longs to return to the lover. It is the deepest desire of creation to do so: eternal life, as Julian of Norwich says, is being "oned" with God, being "knitted" up with God.[2]

In this story there is nothing but God: God in God's self (the Spirit) and God going out from God's self (God embodied). God incarnate means God going out from the divine self to create "another," the world, which in a sense is over against God: the billions of particular, different creatures and entities that constitute it. But the world's "being" and its "well-being" and even its "reason for being" is to live in intimate relationship with God, which, of course, means living in intimate relationship with all other parts of divine embodiment as well.

What, then, of sin and evil? Sin and evil are pretending that we can live outside reality, this reality of interrelationship and interdependence of all things with one another and with God. Sin is refusing to grow into the image of God in which we (and everything else) is made. Sin is refusing to reflect God, become like God, by imagining that we can exist outside of relationship with God and others, living as if one's life came from oneself. Sin is *living a lie.* If God is reality and if reality is good, then sin and evil are a turning away from the ground of our being and our hope for happiness; sin and evil, as Augustine claimed, are *not.* They are a turning away from reality, from the radical, intimate relationships that constitute life and its goodness. Sin and evil are a denial of reality in their false belief that we can live from and for ourselves.

My exegesis of the statement, "Christians believe the world is hidden in God" is, I have suggested, a "likely story" of God and the world for our time. It is not a description, but neither were the medieval or deist stories of how God and the world are related. Rather, all three are Christian retellings of the relation of God and the world in terms commensurate with, appropriate to, different times. The story of God's embodiment and return, of all things evolving from one source that is reality, is congruous with the Big Bang of contemporary cosmology and the resulting unimaginable diversity and interdependence of matter—from the billions of galaxies to the DNA in bacteria, and everything in between. It is a creation story that gives God greater glory than any other that human beings have ever told. It is a retelling of the creation story that underscores God's awesome magnificence and power (God *is* reality) and our total dependence on God (as God's body created to reflect God's glory, each in our own way). It is a story that can be imagined without sacrificing one's intellect, although contemporary cosmology and evolution do not give special support to this religious tale. But this tale can "accompany" the contemporary worldview with minimum strain.

At an important point, however, this story makes a claim that the cosmological, ecological worldview does not: it makes a claim concerning the direction of the universe. This claim, for Christians, is focused on Jesus of Nazareth as the lens or model of God. His life, ministry, death, and appearances are the way that Christians look Godward, the way they dare to speak of the world not as a tragedy, but as a "divine comedy." All of creation, this story says, reflects God, but at one place that reflection is seen (by Christians) in an especially illuminating way. In Jesus of Nazareth, Christians believe they see *what we are meant to be*, and by implication, what we are not meant to be. If the purpose of all of creation is to reflect God, then the story of Jesus is the message and the means for how human beings can do so.

Life as it should be—salvation—is then, for Christians, christomorphic. It is becoming like God by following Jesus. "Following Jesus" is not principally a moral imperative, but a statement of *who we are*. We learn what it means to say human beings are created in God's image for God's glory by looking at Jesus Christ. "The importance of the confession 'Jesus is the Lord' is not only that Jesus is divine *but that God is Christlike*" (italics added).[3] The focus of salvation, then, becomes living in a new way, the way of God's abundance.

This is a deification, not an atonement understanding of salvation. It is an incarnation rather than a cross emphasis, a creation rather than a redemption focus, from the Eastern Christian tradition rather than the Western. It claims that we were created to be with God: creation is the pouring out of divine love toward that end; the incarnation in Christ is the reaffirmation and deepening of that love; the cross is the manifestation of the suffering that will occur, given sin and evil, if all creatures, especially the most vulnerable, are to flourish; and the resurrection is God's Yes that, in spite of the overwhelming forces of sin and evil, this shall be so. We will, all of us, be one with God and with each other. It is an understanding of salvation, of the good life, that reflects and deepens the ecological, economic worldview, for it is communal, physical, and inclusive. It imagines God's work for and with us as the enrichment and fulfillment of all forms of life, with special emphasis on the basics that creatures need for survival and well-being.

This is a different notion of salvation than is typical in most Western theologies. In the West salvation has usually been seen as redemption—God in Christ paying a price for our sins, or ransoming us from the forces of evil, or sacrificing the Son as a substitutionary atonement for us. The focus of these theologies is on redemption from our sin, not on our creation for the abundant life in union with God and others. The focus is on human individuals who are saved from evil (which is often equated with the world), rather than on the whole creation being invited into fuller communion with God and all others. The focus is on "Jesus doing it all" rather than on us, in partnership with God by following Christ, working toward a different way for all of us to live together on the earth.

While the deification view may at first glance appear to take sin and evil less seriously than the atonement view, it actually takes them more seriously. It views them not simply as individual failings for which human beings need forgiveness, but rather as all the forces—individual, systemic, institutional—that thwart the flourishing of God's creation. "Sin" is not mainly or only a personal problem, the solution for which is divine forgiveness. Rather, sin is *living a lie,* living contrary to the way the christic lens tells us is God's desire for all of us. "Evil," in this understanding, is the collective term for the ancient, intricate, and pervasive networks of false living that have accumulated during human history. In the atonement model sin and evil are mainly individual, personal matters; in the deification view they are principally communal, worldly matters: one focuses on individual redemption from sin, the other on the forces, whether individual or institutional, that keep creation from flourishing.

This means, then, that the point of Christology for the deification view is not personal redemption but a "a conversion to the struggle for justice."[4] It means becoming "conformed to Christ" since he is, for Christians, the lens by which we know God. If, however, the goal of salvation is God's glory—every creature fully alive—then becoming christomorphic will involve very mundane work. "Work, land, housing, health, food, and education become the very expression of the glory of God. Likewise, the glory of God is trampled underfoot in any person who suffers hunger, destitution, and oppression."[5] Deification, becoming like God or following Christ, means, then, becoming involved in such matters as ecological economics, the just distribution of resources on a sustainable basis. Deification, becoming like the incarnate God, means making the body of God healthier and more fulfilled. Salvation is worldly work. Human existence "in the Spirit" means working "in the body" so that it may flourish.

Do we do this? *Can* we do this? Some do, and they can do so only by being deeply, personally, profoundly grounded in God. The "saints" who work tirelessly for justice are spiritually alive. Persistent, lifelong cruciform living appears possible only through immersing oneself in God's presence. Justice work and mysticism seem to be companions. To live this way is very difficult; it is, however, what I believe we middle-class North American Christians are called to.

Notes

1. Hans Küng, *Credo: The Apostles' Creed Explained for Today* (New York: Doubleday, 1993), 162.

2. Julian of Norwich, *Revelation of Love,* ed. and trans. John Skinner (New York: Doubleday, 1997), 177–78.

3. Arthur Michael Ramsey, as quoted by Alister E. McGrath, *Christian Theology: An Introduction* (2d ed.; Oxford: Blackwell, 1994), 323.

4. Julio Lois, "Christology in the Theology of Liberation," in Ignacio Ellacuria and Jon Sobrino, eds., *Mysterium Liberationis: Fundamental Concepts of Liberation Theology* (Maryknoll, NY: Orbis, 1993), 173.

5. Pablo Richard, "Theology in the Theology of Liberation," in ibid., 164.

16

Christ and the Ecological Economic Worldview

The previous chapter concluded with an exhortation to cruciform living. This selection, then, looks more closely at the ecological economic Christology that McFague suggests we must embrace in order to "live a different abundant life." As the book title suggests, the nature of this abundant life is at the core of Life Abundant. *McFague proposes that it be understood as not just something that God intends for humans but for all creation. For humans, the way to this abundant life is, as was suggested in the previous chapter, redemption understood in terms of deification.*

Source: 2001:171–80

Aye, here's the rub: how *can* we live a different abundant life? The ecological economic worldview gives few instructions and even less hope. We have suggested that an ecological economic Christology not only fits with this worldview but goes beyond it. How is this the case? How can Christology help us live a different abundant life? As a dramatic and concrete way of answering this question, let us look at some of the interesting results of recent scholarship on the historical Jesus.

The figure who emerges from these studies is peculiarly fitted to help us embrace the ecological economic worldview. More than that, this figure goes beyond and intensifies what living within this worldview means. The conventional image of Jesus (the one we have suggested fits with the neo-classical economic model) and the emerging one are summed up in the two following statements:

> Jesus was the divinely begotten Son of God, whose mission was to die for the sins of the world, and whose message was about himself,

> the saving purpose of his death, and the importance of believing in him.[1]
>
> Rather strikingly, the most certain thing we know about Jesus according to the current scholarly consensus is that he was a teller of stories and a speaker of great one-liners whose purpose was the transformation of perception. At the center of his message was an invitation to see differently.[2]

In the conventional view, Jesus does something for all the rest of us—he dies for our sins—and our role is to believe in him. In the second scenario, Jesus invites us into a different way of seeing—a transformation of perception—and our role is to follow him. We are to see as he sees and live accordingly.

And what is it that he sees? According to a number of contemporary New Testament scholars, Jesus was a social revolutionary—he saw a different way of living in the world. He was not primarily interested in political upheaval, but, as is evident in his parables and wisdom sayings, he was opposed to the various forms of domination and domestication that cast some people in a superior position and others in an inferior one, whether from purity laws, eating customs, gender discrimination, economic disparities, or ethnic/racial divisions. Above all else, he invited people to imagine a different life, one centered in God and inclusive of all others—and then to live it. It is a revolutionary vision because it goes against the conventional hierarchies and dualisms (however these are understood in different cultures) and invites us to see the world in a radically new way—a way that has some similarities with the community model of ecological economics. It is a vision of the world opposed to an individualistic, merit-centered view of human life with insiders and outsiders, haves and have-nots. It is just as clearly on the side of a community-oriented, egalitarian view of human life, inclusive of all living beings.

How is this portrait of the historical Jesus relevant to a Christology for an ecological, economic worldview? If all contemporary understandings of Christ should be grounded in historical judgments about Jesus of Nazareth—if there should be continuity between the Jesus of history and the Christ of faith—then we need to see if the ecological economic context is an appropriate one for reconstructing Christology for our time. Who is the Jesus that grounds our discipleship for planetary living in the twenty-first century?

Let us look at the vivid portrait of Jesus by New Testament scholar John Dominic Crossan. "The open commensality and radical egalitarianism of Jesus' Kingdom of God are more terrifying than anything we have ever imagined, and even if we can never accept it, we should not explain it away as something else."[3] For Jesus, the Kingdom of God was epitomized by everyone being invited to the table; the Kingdom is known by radical equality at the level of bodily needs. Crossan names the Parable of the Feast as central to understanding what Jesus means by the Kingdom of God. This is a shocking story, trespassing society's boundaries of class, gender, status, and ethnicity—as its end result is inviting *all* to the feast. There are several versions (Matt. 22:1-13; Luke 14:15-24; Gospel of Thomas 64), but in each a prominent person invites other, presumably worthy, people to a banquet, only to have them refuse: one to survey a land purchase, another to try out some new oxen, a third to attend a wedding. The frustrated host then tells his servants to go out into the streets of the city and bring whomever they find to dinner: the poor, maimed, blind, lame, good and bad (the list varies in the three versions). The shocking implication is that everyone—anyone—is invited. As Crossan remarks, if beggars come to your door, you might give them food or even invite them into the kitchen for a meal, but you don't ask them to join the family in the dining room or invite them back on Saturday night for supper with your friends.[4] But that is exactly what happens in this story. The Kingdom of God, according to this portrait of Jesus, is "more terrifying than anything we have imagined" because it demolishes all our carefully constructed boundaries between the worthy and the unworthy and does so at the most physical, bodily level.

For first-century Jews, the key boundary was purity laws: one did not eat with the poor, women, the diseased, or the "unrighteous." For us, the critical barrier is economic laws: one is not called to the just or sustainable allocation of resources with the poor, the disadvantaged, the "lazy." To do otherwise in both cultures is improper, not expected—in fact, shocking. And yet, in both cases, the issue is the most basic bodily one—who is invited to share the food—in other words, the issue is who lives and who dies? In both cases, the answer is the same: everyone, regardless of status (by any criteria), is invited.

We North American middle-class Christians may not be terrified by the unclean, but we are by the poor. There are so many of them—billions! Surely we cannot be responsible for all of them! Yet, this historical Jesus appears to disagree: he is not, it seems, interested so much in "religion," including his own, as in human well-being, beginning with the body: feeding the hungry and healing the suffering. Moreover, his message, according to Crossan, had less to do with what Jesus did for others than what others might do for their neighbors.

> The Kingdom of God was not, for Jesus, a divine monopoly exclusively bound to his own person. It began at the level of the body and appeared as a shared community of healing and eating—that is to say, of spiritual and physical resources available to each and all without distinctions, discrimination, or hierarchies. One entered the Kingdom as a way of life and anyone who could live it could bring it to others. It was not just words alone, or deeds alone, but both together as life-style.[5]

The body is the locus: how we treat needy bodies gives the clue to how a society is organized. It suggests that correct "table manners" are a sign of a just society, the Kingdom of God. If one accepts this interpretation, the "table" becomes not primarily the priestly consecrated bread and wine of communion celebrating Jesus' death for the sins of the world, but rather the egalitarian meals of bread and fishes that one finds throughout Jesus' ministry.[6] At these events, all are invited, with no authoritarian brokering, to share in the food, whether it be meager or sumptuous. Were such an understanding of the eucharist to infiltrate Christian churches today, it could be mind-changing—in fact, perhaps world-changing.

At the very least, it is indeed terrifying. It is also absurd, foolish, and utopian. But, as we have suggested, there appears to be a solid link, a degree of continuity, between this reconstruction of society and what we have described as the ecological economic worldview. This worldview is closer to that terrifying picture than is the neoclassical economic model. If this is the case, then for us middle-class North American Christians it may well mean that *sin* is refusing to acknowledge that link, that continuity, explaining it away because we will not accept the consequences for our privileged lifestyle. Sustainability and the just distribution of resources are concerned with human and planetary well-being for all. This is, I suggest, the responsible interpretation of the Parable of the Feast for us. It demands that we look at the structural institutions and systemic forms separating the haves and the have-nots in our time, those invited to the table and those excluded. And it demands that we name them for what they are: evil. They are the collective forms of "our sin." They are the institutions, laws, and international bodies of market capitalism (often aided by the silence of the church) that allow some to get richer and most to become poorer. Our sin is one of commission but perhaps more damningly of omission: our greed camouflaged by indifference and denial—and even by our "charity."

This picture of the historical Jesus suggests some directions for us: it gives us some guidance as we seek a liberation theology for middle-class North

American twenty-first-century Christians. It does so in three ways: it suggests what to do, how to do it, and when and where to do it. It gives us a message, a ministry, and marching orders. At the center of Jesus' message as prophet and wisdom teacher is the vision of a world as an egalitarian community of beings, not a hierarchy of individuals. His parables and aphorisms disorient our conventional expectations and suggest a way of being in the world where all are valued, especially the vulnerable and outcast. He shows us *how* to live this message by doing so himself: his unsettling parables and sayings are embodied in his own practices of living among the marginalized and siding with those considered inferior by conventional standards. He tells us also when and where to do it: now and here. Recent interpretation of Jesus' notion of the kingdom of God shifts it from an otherworldly, existentialist, individualistic abode to a this-worldly, public, and communal vision of new life now for all. The message, ministry, and marching orders that emerge from current historical Jesus research are summed up by Marcus Borg: "As a charismatic who was also a subversive sage, prophet, and renewal movement founder, Jesus sought a transformation in the historical shape and direction of his social world."[7]

This evangelism or good news, however, is not offered as an imperative or as an accomplished fact, but rather as an invitation: it is not telling us to believe something or accept something but inviting us to live differently. It does not appear to be principally a matter of the intellect or the will, but of the heart. The alternative to the conventional hierarchical, dualistic paradigm of life is, according to Jesus, the way of death to the old life and rebirth to the new.[8] At the center of this new life is love to God and others: not just a moderate or "sensible" love, but God-intoxication and compassion for others that knows no limits.

How is this possible? Would such a person be human? Can we be totally engrossed by God and totally and empathetically involved with others? There have been some people who approach this ideal—we call them saints and they appear in all religious traditions. For Christians, Jesus' life is of course the prototype, but it is sometimes easier to argue from the reflection rather than the model (the latter being too overlain with god-like trappings). One of the consistent characteristics of the Christian disciples revered as saints is precisely this combination of God-intoxication and universal compassion for others. Those who have followed Jesus most radically, regardless of their other errors and failings—people like Paul, Augustine, Teresa of Avila, Julian of Norwich, John Woolman, Pierre Teilhard de Chardin, Dorothy Day, Dietrich Bonhoeffer, Sojourner Truth, Martin Luther King Jr., Mother Teresa, and many others less well known—passionately loved both God and the world (and everything in it). Their spirituality and their ethics emerge from excessive dual love, as Teilhard de Chardin puts it, plunging them into God and into matter. These people seem to know no limits, either in their outrageous intimacy with God nor with their borderless love for all living things. They saw things differently because of being grounded in God and practicing compassion for all others, especially the oppressed. The new heart gave them a new mind and a new will: knowing the limitless depths of divine love as that in which all live and move and have their being—including themselves—opened their hearts to others, all others. Here we see examples of human lives lived as reflections of the life we cannot describe but only speak of metaphorically: the life of the historical Jesus who invited us into a new way of seeing, a new way of living.

It is, quite simply, the way of "deification." It is a reflection of God's life and the attempt to become like God. In this way of thinking, Jesus became like us that we might become like him—a human being totally open to God and others. Being God-like is our destiny, but it is not an otherworldly goal. As John Dominic Crossan remarks, "The Kingdom of God is what the world would be if God were directly and immediately in charge."[9] Deification, then, is a worldly matter. We see glimmers and shadows of it here and there, even in something as mundane as the ecological economic paradigm. That model, which underscores the importance of every individual creature, which understands unity only in terms of interrelationship and interdependence, which insists on distributive justice to all beings and sustainability of the earth, is a template ready and open to receive the radicalization of "deification"—the limitless and universal love of God reflected in human lives. This radicalization is expressed by Jesus' cross and resurrection, death to the old way of life and rebirth to a new way, a way that will often involve sacrifice, pain, and diminishment.

The picture of Jesus emerging from recent scholarship and the lives of myriads of his followers over two thousand years give us a sense of the *way* to the new life: it is only possible by relying utterly on God and, by so doing, developing the capacity for selfless love to others. The way to the new life is not by believing something nor by willing something, but by practicing the presence of God in daily communal life. It is not an imperative but an invitation: the invitation to live in God and with others, to live from and toward God here and now with all others, especially the needy.

What, then, of the cross and resurrection as "saving us"? In the traditional, otherworldly, individualistic view, Jesus' sacrifice on the cross for the forgiveness of sins and his subsequent resurrection is the salvific event: it is done for us, and we need only accept it. In the view supported by recent scholarship on the historical Jesus, we are invited into communion with God and partnership with Jesus to bring about a social transformation of life on earth for all creatures. This will involve both cross and resurrection, both sacrifice (especially from us well-off people) and new life (especially for the not-so-well-off creatures). Should we, the favored ones, want to be part of this new way of being in the world? Only if we want to be able to say that reality is good—because, on this reading of Christian faith, we must help to make it so.

Annie Dillard, in her book *For the Time Being*, lays out a grim picture of human existence—from "bird-headed dwarfs," AIDS, and childhood leukemia to tornadoes, earthquakes, and floods. Life is a mess and a misery (but she doesn't indict God—things just are this way, she claims). Now and then, however, to those who seek God, God grants that they see "an edge" of the divine. This gift is so overwhelming that "Having seen, people of varying cultures turn—for reasons unknown, and by a mechanism unimaginable—to aiding and serving the afflicted and poor."[10] These people can say that reality is good, because they have experienced, however briefly, that it is so, and also because they help to make it so.

Finally, then, what does it mean from the context of an ecological economic Christology to say that reality is good? First and most important, reality is good because *God* is with us (Jesus points beyond himself to the source of love and power in the universe); God is *with* us (on our side, working with us, not instead of us, to bring justice and fulfillment to all); and God is with *us* (all of us, not just privileged human beings, but all people and all other life forms, especially the needy). This Christology allows us to say reality is good because it claims that *God is with us* and it claims this in spite of evidence to the contrary—overwhelming evidence. It makes this claim in a strange, involuted way: the claim embraces its opposite. Ecological economic Christology claims that reality is good by way of the cross and cruciform living. It makes the claim by way of diminishment, sacrifice, solidarity with the oppressed, limitation of desires, standing compassionately in another's place. Christianity is not sentimental or naïve: it does not claim that the world spread out before us—the one of inequality, intolerance, greed, genocide, discrimination, and even innocent indifference—is good. Reality can be said to be good only through joining God in trying to make it so. This way was shown by the prophetic, historical Jesus (and his many disciples) to demand such solidarity with all people and the earth itself that it is called "the way of the cross." Here the cross is not the substitutionary, sacrificial death of Jesus of Nazareth for the sins of the whole world, but the *way* of God in the world, always. Jesus is paradigmatic of God's eternal and constant siding with the outcasts and hence the inevitable meeting with diminishment and death that such association involves.

The claim that reality is good does not, however, end with cruciform living: it says also that life conquers death. From the perspective of ecological economic Christology, the resurrection does not say that God raised Jesus from the dead—and us with him—to eternal life. Rather, it claims that the forms of death (physical starvation, mental and emotional deprivation, discrimination, rape, poverty, genocide, ecological destruction) are not the last word. The resurrection is a promise from Reality Itself—from God—that life and love and joy and health and peace and beauty are stronger than their opposites—if we will help make it so, if we will follow the way of Jesus, the way of cruciform living.

What is emerging, then, from ecological economic Christology is a different notion of the abundant life, not the abundance of consumer goods, but the possibility, the promise, of a new life in God for all. This abundant life uses the template of an ecological economic worldview in which individuals live in community on a sustainable earth and with the just distribution of necessities for all. But it goes beyond this worldview, insisting that the *way* to this new life will be difficult, painful, and sacrificial, especially for those who are presently taking more than their share and thus depriving other people and the earth of a good life. But how could the way not be cruciform for us privileged middle-class North American Christians if this new life is "what the world would be if God were directly and immediately in charge"?[11]

Theology, Christology, anthropology: God, Christ, and human life are not three topics but one interrelated matter. Human life under God—the way the world would be if God were directly in charge—is made known to us and made possible for us by Jesus Christ, God with us. Who we are in the scheme of things is defined by God being with us. The prophetic and the sacramental, the historical and the incarnational, the Protestant and Catholic emphases in Christology together declare that God is with us: the glory of God is every creature fully alive. And it is our task to help this happen. In the life, ministry, and death of Jesus we see concretely what is entailed in helping all creatures live fully: it involves, at the very least, distributive justice and sustainability, goals unattainable apart from significant changes by the most privileged human beings. This is the prophetic, historical, Protestant dimension of what God with us in Christ means. The sacramental, incarnational, Catholic side promises all creatures that God is in the world and on the side of the world. In the incarnation and resurrection of Jesus we see more clearly what is the case everywhere and always: *God* is with us, with *all* of us, *with* us in our struggle to give God glory by working for the fulfillment of all creatures. We are not alone as we seek to grow into the image of God—into the image we see in the face of Jesus. "Having seen, people . . . turn . . . to aiding and serving the afflicted and poor."[12]

Notes

1. Marcus J. Borg, *Jesus in Contemporary Scholarship* (Valley Forge: Trinity, 1994), 194.
2. Ibid., 172.
3. John Dominic Crossan, *Jesus: A Revolutionary Biography* (San Francisco: HarperSanFrancisco, 1994), 73–74.
4. Ibid., 68.
5. Ibid., 113–14.
6. See ibid., 179–81.
7. Borg, *Jesus in Contemporary Scholarship*, 13.
8. Ibid., 152.
9. Crossan, *Jesus: A Revolutionary Biography*, 55.
10. Annie Dillard, *For the Time Being* (New York: Knopf, 1999), 168.
11. Crossan, *Jesus: A Revolutionary Biography*, 55.
12. Dillard, *For the Time Being*, 168.

17

God and the World

It may seem odd to conclude this series of excerpts from Life Abundant *with a selection that argues "If reality is defined by God, it makes sense to begin with God." But this spiraling backward through this material—McFague's most extended systematic work outside of* The Body of God—*sets up well the final three chapters of this anthology, which represent McFague's most recent thoughts on God, anthropology, and the God-world relationship. "Beginning with God," then, can mean here to return to the essence of reality, to step back from the ideas about Jesus and of human existence to reassess our assumptions about God—assumptions that, as seen in the early chapters on metaphor and models, are always shaped through human experience. But such reassessment also means confronting other dimensions of contemporary reality, including the economic and ecological models that prevail yet tell a false story about God and the world.*

Source: 2001:135–51

Beginning with God

So, where should we begin—with God, with Christ, or with ourselves? Where can we start finding out what it means to live in reality as defined by love? John Calvin put the issue bluntly when he noted that we could start with either God or ourselves, but we had best start with God lest by beginning with ourselves, we overestimate our importance. Not bad advice. If reality is defined by God, it makes sense to begin with God: we are less likely, as Calvin suggests, to go astray. But how *can* we? What do we know of God? How can we know God—reality—is love? Many have insisted that we do not and cannot know God: hence, we must start with the revelation of God in Christ—here we learn who God truly is. The difficulty with this advice is that "revelation" for Christians usually means the Bible, and the Bible is a collection of peoples' experiences of God. So, we are back to ourselves and our own experience.

Or, are we? One of the oldest and most abiding insights of the Christian tradition is that everything is from God, even our experiences of God's love. These too are gifts, not human works; all knowledge of God, whether "natural" or "revealed" is from God's initiative, God's grace. We can only know God because God makes this possible for us. We were created to know God: intimacy with God is part of our birthright—it comes with our creation, so to speak. In one sense, then, it does not matter where we begin—whether with God, Christ, or ourselves, we are always beginning with God. But *how* we begin with God does matter. Dorothee Soelle says, "We can only speak *about* God when we speak *to* God."[1] What she means is that prayer precedes theology; being in relationship with God (acknowledging this as one's actual state) comes before the conceptual, systematic task of talking about God. She is not claiming that we must each have mystical experiences of God or even affirm the "existence" of God; rather, we must, as many other liberation theologians have also claimed, acknowledge *the presence of God in the world.*

What does this mean? Many things to many people, surely, but at base I believe it means becoming aware that reality is good. It came to me through nature: a sense of unity with the natural world, of give and take with it, of pulsating life of which I and everything else is a part. I felt I belonged and I gradually came to name this sense of belonging as God's love. Nature was the route by which I came to knowledge of God's presence in the world—or, more accurately, the existence of everything within divine love. There are many other routes. Since, for the Christian, God is always incarnate and present, there is no place on earth, no joy or wish that any creature experiences, no need or despair that they suffer, that is not a possible route to God. Wherever reality is seen as hopeful, joyful, and loving, God is there; whenever reality is experienced as despairing, cruel, and hopeless, God must be there also. If God is love, then where love is, God is; where love is not, God must needs be. In nature's health and beauty, I see God; in nature's deterioration and destruction, I see that God is here also. In the first case as a Yes and in the second as No: in the first case as a positive affirmation of God's glory through the flourishing of creation; in the second, as a negative protest against whatever is undermining God's creation.

"Beginning with God" means, then, daring to trust the tiny smidgen of God's liberating love that has come to you, but doing so in light of some criteria—whether it is consonant with Christian faith and whether it would be good for all people and the planet. We come to God through becoming *aware* of

God's presence in one or more of its infinite forms in the world. God is always there (or here); *we* need become so.

Beyond the necessity of starting with God—our experiences of God's love—is the *desire* to do so. The experience of reality as love is one of great wonder and gratitude. It is an experience of worship. We start with God because the realization that love (and not indifference or malevolence) is the heart of reality is overwhelming. The *sanctus* is our response: the deepest religious emotions are awe and thanksgiving. If God is not a being or even just being-itself, but reality as good, then our astonishment and gratitude knows no bounds. It is more than we could ask or imagine; it is complete satisfaction and fulfillment. And we are called to be part of this amazing web of life and love: to praise God by helping all God's creatures flourish.

Now, then, how does all this fit with our two economic models? Can we start with God from both models, and what does it mean to do so? It is very difficult to begin with God from the neoclassical economic worldview. For the most part, God is absent from the world in this model. To be sure, God designed and set the world in motion, as one does a machine, but God is not a ubiquitous presence in the world. The deist God of the model allows for "acts of God" in terms of natural calamities (causing or preventing them) as well as intervention on behalf of individuals in pain, but most of the time, this God can be forgotten—and is. The deist God—otherworldly, distant, uninvolved—suits a worldview of individual aggrandizement. The secularization of the world—the dismissal of God's presence from it—is a necessary by-product of seeing life in terms of individual pleasure and profit, especially if this entails the impoverishment of other people and the planet. The neoclassical economic worldview begins with *us*, we human beings of insatiable desire: this is its primary sense of reality. "God" must adapt to this "relative absolute," this primary commitment of the model.

The ecological economic model, however, is open to beginning with God, because at the heart of this worldview is the individual-in-community: everything *is* because of relationships of interdependence. Individuality emerges in community and the community is nothing but the interaction of individuals. The sense of life intrinsic to this economic model is that our very breath, each breath, depends on others. We live within an unimaginably vast and intricate reality of which each one of us is a part and to which each of us contributes. Is it, then, a great leap to the supposition that this reality is good, rather than indifferent or malevolent? We are not being asked to believe in an otherworldly being, but in the trustworthiness of the whole process that has created and sustains us. In this worldview, starting with God almost comes "naturally"; at the most basic level, it is simply acknowledging that while we are part of the web of life, we are not its creator, its center, or its means of continuation or transformation. We are recipients of a gift.

God Is Love: The Many Ways to Say It

Beginning with God, then, means beginning with that scrap of our own experience of God, our "relative absolute," as understood from various contexts and as congruent with Christian faith. My "relative absolute"—the glory of God is every creature fully alive—means that reality is good. "I believe in God" is what we say when we rest on this assumption, the assumption of the goodness of reality.

But what does it mean to say that reality is good? Is this the same as saying that God is love? I believe it is one way (the best way) but certainly not the only way. The ways of speaking of God's love range from the deistic and monarchical to the dialogic, the agential, and the organic.[2] On the one end of the continuum, the deistic model sees God's love as radically transcendent over the world, so transcendent that God and the world are only externally and occasionally related. At the other end—the organic model—God's love is radically immanent in the world, so immanent that it is difficult to say how God and creation are separate. The monarchical view, God as King and Lord, is also a highly transcendent understanding of God, but with suggestions of greater relatedness, for a king cares for his subjects. The dialogic model is more personal, proposing that God and the individual have an I-Thou relationship: this model allows for divine immanence but only with human beings. The agential model, a variation on the dialogic, broadens God's transcendent love to embrace history, both human and natural, but the agency is all on one side—God's. None of these models is adequate, needless to say. "God and the world" is not a subject we *can* model accurately. The question is which one or ones is/are closer to the Christian paradigm (as understood in our time) and better for the planet and its inhabitants?

The monarchical model, while deep in the tradition and still popular in many quarters of both church and society, has come under severe criticism from philosophers and feminist and other liberation theologians, as well as process theologians.[3] From the perspective of an ecological economic worldview, it is especially problematic because it sees the God-world relationship as entirely one-sided: God is an imperial, patriarchal figure whose transcendence is manifest in his total control over the world and whose immanence is shown by divine sacrifice for the sins of the world. The model views power as control, is anthropocentric to the neglect of the rest of creation, understands relationships externally, and removes responsibility from human beings. God's love *is* transcendent—as is a king's or absent father's—but it is not immanental: we do not live and move and have our being in this God.

The dialogic model has been an attractive way of modeling God's love, especially during the twentieth century, though the model is also ancient, going back to the earliest Hebraic roots where God speaks with human individuals. It is a way of talking of God's immanental presence as close to us (we pray to and are addressed by God), while at the same time insisting that this conversation partner is pure spirit and hence not overly interested in the world. From the perspective of our ecological economic model, it is even more anthropocentric than the monarchical model, limiting divine concern to the inner joys and fears of individual human beings.

The deistic model is, as I have suggested, the one that fits best with the secularized, consumer-oriented economic worldview: it so emphasizes, overemphasizes, the transcendence of God that God becomes irrelevant. The last thing this worldview needs is a "sacred universe," the sense that God is in, with, and through all that is. This model is often joined with the dialogic one, creating at least one place—the inner individual—where God and the world meet. This meeting place, however, is protected from the physical needs of either other people or the planet. It is bodiless and individualistic: the sins confessed here are mainly personal failures and the love given mainly a forgiving, comforting one.

Is this enough? Should God's love be no more than radical transcendence mitigated by care for persons? Is this what we mean, should mean, by "God"—that God is the One who designs and starts the world, controlling it through natural laws while intervening now and then to aid needy individuals? The ecological economic model says no: God is much more than this. God is radically transcendent *and* radically immanent: God's love is the power that moves the galaxies and that breathes in our bodies. One way to imagine this relationship between God and the world is with the metaphor of the world as God's body.[4] This metaphor is a combination of the classical agential and organic models. It suggests that we might think of God's transcendence as radical immanence; that is, God's love is totally, though not exhaustively, incarnated in the world. The world, the universe, is the "body of God": all matter, all flesh, all myriad beings, things, and processes that constitute physical reality are in and of God. God is not just spirit, but also body. Hence, God can be thought of in organic terms, as the vast interrelated network of beings that compose our universe. The "glory" of God, then, is not just heavenly, but earthly: we can praise God by marveling at and caring for people as well as everything else. But God is not only the universe; God is also (and primarily) the breath that gives it life, the spirit that transforms it. Just as we are not primarily our bodies (though we are thoroughly bodily), so also God is not reduced to the body of the world but is also and primarily, the life and power, the breath and love, that makes the universe what it is. By combining the agential and organic models, we have a way (a feeble, inadequate way, of course) of expressing what it means to say that reality is good, that God is love.

It is a way that combines being and goodness: if we say only that God is being-itself and exclude goodness, then perhaps reality is indifferent or malevolent; if we say only that God is good but not being-itself, then perhaps God is just a being—a good one—but what about the rest of reality? With the metaphor of the world as God's body, God as the agent or spirit in and through all that is (as our spirits are the energizers of our bodies), we can imagine a unified view of God and the world, which does not, however, identify them. Moreover, this view gives us a way of imagining reality as good, as having value: every creature, thing, and process in the universe has value because it is an aspect of God, it is part of God's body. Another way to express this is to say that since everything derives its existence from God, everything has value. H. Richard Niebuhr says that seeing being and value together is "the assurance that because I am, I am valued, and because you are, you are beloved; and because whatever is has being, therefore it is worthy of love. . . . In [God] we live and move and have our being not only as existent but as worthy of existence and worthy in existence."[5]

The world as God's body or the agential/organic model of God and the world is a form of panentheism. Whereas deism is an extreme form of theism (God as external to and distant from the world) and organism is an example of pantheism (the identification of God and the world), panentheism is an attempt to speak of God as both radically transcendent to *and* radically immanent in the world. It is a corrective to the classical view, which, while affirming both divine transcendence and immanence, has tended to emphasize the former, undercutting the sense of God's presence in and to the world. While the world as God's body tends in the other direction, toward highlighting God's immanence, it is an emphasis that we need, given our long history of transcendence understood as divine distance from the world. We recall that *no* models are adequate; they are not descriptions, merely an attempt to express something of God's being and nature. Moreover, many, if not most, contemporary doctrines of God are, to one degree or another, panentheistic. Monarchical or deistic theism, even when softened by the dialogic model, results in a supernatural being who wields power in unilateral and oppressive ways. This is not a model of God that most people today can believe in, nor is it a model that is good for the earth and its people. Its credentials as Hebraic and Christian are also doubtful, for the God of both traditions is Emmanuel—God with us—the compassionate, available, and caring source and renewer of life.

We are suggesting, then, that the understanding of God that is compatible with an ecological economic worldview (and one that is consonant with Christian faith) is not the popular image of God as a supernatural individual, the designer of the world and redeemer of human individuals, a God who can be forgotten most of the time and who is mainly concerned with "religious" or personal moral matters. This God, while a caricature of the Enlightenment and Protestant legacies, is nonetheless a powerful force in civil society and the model of God that fits best with the conventional economic worldview. On the contrary, in the model of God for an ecological economic view, God is radically present in and to the world and is concerned with everything that goes on in it, especially with bodily needs and pain. This is a "God of the basics," a God who cares about those things that keep beings alive, healthy, and flourishing. This is, in other words, the God who cares about the *oikos*, the management of the entire planetary household, so that all will have a fair share and the house will be in good shape for future inhabitants. This God cares so much about the *oikos*, the inhabited world, that we are allowed to think of it as God's *body*. It is an outrageous thought, but both the Hebrew and Christian traditions suggest it is a better way to think than of God as a heavenly spirit who is indifferent to the world. It is better, say these traditions, to err on the side of God loving the world "too much," than of not loving it very much.

If, then, we were to accept the agential/organic model, the world as God's body, as a helpful way to speak of God and the world from an ecological economic context, what would our basic response be to both God and the world? I suggest we would address both as "Thou," as living subjects who have being and value; not as "objects" that we can manipulate or use, but ends in themselves to be honored.[6] In other words, our primary stance toward God, other people, and nature would be one of appreciation and gratitude. We would value each being—and the source of all being—in itself, for itself we would value each just because it is. We would also be grateful for these others whom we desperately need and in whom we take joy. If we are individuals-in-community, then we live and flourish with and by means of all these others, as well as the Other. In summary, this way of saying that God is love or that reality is good places us in a position of reverence toward God and the world: in the model of the world as God's body, there is no way to separate them.

God as Creator, Liberator, and Sustainer

The "God of the basics," the God who cares about the management of the household, is its creator, liberator, and sustainer. The radically transcendent *and* radically immanent God is the source of everything that is, the power that frees creation from what would destroy it, and the love that nourishes it in every moment. The God whose glory is every creature fully alive cannot be a solitary, distant being. The "trinity" is a *model*, a way of speaking of God, that tries to express God's profound involvement in, with, and for the world. It claims that the universe originates in God, owes whatever signs of hope and goodness appear in it to God, and depends on God continuously for all forms of nourishment. The trinity is certainly about God, but just as important, it is about God and the world; it is a way of talking about God's transcendence and immanence in relation to the world.

The notion of the trinity has been a source of misunderstanding and mystification for most of Christian history: How can three be one or one be three? Which of the three is responsible for what actions? We are not interested in such puzzles, but rather in the way the trinitarian model of God gives us a language for speaking of what we know from our own experience and what the Christian tradition upholds; namely, that God is our ground, our savior, and our nurturer. The trinity is an attempt to express the full dimensions of the experience of God as the One in whom we live and move and have our being; the One from whom we come, to whom we return, and in whose presence we live every minute; the One who is no more alone than we are—as Martin Buber puts it, "In the beginning is relationship."[7] From the "beginning" God is relational as we are, all the beings and things God has created. As we are not solitary individuals, neither is God: in the ecological, economic worldview and in Christian faith, beings are individuals-in-community. We *are* because of relationships. The trinity, then, is not a conundrum or theoretical obscurantism; rather, it is the most basic affirmation we can make about God. The trinity is about relationship, about God with us in every way, at every level, in every moment. In Catherine LaCugna's words, the trinity "expresses the one ecstatic movement of God whereby all things originate in God and are returned to God."[8] The trinity, so understood, is a way of speaking of creation, incarnation, and deification; that is, our beginnings from God, our salvation in God, and our movement toward God. The trinity, then, far from being irrelevant, is central to Christian faith: it expresses the entire God-world dynamic. This dynamic graphs the movement of God with us and us with God as a going out and a return: as God goes out to the world in creation/incarnation, so the Christian life is a return to God. Since God's life penetrates ours in creation and salvation, so Christian life becomes a participation in the divine life: ". . . orthopraxis means right practice, right acts, in response to God's life with us."[9] The trinity, so understood, is not a Christian doctrine in a narrow sense. It is not the claim that Jesus of Nazareth is "the second person of the trinity," although, as we shall see, for Christians Jesus is an affirmation, deepening, and clarification of the trinity. More basically, the trinity is about God's love for the world and the world's response.

Let us look, then, at the substance of this doctrine—God's activity as creator, liberator, and sustainer—to see how they fit with and illumine the ecological, economic worldview. These three "activities" of God spell out what the God-world relationship is from our side, the world's side. Most broadly, these divine activities mean that God does everything for us: we owe our existence, our happiness, and our daily nourishment to God. These are not, however, one-time events, nor do they conflict with or replace scientific explanations. They are ways of speaking of our radical dependence on God for life, for love, for all the things we need to exist and flourish. They are a doxological statement, not a scientific one. They are perfectly compatible with an evolutionary view of the universe; in fact, the Big Bang creation story *enhances* our praise to God. To remythologize Christian faith from that perspective is to make God all the greater, as Job would have well understood.[10]

Understanding God's love in creator/liberator/sustainer terms is especially relevant to us today if we want to live within an ecological economic worldview. These three divine activities are about creaturely flourishing; they are concerned with the gift of life, its maintenance, and its liberation from forces that would destroy it. The ecological economic model is similar: it is a vision of planetary living in which justice and sustainability are priorities. Both are radically relational understandings of existence; neither sees either human beings or God in solitary, individualistic terms. They are commensurate, though by no means identical, perspectives. The ecological economic worldview and the understanding of God we have been depicting are compatible and mutually enhancing.

How is this the case? The creator/liberator/sustainer God—the One whose glory is every creature fully alive—is concerned about the well-being of all creatures, not just the moral rectitude of human beings. This is a radically physical, inclusive, democratic God who gives religious backing to the ecological economic model. This God cares that those to whom she gives birth have enough to eat; that those who are sculpted by the divine hands retain their beauty; that those whose existence he calls into being with a word continue to flourish. God the creator is fiercely protective of his/her creation, just as any parent or artist. We, all of us, belong to God: we are the precious creations of God's hands and words, and we are the fruit of God's body. No metaphors are too strong or too intimate to express the loving relationship between God and creation: parenthood and artistic creation can give us only a *glimmer* of how God the creator feels about all of us. Just as human parents would give their life for their children (and sometimes do), so God's love for creation is particular, boundless, and total. Just as artists feel that they are embodied in their work, that who they are is expressed in their creations, so also God's glory is reflected in each and every creature, from the mite to the whale, from the acorn to the mountain, and in each one of us human beings. The doctrine of creation is not primarily about whether God produced matter from nothing, nor is it about a moment in time when the universe appeared. The doctrine of creation is about God's total graciousness in the gift of life and total commitment to the life so created.

God as liberator and sustainer does not tell us something new or different about God. God as liberator underscores that God is there for us no matter what. God the savior does not mean that in the incarnation, ministry, death, and resurrection of Jesus of Nazareth, God does a new work, something different from God's work in creation. God as savior or liberator continues the work of God as creator; it is God's sign and seal that *nothing* can separate the world from God's love, not even the most perverse and evil acts of human beings. The creator God *must* also be the liberator God, for since creation in the ecological economic model is an infinitely old and infinitely complex reality, it is an ongoing event that meets with all sorts of natural, historical, and increasingly human forces that would destroy it. God the liberator is always Emmanuel, God with us, as the Hebrews well know in their exodus from Egypt and the long journey toward the promised land. God the creator has to be God the liberator; the parent will do whatever is necessary to protect from danger the products of its own being.

Likewise, God the sustainer is a further elaboration of how the creator and liberator God operates to insure planetary well-being. The sustenance—breath and food and all needful things—that creation must have to survive are provided daily and concretely by God. God the liberator will not only protect us against great evils and dangers—whatever would enslave and undermine us, but God the sustainer will also give us the most mundane, basic things we need to thrive.

This God—the creator, liberator, and sustainer of everything—is a down-to-earth householder. This God cares about just and sustainable planetary management, so that all creatures may flourish. This God will judge harshly those who do not consider the lilies or who kill a sparrow or who take extra helpings at the table when others are hungry. Economics and God are interrelated topics: an ecological economic worldview demands an understanding of God such as we have been sketching. Likewise, this view of God enhances the ecological economic worldview, providing depth and a sense of appropriateness to it. The ecological economic worldview helps us see how we can serve God, for it means that we do *God's work* as we labor to incorporate this economic view on our planet. The ecological economic model also benefits because we can now see that it is not just an idealistic fantasy, but a partial reflection of God's will for the world. This economic view is closer to the love that God has for the entire creation than are some other economic views.

And this brings us to the neoclassical economic worldview. How does it fit with the model of God as creator, liberator, and sustainer that we have been sketching? Are they mutually compatible and enhancing? Not likely, since one's view of God and of the world go together. The neoclassical economic worldview highlights the importance of the individual and his or her desires. It is atomistic and dualistic. It understands reality as composed of discrete, individual units and beings that are externally related, either as parts of a machine or by human decisions and contracts. Reality so understood is divided into mind and body, spirit and flesh, humanity and nature. Individuality and not relationality is basic in this picture; likewise, mind—not body—is primary. The *sensibility* of this worldview—its basic awareness of who I am, who we are, in the scheme of things—is very different from that of the ecological economic worldview. In the neoclassical picture each creature and thing is alone, independent, and whatever has "mind" is superior to all bodily functions and needs. Whereas in the ecological economic model the basic awareness is of a spirit-filled bodily existence that all people, creatures, and things share (even God!), in the neoclassical picture the basic awareness is of disembodied, solitary individuals over against a purely physical world composed of animals and matter.

Where does God fit into this picture? God is the super-individual, the utterly transcendent designer and creator of the world-machine, who, like humans, is disembodied, a mind/spirit who is external to the world but in charge of it. This God is creator, the One who originates the world process; and also savior, the redeemer of human beings who fall into sin by not loving God and neighbor; but this God is only marginally sustainer, for this God is not continuously and constantly in and with the world. Rather, the deistic God is at most present just once: in Jesus of Nazareth whose death was a sacrifice for the sins of the world and whose life was an inspiration for all to follow. This is not the God in whom we live and move and have our being; this God is to be worshiped on Sundays and provides some ethical guidelines for treating other people fairly and even for conserving natural resources for future generations. But unlike the understanding of God that accompanies the ecological economic worldview, this God is not a statement about reality. Believing in this God does not mean that one trusts that reality is good; rather, it means that one enters into a contract with the supernatural divine force that is the mind behind the world machine, a contract to live decently and virtuously with other rational beings and in a world composed of matter. This God is distant from worldly events, both physically and emotionally; it is a detached God who views the world from "the sky," protected from the mundane agonies of starvation, persecution, pain, war, and death.

It would, in fact, be impossible for the God of the ecological model to fit with the neoclassical worldview. That God is constantly, annoyingly present in the world and concerned with basic and ordinary physical well-being. That God cares about lilies and sparrows and hungry stomachs, not just about mental anguish or spiritual alienation—or even moral peccadilloes. That God is the busy householder, insisting that all family members deserve a fair share at the table and that the house must be kept in good order for others. That God is intrinsically and permanently worldly. Such a God is very difficult to escape or forget, for this God is always present.

How Is God Present in the World?

This simple question is, among all other questions about God, one of the most difficult. It did not used to be. Until the Enlightenment, many events were seen to be "acts of God," from unwanted babies to illnesses and earthquakes. Until the scientific revolution, people did not ask *how* God could act in the world, but simply assumed that unexplained events as well as extraordinary ones, whether good or bad, were from God. Moreover, before scientific empiricism insisted that only matter is real, spiritual acts and actors were seen to be just as real. In other words, God was a presence in the personal and public lives of people as well as in nature in ways we can scarcely imagine.[11]

But those days are long gone. For many if not most contemporary people, God's *absence* is a far more common experience. This is not necessarily felt as an absence; it is not the experience of the loss or "death" of God, so much as it is the experience of the irrelevance of God or simply the lack of any experience of God. The neoclassical economic worldview, the reigning paradigm of our time, suggests how this has come about. As we have noted, the deistic God of this paradigm is absent from the world. This God resides elsewhere and has little connection with worldly pains and pleasures. Apart from starting up the world as creator and intervening now and then, mainly in the inner life of individuals, God is not a factor to be reckoned with in world events. Everything, or almost everything, goes along just fine without God—the scientific, economic, and public worlds. No explanations or interference from God is necessary; in fact, it would be inappropriate and intrusive. "Religion" is one discrete area of life that deals with personal issues of morality and mortality; it is not part of economic or public life. The scientific revolution and the Enlightenment dealt with religion by compartmentalizing it; God was no longer always and everywhere present as had been true in medieval times. Now God was pushed to the margins of the world and especially into the inner person. The deistic view of God is a convenient one for a consumer society that does not want interference in matters of the distribution of necessities or the sustainability of the planet. This God stays out of the political arena, finding its only abode in the inner recesses of human beings. This God is not a householder, butting into every nook and cranny of the planet, concerned about its well-being at every level. To the householder God, nothing is off-limits, and especially not politics and economics.

So, how is the householder God present in the world? We recall that the God who fits with the ecological economic view is the world's creator, liberator, and sustainer, the One upon whom everything is dependent for everything: each creature's first and last breath, the billions of species of living things and billions of electrons and quarks that constitute all things, the stars and galaxies, and so on. "God" is the source of all power, all love, all good in and with and for everything, at all times and places. This is the "ubiquitous God" *par excellence*; this God is never absent. If this God were absent, nothing else could be present: everything would collapse or disappear, for God is being-itself, the source of all being without whom nothing else is. This God is also the source of all goodness and love: reality is good because God is the "direction" of reality, its direction toward love and goodness. "God" means reality is good.

The radical intimacy of God and the world in the ecological model means that we can experience God's presence anywhere and everywhere. There is no place where God is not. Is this pantheism? Are we saying that God and the world are identical? No, they are not, but we are suggesting that one needs "double vision" to distinguish them. By "double vision" I mean that God is always present in mediated form, through something or someone else. We do not meet God directly "face to face," but we do meet God in the world. As the body of God, the world is a sacrament, *the* sacrament, the incarnation, of God, so that while each thing is itself in all its marvelous particularity and uniqueness, *it is at the same time and in and through its own specialness,* the presence of God.[12] This is not pantheism because the world is not simply a manifestation of God; on the contrary, by means of each being's uniqueness, each rock's concrete contours, each tree's particular form, each galaxy's unique constellation, God is glorified. The God whose glory is each creature fully alive revels in differences, not in sameness. The God that fits with the ecological paradigm is the God for whom oneness is only achieved through the infinitely complex interrelationships and interdependencies of billions of different constituents, beings, and events. So, it is in and through this world, the very one that lies before us, that God is present, if God is present at all.

We have found it helpful to think of this relationship of God and the world in terms of agent and body, in terms of a body (the world) inspired by God, a body made alive, kept alive, and protected from destruction by God. One can imagine these processes of creation and its fulfillment occurring in many ways. Contemporary theologians have suggested some of these ways with the help of evolutionary and process thought. The effort in most of these cases is to suggest how God's presence can be imagined in light of an evolutionary, ecological worldview without identifying the two or even necessarily suggesting that evolution is guided or directed by God. Rather, the intent is to remythologize the world's story from the perspective of a particular religious tradition. That is, given belief in God as love, how can this belief be seen in terms of the current evolutionary worldview? Evolution does not prove or disprove the "existence of God" or the "goodness of reality." Rather, we ask, if one does so believe, can the ecological paradigm fit with such belief? We have here suggested that it not only fits, but that this view of God enhances the ecological, *economic* worldview even as this worldview gives concreteness, meaning, and detail to the belief in God's worldly presence.

In addition to God's presence in and through the natural processes of the world—as incarnated in everything—we can also speak of this God, the agential/organic God, as particularly present wherever and whenever creatures are helped to flourish. And this places a special vocation on us human beings as the self-conscious part of creation who know when we help others to flourish and when we participate in their destruction. (Here is this view's definition of right action and of sin: helping others to flourish versus participating in their destruction.) If God's presence is to be found sacramentally everywhere, it is to be found especially in those human beings who, as God's co-workers, improve the well-being of some aspect of creation. Liberation theologies have been especially insightful on this point, insisting that God cannot do all the work of salvation (that is, helping the world and especially the oppressed to flourish). *We* human beings are the hands and feet of God, manifestations of God's loving presence. If God is absent from the world, it is because we are; made in God's image, as agents of our own bodies, we are also God's auxiliary agents in and for the body of the world—our lifework is to further the divine purpose of planetary prosperity.

This means, of course, that we love God by loving the world, but such loving can only be done in public, political, and economic ways. The well-being of the planet is not a private, personal, or "religious" matter; it has to do with public debate, political laws, and economic policies. Theologians—and all religious people who accept this understanding of how we should love God will become public advocates for political and economic policies that promote fair distribution of necessities and the sustainability of the planet. Theology is about these matters, about the well-being of the earth, not about how to win eternal salvation or even how to find personal peace and serenity.

Notes

1. Dorothee Soelle, *Theology for Skeptics: Reflections on God,* trans. Joyce L. Irwin (Minneapolis: Fortress Press, 1995), 12.
2. See McFague 1993:136–41.
3. For one critique, see McFague 1987, ch. 3.
4. See McFague 1993, esp. chs. 5, 6.
5. H. Richard Niebuhr, *Radical Monotheism and Western Culture* (New York: Harper & Row, 1943), 32.
6. See McFague 1997, chs. 4, 5.
7. Martin Buber, *I and Thou* (New York: Scribner's, 1970), 18.
8. Catherine Mowry LaCugna, "The Trinitarian Mystery of God," in Francis Schüssler Fiorenza and John P. Galvin, eds., *Systematic Theology: Roman Catholic Perspectives,* vol. 1 (Minneapolis: Fortress Press, 1991), 177.
9. Catherine Mowry LaCugna, *God for Us: The Trinity and Christian Life* (San Francisco: HarperSanFrancisco, 1991), 16.
10. See McFague 1993, chs. 2, 3.
11. For further elaboration of this point, see McFague 1997, ch. 3.
12. See McFague 1997:164ff., and McFague 1993, chs. 2, 6.

18

"The Dearest Freshness Deep Down Things": The Holy Spirit and Climate Change

Having worked through McFague's detailed theological thoughts on anthropology, Christology, and God in the previous three chapters, this excerpt, the final chapter in A New Climate for Theology (2008), *reconsiders the identity of God and of humans in light of the crisis of climate change. What is new here—or at least, has not featured prominently in earlier selections—is McFague's understanding of the importance of the Trinity for contemporary Christians, and what hope can look like in light of the climate crisis. Despite the title, McFague does not have a strongly stated pneumatology in her work (at least within a traditional trinitarian framework, as it is usually expressed). However, this is perhaps her strongest eschatological statement since* The Body of God. *What is particularly notable is how she once again uses Gerard Manley Hopkins's "God's Grandeur" (which appeared earlier in ch. 1), but here for very different purposes—not to explain metaphor but to urge us toward caring for creation.*

Source: 2008:159–76

> The world is charged with the grandeur of God.
>   It will flame out, like shining from shook foil;
>   It gathers to a greatness, like the ooze of oil
> Crushed. Why do men then now not reck his rod?
> Generations have trod, have trod, have trod;
>   And all is seared with trade; bleared, smeared with toil
>   And wears man's smudge and shares man's smell: the soil
> Is bare now, nor can foot feel, being shod.
> And for all this, nature is never spent;

> There lives the dearest freshness deep down things;
> And though the last lights off the black West went
> 	Oh, morning, at the brown brink eastward, springs—
> Because the Holy Ghost over the bent
> 	World broods with warm breast and with ah! bright wings.
> —Gerard Manley Hopkins, "God's Grandeur"[1]

Twenty-five years ago, a conversation about the Holy Ghost rescued me from an embarrassing social event. I was sitting across from the wife of Italy's ambassador to England at a high table dinner at an Oxford college. I was definitely out of my comfort zone and wondered how I could manage over the next several hours of elaborate cuisine, copious wine, and clever conversation. The ambassador's wife asked me what I "did." I hesitated, knowing that "being a theologian" is comparable to "being a nuclear physicist" to most people. But I mumbled what I "did." She smiled warmly and replied, "You know, when I was a child, I always prayed to the Holy Ghost because I figured he was less busy than the other two." The rest of the evening was a smashing success.

But within this story lies an interesting historical note: the Holy Ghost (Spirit) has been the neglected third party of the Trinity—at least until about fifty years ago. Even in my own early writing, I disparaged the "spirit" metaphor as "amorphous, vague, and colorless," "ethereal, shapeless, and vacant," concluding that "Spirit is not a strong candidate for imaging God's sustaining activity."[2] But how wrong I was! I should have known better, since I have loved Hopkins's poem about the Holy Ghost since I was in college. However, it was only recently as I reread the poem in the light of climate change that it began to take on new depth and meaning for me.

"God's Grandeur," written in 1877, bemoans nature's fate at the hands of Western industrialism: the separation of human beings from nature via shoes and the desecration of nature by human activity ("seared with trade"). What should be a world "charged" with God's glory, so that every single scrap of creation tells of God in its own way, has become smudged, bleared, and smeared, camouflaging the particular reflection of God in all things. Hopkins's vision of God and the world in which each and every iota of creation shines with some aspect of divine glory has faded in the last lights of a dark Western culture. But the hope for the "bent world" does not lie in nature's own restorative powers; rather, it rests in the warm breast and bright wings of the Holy Ghost. God's power of motherly brooding that hovered over the chaotic waters at creation is with us still in the bright, rising wings of each new morning. In this poem we have an argument for, a confession of, hope. Hopkins could not envision the destruction of nature that we now know, and which is epitomized in global warming, but the witness of this poem is that *no matter how bad things get*, there is hope—not because of human beings or even of nature, but because the power of life and love that was at the beginning of creation is with us still as our source and our savior. "Nature is never spent" and "there lives the dearest freshness deep down things" *because* of the sustaining power and love of God's Spirit. The sextet of the sonnet could not be stronger, more intimate, or more hopeful. We who can now imagine, given climate change, the end of civilization as we know it, brought about by Western carbon dioxide emissions, shiver at the ominous line, "the last lights off the black West went," but take a breath of hope with the final three lines. Here, the "bent world," our world indeed, is nonetheless the place where divine love is incubating new life after the terrible destruction we have brought to our planet. Like a mother bird tucking the new life under her own body and earnestly protecting it, God sustains and renews us, *no matter what*. The final four words are more than we could ask or imagine: "with ah! bright wings." We do not deserve this; we could not have expected it; we can scarcely believe it, but it is the one thing necessary as we face up to climate change and the needed changes in our behavior.

Surely, this image of God is the one for our time. Nothing less can speak to the depth of our despair as we well-off humans contemplate what we are doing through our reckless, selfish, out-of-control consumerism to the poor of the planet and to the planet itself. We now know that climate change, which will affect every plant, animal, and person on earth, is the most serious crisis of the twenty-first century. If we ever thought ourselves in charge of the earth, capable of "managing" the planet, we now know that we have failed utterly. We must undergo the deepest of all conversions, the conversion from egocentricism to theocentrism, a conversion to what we truly are: reflections of God, as is everything in creation. The only difference between us and the rest of creation is that the others reflect God, tell of God, simply by being, whereas we must *will* that it be so. We must desire to be what we truly are—made in the image of God, and thus able to live justly and sustainably on earth with all other creatures.

GOD AND THE WORLD: A SACRAMENTAL SENSIBILITY

The reason for Hopkins's hopefulness is his belief that the world lives within God. Hopkins has a sacramental religious sensibility: God and the world are not two separate realities that exist independently and must somehow find each other. Rather, the world is "charged" with God as if with electricity. "All things therefore are charged with love, are charged with God and if we know how to touch them give off sparks and take fire, yield drops and flow, ring and tell of him."[3] Hopkins's sacramental sensibility, in which each scrap of creation becomes *more itself* as it lives more completely within God, can most adequately be expressed with the metaphor of "spirit." God is the empowering Spirit who brings all things to fulfillment, or in a gloss on Irenaeus, "The glory of God is all things fully alive." This is not a view of the God-world relationship in which the more power the one has, the less the other has; rather, God is the "wild air, world-mothering air" in which all things grow and flourish.[4] Hopkins agrees with the medieval mystic Mechthild of Magdeburg: "The day of my spiritual awakening was the day I saw—and knew I saw—all things in God and God in all things." We live within God; hence, metaphors such as water, breath, milieu, ocean, and air are our weak attempts to express the utter dependence *and* radical uniqueness that lie at the heart of an incarnational understanding of creation. This understanding says that we live within the body of God; that the world is/is not the body of God; that all things exist within the one reality that is, and that reality is on the side of life and its fulfillment. God as Spirit is the power of life and love within which all bodies exist. Most creatures live instinctively as the sacraments they were meant to be: they reflect God's glory, each in its own illimitable way. We humans have a choice: to live in reality, in and for God, or to live in and for ourselves—nowhere—outside of reality. We have the choice *to live a lie*, to live what we were not meant to be, in and for ourselves.

This ontology—the world within God—provides a picture of the God-world relationship that is the ground of our hope. It gives a reason to hope at a time when our planet seems doomed to destruction. Let us look at some of the features of this picture of God and the world.

Who Is God?

If the world exists within God—if in the lovely words of Julian of Norwich, God holds the world as one holds a hazelnut in one's hand—then God is everywhere. God is either everywhere or nowhere. God cannot be in "one place" and not "another place"; a "being" might do that, but not God. God is right under the surface in everything. God "accompanies" us when we travel to the ends of the earth—we may have to leave our loved ones behind, but not God. Moreover, prayer is merely the acknowledgment that God is always there, always available. *We* may not be present; in fact, we are often absent, but God is always present. God the Spirit is ubiquitous, everywhere at the same time, always hovering with warm breast over every inch of the earth (universe). God is the liminal presence in all things. The divine presence announces itself in a breeze rustling through leaves, in the sound of a bird's call, in the face of a starving child (or a happy one), in a clear-cut forest. God is in all things because all things are in God—in all shapes and shades, all conditions and crises, all joys and sorrows. God is in birth and death and everything in between. God is ubiquitous: God is wherever I am, wherever each and every iota of creation is.

But God is not a being, even the highest being: God is reality. This is another way of saying God is "being itself," or the ground of all that is real, is actual, exists. The Christian tradition can lead us astray when it suggests that God is a supernatural being who is the only reality. This paradigm suggests unilateral divine power, power that takes over and sucks everything into itself. Here God is both not great enough and too great: not the source of all life and love, but the highest being, the only power in the universe, choking off all other powers. But if God is reality, in whom we find our own distinctive realities, then trees can still be trees and mountains can be mountains and even I can and must be myself. God is the Spirit, the breath, the ether, the atmosphere in which each and every thing grows and flourishes. Here there is no competition for power: the world is charged with the grandeur of God, and it is so by *being most fully itself*. God as the body of the world *is* that body by way of all the zillions of bodies that compose the universe. There is one reality: God visible (body) and invisible (spirit), but the latter is known *through* the former. Everything is suffused, infused, with God's breath and light and power. The world is alive with God—but indirectly, incarnationally.

Christian mysticism—seeing God in all things and all things in God—is incarnational. We live *in God through the world*. Everything exists within God's "womb," within God as womb. This womb, the earth, is the body from which we derive breath, food, water, and habitat. There is not God *and* the world, but the world *as it exists and only exists in God*. We become aware of God *through the earth*: we develop "double vision," the ability to see God *in* the world, in its beauty and its horror, and even in the most ordinary things on ordinary days. Mysticism is this double vision, seeing everything as it is *and* as in God, both at the same time. Mysticism is radical incarnationalism, seeing God in the flesh *everywhere*. Mysticism is delight in things and in God; it is seeing, hearing, tasting, smelling, touching God everywhere and in everything, but *only* in and through all of these wonderful creatures. Who would want a disembodied mysticism? "The world is charged with the grandeur of God"—indeed, it is. God is in all things incarnationally: God tells us of life, love, truth, beauty, and goodness as each of these qualities is realized in the world. Thus, the exquisite beauty of an alpine forget-me-not is the way we experience God's beauty; the energy and joy of a young child is the way we experience God's vitality and life. "Everything is God," God is reality, but *only* as everything is exquisitely, precisely, idiosyncratically itself. "The glory of God is every creature fully alive." God and the world are not in competition: an incarnational theology does not say, "The more God, the less world," or "The more world, the less God." Rather, it says, "The more God, the more world," and vice versa. We, the world, flourish *in* God, *only* in God, and *fully* in God.

God is not a being, then, but reality: God is the "stuff" out of which everything comes and to which it will return. Life emanates from God and is more "like God" than like anything else. All creation was made in God's image, as a reflection of God, and this is what we humans must acknowledge and live into. There is not "God and the world," but "God and God in the form of the world" (the world as God's body, God's incarnation). The world (all matter) is a manifestation of God, for God is reality. If the world were "outside" God, then there would be something greater than God, that is, "God and the world." A dictionary definition of *reality* is "something that exists independently of all other things and from which other things derive."[5] Hence, "God" is being-itself, or existence-itself, the source of all other forms of existence. So, to say that God is reality is not to say that God contains or includes all that is in a pantheistic fashion. Rather, it is to say that God is that from which all else derives its being, its reality. If we then say that reality is "good," we make a faith statement about the hopeful, life-giving direction of what "really is," in contrast to appearances, which do not support such a statement.

And this is the most astounding thing of all—that reality is good, that God is love. God is in, with, and for everything. The "with" and "for" part is what Christians read about reality in the face of Jesus: in his ministry of love and healing and in his death for the oppressed, Christians claim that reality (God) is on the side of life and its fulfillment. This is the "direction" of reality, something we could not figure out on our own; in fact, most evidence appears to be contrary. God is like Jesus: "For it is the God who said, 'Let light shine out of darkness,' who has shone in our hearts to give the light of the knowledge of the glory of God in the face of Jesus Christ" (2 Cor 4:6). Thus, reality (God) is not a being, but is "personal" in that we can use words such as *love* and *fulfillment* regarding reality's "intention." This assertion about reality's intention is what faith, rock-bottom faith, is: trust that love and not indifference, neutrality, or malevolence is at the heart of things. It is not "belief in God," but trust that things will be all right or, in Julian's words, "all things shall be well."

Another way to express this understanding of the God-world relationship is the Trinity—not the conundrum of "three persons in one substance," but the truth that God (reality) is a giving and a receiving God. The Trinity suggests what reality is: a continual flow of giving and receiving, of sharing, of living in one another, of counting on one another. We see a form of this reality in ecology: the interrelationship and interdependence of all things. Nothing is itself alone—even God, or perhaps most eminently, God. In the beginning was relationship, so says the Trinity. There is no beginning or end to this process—no self (God or creature) that is itself by itself. We become through relationship—with God and with our billions of neighbors. The Trinity reminds us that God is not an isolated individual—nothing is. Thus, God is not a being outside of other things; rather, God is the reality of all things, or all things become real (exist and are fulfilled) by living in God. Trying to live anywhere else is false, a lie, hopeless. Things *are* themselves as and to the extent they acknowledge the source of their being. This is an extraordinary thought: life and grace are the same thing. Grace is the gift of acknowledging one's total dependence on God, who is life and gives life.

Who Are We?

If God is reality, in whom we live and move and have our being, from whom we come and to whom we return, then our time on earth is also lived within God. We are not on our own; we belong to God. Believing in God is not primarily asserting that "God exists"; rather, it is acknowledging that I know who I am. I am a contingent, unnecessary, transient creature who has been given the gift of life and love. I am aware of being totally and gratefully dependent on the earth and all its interlocking support systems, on others whom I love and who love me, and on whatever is in, through, with, and for life and love—what we call "God." I did not create myself; I cannot sustain myself; I cannot transform myself. I live within the womb that gives me birth, feeds and nurtures me, gives me delight and joy, strengthens me through loss and suffering, and will be my tomb when I die.

Remembering daily and in particular ways who I am and where I fit in the scheme of things is a central spiritual discipline. Coming to faith is not so much knowing who God is as knowing who I am. I am not the center of things; I do not live by my own merit or means; I am finite, mortal, and small. And yet coming to faith as this dependent, vulnerable creature means that I trust ("know") that I live in God: God is my reality. I am not on my own; I cannot account for my own existence, let alone its moments of flourishing, from myself. I belong to something outside of myself that is at the same time inside and all around me. I belong to the source of my breath, my delight, my need, my hope. And in pain, loss, sorrow, disappointment—and even destruction and death—I still belong to God, though I often do not know how.

The acknowledgment of who we are (our "faith") means a dual realization: of gratitude and responsibility, of delight and duty. The primary religious emotions are wonder, amazement, and thankfulness. Simply to be alive, along with all of the other fascinating, diverse, beautiful, and wonderful creatures is a gift beyond imagining. Once we wake up to the glory of planet Earth in all its spectacular particularity and complexity, we are blown away. Once we "see" the world—and ourselves as part of it—with "double vision," as grounded in God and resplendent with the individuality of each thing, from slugs to forget-me-nots, from whales to big cedars, from crouching tigers to fields of waving wheat, we want to shout, "Hallelujah!" To see creatures, including human beings, becoming their illimitable selves *as* they live within and for God—this is a great joy. We realize that there is no either/or, but a both/and: it is not God versus us, but rather God as the ground, source, breath, water, womb, bath, air, breast, and tomb within which we become who we truly are. Each scrap of creation, including us human beings, becomes the unique individual that in its own distinctive way tells of God's glory.

And our peculiar, distinguishing characteristic is seen in the choice that we humans have to tell of God. We are the one creature that has to decide to reflect God. What is becoming increasingly clear is that the way we must reflect God is to accept responsibility for planetary well-being. Accepting this responsibility is an awesome task. Never before have human beings *known* that they are responsible for planetary health. Until the second half of the twentieth century, human beings could, with good conscience, still claim that our behavior might not be the cause of the earth's increasing deterioration. But that is no longer the case. The first step in accepting responsibility as God's partner in sustaining creation's health is to admit that *we* are a major cause of the crisis facing the twenty-first century: global warming. Denial is no longer possible. This first step is finally occurring, even in Western governments and oil companies.

The second step is to become informed about climate change. Doing so is not easy. Global warming is an incredibly complex phenomenon; in fact, it involves the most complicated, profound, and important systems on earth. It has no one cause; it has many feedback systems; and it has some unknowns. It is not something we *want* to be responsible for—any more than the generation that fought the Second World War wanted to do so. But it is our calling, our destiny, and our duty. It is the planetary agenda that faces all people, all religions, all fields of expertise, all professions of our time. The consequences of global warming will reach into every corner of the earth, from the decline of biodiversity to the desertification of land, from the spread of tropical disease to the flooding of cities, from the melting of ice caps to wars over food and water and the retreat of the wealthy to fortified spaces as the poor cry at the gates. The prospect of the earth's future in light of uncontrolled global warming by a number of sources is frightening, if not terrifying. But do we have a choice? Once we see who we are in the scheme of things—the neediest of all creatures and dependent on our planet's health for every breath we take, every cup of water we drink, every piece of food we eat—we realize that we *must* take care of the earth that is taking care of us.

One of the central tasks for the world's religions, including Christianity, is to attend to the image of human beings that functions in our society. Anthropology, the study of human beings and their place in the scheme of things, is the business of religion. Religions are central in forming the most basic assumptions about God and the world, and especially about human beings, for the cultures in which they exist. It is for this reason that we have undertaken in these pages a Christian vision of God and the world that is both deep within the tradition and relevant to our time. *If* people were to see themselves as living within God along with and for all other creatures, might we not have a vision of humanity that would encourage both responsibility and hope? Would we not see that *we are not alone*; rather, we are part of a magnificent creation in which all creatures are interdependent and all radically dependent on the source of their life and well-being? Would we not take courage—along with the great responsibility we now feel—*because* "there lives the dearest freshness deep down things," the Spirit of God, whose warm breast and bright wings are the hope of planet Earth?

What Is Our Task? Care and Hope

Surely, the most difficult task facing us as we finally acknowledge our responsibility for planetary health is summed up in one small word: *hope*. Is it possible to have any? The more we learn of climate change—the apocalyptic future that awaits us unless we make deep, speedy changes in our use of fossil fuels—the more despairing we become. Whether it is a 50 percent, 70 percent, or 90 percent reduction in carbon dioxide emissions worldwide that must be reached by 2050, it is a task that seems beyond our physical—and more important, our moral and emotional—capacity. It appears that we human beings do not have the *will* to live differently—justly and sustainably—to the degree necessary to save ourselves and our planet. The single most difficult obstacle to overcome is, then, our own lack of hope. This issue cannot be brushed aside. It is important to face the facts.

Increasingly, in popular media such as films and novels, we see pictures of the dystopia that awaits us in a future of profound environmental degradation. It will not be a world simply of less water, more heat, and fewer species of plants and animals; rather, it will be one of violent class wars over resources, the breakdown of civilization at all levels, and the end of certain facets of ordinary life that we have come to expect—the opportunity to have meaningful work, to raise healthy children, to enjoy leisure activities.

"Life as we know it," as we well-off North Americans have come to expect as "natural" and as our "right," will come to an end. The most ordinary activities that rely on access to basic resources will disappear: going to school, putting on parties, enjoying concerts, taking vacations, watering the flowers. The ordinary things that make up the fabric of our days and that we love are at stake. An environmental dystopia will be not only piles of garbage in the streets, violent gangs of thugs, new dangerous diseases, and constant fear for one's safety. It also will be the fraying of the most basic civilities between people, the undermining of solidarity and community, and in its place we can expect a raw, radical, and very sad form of individualism.

As we imagine this dystopia, as we begin to feel what life will be like on a daily basis, we are horrified. Most people do not allow themselves to imagine this possibility, claiming that it is an exaggeration, that human ingenuity can cope with the situation. But dismissal of the facts is becoming increasingly difficult: denial and rationalization appear to have had their day. We must allow our imaginations to begin to live within the world that responsible science is telling us will be our fate unless drastic changes are made soon. We must do this so that we can acknowledge where our hope really resides—not with us, but in the power of love and renewal that lives within the universe, the Holy Spirit, the Spirit of God.

As we consider the basis for our hope, let us recall who God is. We must and can change our ways, live justly and sustainably on our planet, because of God, not because of ourselves. The hope we have lies in the radical transcendence of God, a transcendence so transcendent that it exceeds all of our notions of transcendence. A "supernatural" transcendence—God as the highest being who controls the world—is a paltry view of transcendence compared with God as radically immanent to and with and for *everything that is*. God's transcendence—God's power of creative, redeeming, and sustaining love—is closer to us than we are to ourselves. God is the milieu, the source, of power and love in which our world, our fragile, deteriorating world, exists. The world is not left to fend for itself, nor is God "in addition" to anything, everything. Rather, God *is* the life, love, truth, goodness, and beauty that empower the universe and shine out from it. God is the reality of everything that is; hence, without God, nothing would be. Therefore, God is always present, always here (and there); we simply have to open ourselves to become aware of and acknowledge God's presence. This is the basis of our hope: the world is created, loved, and "kept" by God, as Julian puts it.

Thus, "mysticism" is simply this awareness of God's presence in and through and with everything for its well-being. Mysticism is not—or need not be—a one-on-one relationship between a human individual and God; rather, it is the acknowledgment that everything lives and thrives and rejoices—and grieves and dies—*in* God. Mysticism is radical incarnationalism, seeing God in the flesh *everywhere* and in all conditions of embodied life. Mysticism is the recognition that we are never alone—nothing is—for God is ubiquitous.

Julian's lovely story of the hazelnut sums up our hope: hope for the world lies with God, its maker, lover, and keeper.

> At the same time, he [God] showed me something small, about the size of a hazelnut, that seemed to lie in the palm of my hand as round as a tiny ball. I tried to understand the sight of it, wondering what it could possibly mean. The answer came: "This is all that is made." I felt it was so small that it could easily fade to nothing; but again I was told, "This lasts and it will go on lasting forever because God loves it. And so it is with every being that God loves." I saw three properties about this tiny object. First, God had made it; second, God loves it; and third, God keeps it. And yet what this really means to me, that he is the Maker, the Keeper, the Lover, I cannot begin to tell.[6]

This is the religious sensibility that allows us to hope, a sensibility that imagines the world as a hazelnut, held within divine love, trusting not in its own powers to "last," but in the never-ending creative, redeeming, and sustaining love of God. Surely we feel about our sorry, beleaguered planet as Julian did holding the hazelnut: "I felt it was so small that it could easily fade to nothing," but she was told that it *will survive* because God loves it. This is certainly an astounding statement of faith, a statement of radical hope. Hope is trust, trust in God—not in things, events, or people. To trust in God means God can be counted on to hold one's life and all life in trust, in safekeeping. It means that one can rest one's life—and the life of the whole planet—in God, knowing that this trust will *somehow* be honored. Although, as Julian acknowledges, what it means to say God makes, loves, and keeps the world, we "cannot begin to tell."

This, then, is an odd kind of hope. It does not mean that things will necessarily turn out "as we hope," nor does it mean that we will be successful in our attempts to "save" the planet, but it does mean that God will "make all things well," as Julian writes in her mysterious, enigmatic, and profoundly hopeful words. "It was in this way that our Good Lord answered all questions and doubts I might make, comforting me greatly with these words: 'I may make all things well; I can make all things well, and I will make all things well, and I shall make all things well; and you shall see for yourself that all manner of things shall be well."[7] Faith in God is the conviction that since everything lives within God—that the reality we inhabit is love—things will be "all right." But this sounds absurd, if not morally repugnant. How can "things be well" if people and the planet are dying from global warming? We do not know. We believe, however, that it is so, not because we will make it so, but because of God. This is not a sentimental or romantic hope that things will turn out okay, but rather the faith that *however they turn out*, the world and all its creatures are held, kept, within God.

Since reality is oriented, however obscurely, mysteriously, and circuitously, to the world's well-being, we *can* hope. We live toward this future, because we already know something of it—if we did not, we could not hope. We know it every day as "morning, at the brown brink eastward, springs." The small glimmers we have of hope—the return of flowers, the birth of a child, a compassionate deed—make us certain that this is the way things were meant to be and will be, *because* these reflections of God's love are shining forth in our world. Having hope is a sign that we are already on our way: we cannot know God apart from God; we cannot hope in God apart from the gifts of hope that God gives us in the most ordinary—and precious—moments of our lives. If we have hope, we have all things, for trusting in God means that nothing can separate us from the source of power and love in the universe.

Curiously, this faith, not in ourselves, but in God, can free us to live lives of radical change. Perhaps it is the only thing that can. We do not rely on such hope as a way to escape personal responsibility—"Let God do it"—but rather this hope frees us from the pressure of outcomes so that we can add our best efforts to the task at hand. It allows for a measure of detachment from goals so that we can focus on doing our part. It allows us also to reflect on God's way of loving the world, a way expressed in the Christian doctrines of incarnation, cross, and resurrection: God loves the world totally and completely. God gives everything, goes the limit, to be on the side of life and its fulfillment. But God does this in a way suited to us embodied beings who live in our physical "house." The story of Jesus Christ is the story of God incarnate, facing the worst that the world (human beings) can offer in terms of oppression and destruction, and rising to new life—the cross and the resurrection. It is a story that goes *through* physical horror, physical death: it is inclusive of the worst dystopia that we, in the twenty-first century, can imagine for our deteriorating planet—and yet it is the story of "the dearest freshness deep down things," of the bright wings of the Holy Spirit. The two major days of the Christian calendar—Christmas and Easter—are about hope and renewal. They are about new life. Christmas is the celebration of birth, the incarnation of God in the world; Easter is the celebration of rebirth, the world's rebirth. The resurrection is a yes to life against death, or perhaps more accurately, it is the recognition that death and life, life and death, are parts of God, who is all yes. Even death takes place within the Great Yes (though what this means, we "cannot begin to tell").

So on the one hand, it appears that it is impossible to despair, since we live (and even die) within God, within reality, which is love. Whether we are joyful or despairing, healthy, sick, alive, or dead, we live in love. Nothing can be totally negative or final or fearful (even despair and death), because everything happens *within* God's love. There is always hope that something else, something more, something good might happen (yes, even in death), because we live and die in God's world. In a sense, then, everything that happens, good or bad, happens to God also. There are no scraps, no leftovers, no tail ends of creation that do not rest in God; nothing is neglected or passed over.

But on the other hand, what of the evil, perverse, murderous, greedy events that we humans are responsible for? Even here, God is present—not as the power behind such events, but as the negative critique of them. God is incarnate as the Yes beneath all that is life and love and goodness and truth and beauty, and as the No in all that is cruel, perverse, false, greedy, and hateful. To practice the presence of God means to embrace what God embraces: life and love. But we must not shy from imagining the worst possible outcome of human behavior, a sickening, hopeless dystopia, and then we must put even this picture of the world where it belongs—within God. Whatever happens to us and to our world, however horrendous, happens to God as well. We are cupped within the divine hands, warmed in the divine breast, held close through our greatest fears, comforted when things go wildly wrong. If this were not the case, then we are indeed forsaken. When we need God the most, as we earthlings surely will in this precarious twenty-first century, we cannot *not* trust. Faith in God is faith that *no matter how bad things get*, somehow or other, it will be all right.

Julian's hazelnut story tells us that God made the earth, God loves it, and God keeps it—three phases of the ever-widening contemplation of the trustworthiness of things, of reality. The hazelnut story is a metaphor of rock-bottom trust that reality is good, that the direction of things is Yes. Everything is loved—the lamb *and* the tiger, the messiness and cost of evolution, all of the contrary events (from any particular perspective), and all of the darkness of life—and everything is "kept" by God (whether it lives or dies). These three moments are the ever-widening contemplation of the world as within God. Each moment is more difficult because it is more inclusive: it is hard to believe that everything is created by God, harder to claim that everything is loved by God, and harder still to trust that everything is kept—protected and cherished—by God. And yet this hope is the one thing needed as we face planetary living in the twenty-first century. "Nature is never spent" and "there lives the deepest freshness deep down things" *because* of the sustaining power and love of God, within whom the earth, our bent world, lives.

If we overcome denial concerning climate change and accept responsibility for it, we face the possibility of incapacitating despair. What Julian and Hopkins—and Christian faith—say is that we should not despair. God "keeps" all things, a new morning springs, the resurrection occurs. In the worst of times, people often say, "All we have is God." Indeed. Here "God" is the thread of hope that desperate people hold on to. God is that scrap of life and goodness still in us. God is what keeps us from giving up. God is not a being, but whatever life or love there is, no matter how small. We hold on to whatever shred of hope is left. It is very small indeed sometimes—but it is enough. "Because the Holy Ghost over the bent / World broods with warm breast and with ah! bright wings."

Notes

1. John Pick, ed., *A Hopkins Reader* (New York: Oxford University Press, 1953), 13.

2. McFague 1987:169–71. However, in *The Body of God*, I realize the importance of the model; see 1993:141ff.

3. Christopher Devlin, ed., *The Sermons and Devotional Writings of Gerard Manley Hopkins* (New York: Oxford University Press, 1959), 195.

4. Gerard Manley Hopkins, "The Blessed Virgin Compared to the Air We Breathe" (1883), in Pick, *Hopkins Reader*, 21.

5. *Random House Webster's College Dictionary* (New York: Random House, 1997), 1053.

6. Julian of Norwich, *Revelation of Love*, ed. and trans. John Skinner (New York: Doubleday Image, 1997), 10–11.

7. Ibid., 60.

19

Who Are We Human Beings?

This selection, from the final chapter of McFague's latest book, Blessed Are the Consumers, *brings together a number of strands from earlier writings and adds some new textures. In* Life Abundant, *she writes of God—reality—as love. Here, she expands this to speak of God as* kenotic *love, in keeping with the overall emphasis of this volume. Moreover, hearkening back to* Metaphorical Theology *and* Models of God, *she speaks of God in terms of friendship. What is most striking here, however, is not only how she uses these metaphors to speak of how we as human beings should be in the world but her introduction of yet another new metaphor, growing from her exploration of John Woolman, Simone Weil, and Dorothy Day: food.*

Source: 2013:199–203

We come, then, to the other crucial question of Christian theology: If God (reality) is kenotic love and creation is the pulling back of the divine to give others the chance to live and practice kenoticism in all its many forms, including the minimal ones of evolution, then who are we in the scheme of things? Again, I do not ask this question in general or "from above," but only from on the ground (looking at the experiences of our saints and our own experience) and only within the environment of "deep incarnationalism" or from the face of Jesus.

Archbishop of Canterbury Rowan Williams helps begin our conversation with his suggestive remark: "God gives God, having nothing else to give."[1] Hidden within this enigmatic sentence is a wealth of insight for a Christian anthropology. As we clearly see in the stories of our saints [John Woolman, Simone Weil, Dorothy Day], this is precisely what they "give." It is not only what God has to give, but also all that we each have to give. That recognition is the beginning of an understanding of who we are that emerges from seeing God as kenotic love. Since we are made in the image of God, then what we say about ourselves must be based on what we say about God. As we have discovered, God is love—not a "what" but a "who," not a being or object or individual but one who relates as subject to other subjects in a totally outgoing, self-emptying way. God is more a process than a thing: the concept of the Trinity is an attempt to describe this most basic activity at the heart of things. It is probably more appropriate to say with the early theologian Irenaeus that "God" is friendship rather than that "God" is an entity or substance. While I have insisted that only God can define *love*, friendship contains a suggestive characteristic that points us in the right direction. The singular characteristic of friendship is deep and abiding concern for the well-being of another. While erotic and even maternal love are dramatic and profound kinds of love, they still contain a note of egotistic satisfaction. Simone Weil calls friendship the highest form of love, for friendship alone focuses solely on the other, wishing the best for the friend even at one's own expense . . . [F]or her, "God is . . . the perfect friend," for the "infinite" nearness and distance of the Trinity epitomizes friendship.[2] In friendship, one gives oneself, for there is nothing else to give that matters, as the well-known comment from the Gospel of John states: "This is my commandment, that you love one another as I have loved you. No one has greater love than this, than to lay down one's life for one's friends" (John 15:12-13). The suggestion here is that "friendship," not erotic or maternal love but rather a more-or-less "cool" and "impersonal" relationship, is the closest human analogy to both Jesus' love for his disciples and God's love for the world (trinitarian love). The love that before all else is focused *on the other* regardless of the expense to the self appears to be the best hint we have of kenotic love.

Hence, . . . we begin our discussion of who we are with a *relationship*, the activity of self-giving that we see in our saints and that is epitomized in the life, message, and death of Jesus of Nazareth. Jesus, as the face of God, tells us that who Jesus "is" manifests itself in friendship with God—his will is totally open to God's will, wanting to do only what God wishes, no matter the cost to the self, even death on a cross. I have noted that the mysterious doctrine of the hypostatic union is a oneness of intentionality between God and Jesus, in which Jesus empties his own will in order to be filled with the will of God. Just as Jesus became one with God by living within and for God, so also the saints practice "deification," becoming "like" God by loving others with a total lack of self-regard. The implication here is not that we become God but that we become fully human, that is, capable of empathetic love to all other creatures, becoming true friends with God and all fellow creatures.

There are several characteristics of deification as an interpretation of authentic human living that help to flesh out what is meant by the term. It originated in Eastern theology, based on the cryptic statement by Irenaeus and used extensively by Athanasius and other early theologians—"God became man in order that man might become God." It is not meant to be taken literally: it does not mean that we will all become little "gods" and lose our humanity. Rather, the central insight was to stress continuity between who God is and who we are: in both instances, the intention is to underscore that God and human beings are not individuals, objects, or entities, but persons, subjects, and processes. According to this interpretation, God and human beings are not in competition but are part of the same story, a surprising tale that, contrary to our fears and expectations, claims that life is not meaningless, indifferent, or malevolent but good news, the friendship of God and the world. The real mystery and hiddenness of God is, as one theologian puts it, "the heart-stopping, breath-taking freedom of the three divine Persons to give themselves away in love to each other, and so to us and all creation—it is this which is truly incomprehensible."[3] And he adds a word about who we are in this story: "We become who we are as Christ came to be who he is, by giving self away freely in love."[4] Here we have the whole Christian story about God and human beings in a nutshell: what we learn from the story of Jesus about total self-giving love as the heart of the divine (as expressed in the Trinity) is also the heart of the human (as seen in Jesus and in the saints): empathetic, self-emptying love. Thus salvation is deification in the sense that to be fully human is to grow into what we were created to be—the image or reflection of God. We attain this slowly through the journeys of our lives, as we learn through voluntary poverty to diminish the ego, opening ourselves to the friendship of God—divine self-emptying that we might flourish—and hence become, like God, instances of empathetic attention to all others at every level of our personal and public lives. We do not do this on our own—our wild space gives glimmers of it that, if we will accept the invitation to live outwardly, for the world and others, rather than just inwardly, for ourselves, can be the beginning of a friendship with God in which we are gradually able to invite all others into this circle of friends.

In addition to deification being a story of continuity between persons (the "I" and "Thou" of all subjects in the universe), it is also an ontological rather than just a moral story. That is, this story tells us about reality, not just about how to behave. It claims that reality is this way: from its primordial cosmic beginnings with the simplest of "subjects" to its ultimate Subject, the Trinity, deification is the attempt to express the pattern of becoming like God through the various levels of kenotic foreshadowing in the give-and-take of evolution. We human beings are part of this story, and at least on our planet, an increasingly important part since we are the only creatures capable of living consciously according to the critical law of reciprocity, which allows earthly flourishing.

Friends give themselves, having nothing else to give. This could be a mantra for the three saints that we have been following throughout this book. This is perhaps the most astonishing and persuasive characteristic of the lives of Woolman, Weil, and Day. It is also at the heart of the enigmatic kenotic statements that in losing one's life, one finds it, which has been the thread we are following as religion's most important contribution to our twin crises of climate change and the unfair distribution of resources for survival. If a critical difference between the market-capitalist view of human life and a kenotic view is that the former claims that human beings are basically insatiable individuals concerned with the satisfaction of their own narrow egotistic desires, while the latter view claims that human beings, made in the image of God, can only find fulfillment by giving up themselves for the well-being of all others, then we can clearly see that giving oneself is the heart of the matter. The doctrine of the Trinity tells us that we have nothing to give but ourselves; friendship tells us the same thing. As we seek to understand the most central thing Christians say about human beings, we have to ask, What does it mean to give *oneself*? It can only mean our bodies; it can only mean food for other bodies. At the most basic level, the saints do not preach a gospel of sharing with needy others; rather, they give their own bodies that others might live. Thus, as Edith Wyschogrod puts it: "The saintly response to the Other entails putting her/his own body and material goods at the disposal of the Other."[5] Thus, at both ends of the giver-receiver relationship, it is not words or encouragement or gifts that are exchanged, *but the body itself and the means to keep bodies flourishing*. A deeply incarnational understanding of Christianity claims that at every stage—who God is, what creation is, who we are, and how we should live—the focus is on *embodiment*. Jesus gives himself in his life and message of empathetic love to others, gives his body on the cross in solidarity with all who suffer, and thus points to God as the divine giver par excellence, whose being is composed of persons, as movements of interweaving love. Likewise, creation is the pulling in of the divine self to allow space for others to live fully embodied, physical lives, and Christian discipleship is following the pattern we find in Jesus' life and in the Trinity of limitation, restraint, self-sacrifice of one's own body that other bodies might flourish.

If we were to reach for a single word that summed up kenotic love as the heart of Christian faith, it would be *food*. This lowly, mundane, physical, nonspiritual word appears again and again in the stories of our saints and in the Christian story itself. Food is the sine qua non of existence; it sums up the entire corporeal planet, which is created by energy and is sustained by food; the evolutionary story is the tale of who gets food and who does not; and wars increasingly will be fought over food. As we consider the dual crises facing our planet—climate change and unjust resource distribution—we see that they are all about food. If we take the mother-child relationship as a quintessential example of what we mean by compassion or empathy—responding to the deepest need of another—then the mother's giving food from her body to the infant can be seen as the model of radical kenotic love. It is no accident, then, that food appears so frequently in the Christian story and that its central ritual, the Eucharist, is a common meal in which the disciples give food to one another as Christ gave his body as bread and wine for all. As we recall the four stages of conversion from an individualistic view of the self to a universal view, we see the centrality of the body and of food: the first step—the wild space of voluntary poverty for well-off middle-class people is followed by a self-emptying that allows one's attention to move from its conventional focus on the self to the needs of others, especially deprived others, whether human or nonhuman. The defining characteristic of the universal self, the inclusion of all others in one's understanding of who one is, points to the stretching of one's own body (and bodily needs) beyond the limits of one's own skin: the world becomes my body, and I must therefore consider all the world's physical needs and not just my own.

We have seen this pattern time and again in Woolman, Weil, and Day. Woolman's dream could not be more physical, more bodily: he sees a "mass" of "human beings in as great misery as they could be, and live . . . and I was mixed with them, and . . . henceforth I might not consider myself as a separate being."[6] Weil's paralytic prayer expresses the body-food connection with eerie power: "May this love be an absolutely devouring flame of love of God for God. May all this [her mind, powers of sensation, and experiences] be stripped away from me, devoured by God, transformed into Christ's substance, and given for food to afflicted men whose body and soul lack every kind of nourishment."[7] Added to these comments is Day's little way, in which every last crumb and corner of her life at the physical level, from bad food to lack of privacy, is given to others, summed up in the most mundane of comments: "Above all the smell of the tenements, coming up from basements and areaways, from dank halls, horrified me. It is a smell like no other in the world and one never becomes accustomed to it. . . . It is not the smell of life, but the smell of the grave."[8] As Day apparently mentioned many times, Dostoevsky was painfully acute when he wrote: "Love in action is a harsh and dreadful thing compared to love in dreams." More than anything else that we could imagine, embodiment of the "dream" in one's own flesh is what is called for today. It is the central focus of Christianity's incarnationalism and should be, I suggest, the central focus of an ethic for our time of climate change (which will undermine the ability of the planet to feed its inhabitants) and unjust distribution of the food that the planet can provide. The classic doctrine of Christian discipleship, that, made in the image of God, human beings should embody the kenotic love of God, means that our own bodies must be on the line. In other words, food (and the whole planetary apparatus that goes to produce food for the billions of creatures) should become the central task at all levels, personal lifestyle changes, and public policies.

Notes

1. As quoted in Mark A. McIntosh, *Mystical Theology: The Integrity of Spirituality and Theology* (Oxford: Blackwell, 1998), 166.

2. Simone Weil, *Waiting for God*, trans. Emma Craufurd (New York: Harper and Row, 1951), 214.

3. Ibid., 194.

4. Ibid., 208.

5. Edith Wyschogrod, *Saints and Postmodernism: Revisioning Moral Philosophy* (Chicago: University of Chicago Press, 1990), xxii.

6. John Woolman, *The Journal of John Woolman and A Plea for the Poor* (New York: Corinth, 1961), 214.

7. Simone Weil, *First and Last Notebooks*, trans. Richard Rees (London: Oxford University Press, 1970), 244.

8. Dorothy Day, *The Long Loneliness* (New York: Curtis, 1952), 58.

20

Falling in Love with God and the World: Some Reflections on the Doctrine of God

This final selection, a 2013 essay that appears in Ecumenical Review, *in many ways summarizes much of what has been covered in this volume and brings it full circle. We hear more of the autobiographical experiences that have shaped McFague's understandings of God, including references to such influences as Karl Barth and Teilhard de Chardin. Issues of panentheism, the problems with traditional understandings of God, the world as God's body, and the more recent concern with kenoticism reappear. And, echoing the quotation that served as the epigraph for this volume's introduction, she asks once again, "What is the task of theology, and thus of theologians?" Here, she suggests that "theology at a time of deterioration due to climate change and financial inequality must focus on deconstructing and reconstructing the doctrine of God. . . . A primary task of theologians is to guard and encourage right thinking and talking about God and ourselves." And so, once again, the God-world relationship is set front and center, never reduced to a matter of just one or the other. The questions continue to be explored. The journey, the hike, proceeds onward.*

Source: From *Ecumenical Review* 65, no. 1 (2013): 17–34.

I have been asked to write an essay on the doctrine of God and ecology. It is a monumental task; it is also one that could be done in a number of different ways. But since I am almost eighty years old and my horizon is shrinking, I have decided to use my own story as the context of how the standard doctrine of God has changed into an ecological one over the last seventy or so years. My story and the rising up of the "ecological God" cover approximately the same time frame; hence, sketching the journey of the big story within my small one may provide a few modest but hopefully honest insights.

Seventy-three years ago I was seven years old and experienced God for the first time. Coming home from school one day, I suddenly realized that some day I would not "be here" for Christmas, and even more shocking, I would not be here for my birthday. I was becoming conscious that I was contingent, that I did not create myself, that I would not live forever, and that I was dependent on something else. I believe now that such a radical sense of nonbeing with the accompanying gratitude and awe at what did create me—and sustains me in life—is one of the quintessential religious emotions. It underlies a profound sense of radical transcendence and radical immanence that has been the theme of my religious journey and I believe is the central issue facing any Christian doctrine of God.

For me and for most of my cohort seventy years ago, it was the transcendent dimension that dominated our view of God and did so in a comfortably personal and often individualistic way, with a picture of God as a supernatural father who both judged and forgave his wayward children. My "theology" and the implicit theology of this era, the forties and fifties in the Western, Christian world, was unapologetically anthropocentric and anthropomorphic. God was the God of human beings, and especially individual human beings in their personal and public joys and woes. "Human beings" were essentially all the same under the skin as the *National Geographic* instructed us and loving your neighbor was practiced through charity and the Social Gospel.

At about the same time as my first experience of transcendence, I was also opening up to the natural world. My family owned a one-room cabin without running water or electricity on Cape Cod and I was free to run wild all day in the woods as long as I turned up for dinner. I fell in love with the world in a way similar to Annie Dillard's description of her waking up to it: "Children ten years old wake up and find themselves here, discover themselves to have been here all along.... They wake like sleepwalkers, in full stride; they wake like people brought back from cardiac arrest or from drowning . . ."[1] Such an awakening to the world was a conversion of equal strength and importance to my sense of radical contingency. Simultaneously, I was waking up to experiences of transcendence and immanence, but they were not connected. Years later when I read that Pierre Teilhard de Chardin at seven years old wrote that he had a passion for God and a passion for the world and could not give up either one, I knew my theological journey mirrored his.[2] However, it took many years before I could see the way that radical transcendence and radical immanence might be one. Along the way I met once again the transcendent God when, as a college sophomore, I read Karl Barth's preface to the second edition to his commentary on *The Epistle to the Romans*. Here he identifies himself with Kierkegaard's "infinite qualitative distinction" between time and eternity, "God is in heaven, and thou art on earth," claiming that this is the "theme of the Bible."[3] When I read these words I can recall feeling a conversion to a whole new level of what divine transcendence meant, blowing wide open my cozy view of a supernatural father who judged and forgave his wayward children. Radical transcendence meant the otherness of God in ways I had never imagined. But soon, while studying theology at divinity school in the fifties and sixties, I met the feminist critique of the distant, patriarchal, transcendent God and had my faith shaken: a supernatural being who controlled the world "in heaven" was not only not credible to me, but oppressive. Barth had given me the cold mountain wind of radical transcendence, but what of the world—that wonderful feel of earth on my bare feet as I ran in the woods, hunted turtles from a tipping canoe, and had close encounters with caterpillars and pine trees? What of my other love? There was no connection. Soon, however, with the help of my undergraduate degree in literature, I began to question the type of language that we were using to talk about God. It sounded like description, but I began to suspect it was metaphorical.

And it has been a long journey for me (and for many others over the last fifty years) to move toward an understanding of God and the world in which one's passion for the world and passion for God can come together. Like Teilhard de Chardin, I discovered that I did not have to give up either; in fact, as I experimented with the model of the world as God's body I came to see how loving the world *is* loving God. As a Christian, I no longer see God off in the sky (or even as an infinite abstraction), but as the spirit of the body we call the earth. God is always everywhere with each and every smidge of creation as the loving power of life to all in their sufferings and joys.

The world as God's body is a "panentheistic" understanding of God, in contrast to both theism (deism) and pantheism. In theism (and deism) God and the world are separate, abiding in different places (heaven and earth); in pantheism, God and the world are the same, without distinction. But in a panentheistic view, the world lives "within" God, insisting on the most radical transcendence and the most radical immanence. Teilhard's passions (and mine) are one, as expressed in the lovely prayer he wrote while contemplating his own death.

> After having perceived You as: He who is 'a greater myself,' grant, when my hour comes, that I may recognize You under the species

of such alien or hostile force that seems bent upon destroying or supplanting me. When the signs of age begin to mark my body (and still more when they touch my mind); when the ill that is to diminish me or carry me off strikes from without or is born within me; when the painful moment comes in which I suddenly awaken to the fact that I am ill or growing old; and above all at that last moment when I feel I am losing hold of myself and am absolutely passive within the hands of the great unknown forces that have formed me; in all those dark moments, O God, grant that I may understand it is You (provided only my faith is strong enough) who are painfully parting the fibres of my being in order to penetrate to the very marrow of my substance and bear me away within Yourself.[4]

When I first read that prayer I realized that it not only brought God and the world together in the most intimate and total way—taking my "matter" into God's own self, but it also "solved" the eternal life problem in a satisfactory way (at least for me). If we live within God now, then surely when we die we will simply live more *fully* in God, as God "bears me away within Yourself." What we cherish now—the God who is closer to us than we are to ourselves here on earth—will be even closer when we die. What more could we ask for or imagine? And what could convey better the passion for the world (in the form of one's own precious body) and the passion for God that is, I believe, the litmus test of a Christian doctrine of God. It is, in a nutshell, what the "incarnation," the central faith of Christianity, is all about. So, how does this religious journey translate theologically, and what pertinence might it have for ecology and climate change?

The Task of Theology

I propose now that we back up and ask the central question regarding a doctrine of God in and for our time. Whose responsibility is it to attend to such a task and what would a sketch of such an understanding of God look like? These two issues will occupy us for the rest of this essay. I will suggest a few preliminary comments. First, while the understanding of God in a culture comes about in a vast number of ways, I will take a narrow focus: What is the responsibility of a theologian in this task? I want to suggest that theology at a time of deterioration due to climate change and financial inequality must focus on deconstructing and reconstructing the doctrine of God. If theologians, who are some of the keepers and interpreters of this deep knowledge, allow false, inappropriate, unhelpful and dangerous notions of God to continue as our society's assumptions, we are not doing our job. A primary task of theologians is to guard and encourage right thinking and talking about God and ourselves. This, of course, is but one small task needed for the planetary agenda to change. Other people—doctors, car manufacturers, teachers, parents, corporate leaders, lawyers, politicians, agriculturalists, and so on—also have important offerings to make in our struggle against climate change. The particular task of theologians is prior to our action; it is at its roots. It is a limited task and mainly a linguistic one: suggesting different language for talking about God and ourselves—with the hope that different action might follow. The limitations and possibilities of this task are perhaps best seen in the negative: if we do not change our basic assumptions about God and ourselves from one in which God and the world are separate and distant, can we expect people to change their behavior? If we know nothing else, do we have a choice?

Deep down, beneath all our concepts and ideas about ourselves, is a sense, a feeling, an assumption about "who we are." This is not a question people commonly ask of each other—or of themselves—anymore than they ask one another, "Who is God?" These questions are seen as too personal or too abstract or too intimidating for civil conversation. Nonetheless, they are the deepest questions of human existence and lie uneasily beneath any glib answers we might give, were we to be asked. However, we act all the time on the basis of these deep assumptions of who we are and who God is, even while not acknowledging that we even have such assumptions. When we respond with approval to an advertisement for an expensive car telling us that "we deserve the very best," we are implicitly acknowledging that privileged individualism is our assumption about human nature. When we say that God is interested in spiritual not secular matters (and therefore not in cars), we are implicitly confessing that we believe in a distant, uninvolved God.

Who I am and who God is are taken for granted in a culture: the answer lies with the unacknowledged and accepted conventions of what is meant by "I" (a human person) and "God." But it is the false conventional views of God and human beings that permit the continuing destruction of our planet and its inhabitants. The environmental crisis is a theological problem, a problem coming from views of God and ourselves that encourage and/or permit our destructive, unjust actions. For example, if I see myself (deep down) as superior to other animals and life-forms—a privileged individual (Western, white, educated, and so forth)—then of course I will act in ways that support my continuation in this position. If, as a human being, I am basically "on my own," then it is also "up to me" to maintain my superiority. This sense or feeling of separate and responsible individualism need not be conscious; in fact, it usually is not. Rather, it is considered by most privileged Western human beings to simply be the way things are. It is seen as "natural" rather than as a personal belief.

Likewise, if I imagine God (deep down) to be a superbeing, residing somewhere above and apart from the world, who created and judges the world but otherwise is absent from it, then I will conduct my affairs largely without day-to-day concern about God. If the God I believe in is supernatural, transcendent, and only intermittently interested in the world, then this God is not a factor in my daily actions. Whether or not I treat myself to that expensive car is certainly not relevant to such a God.

So, we are suggesting that *who* God is and *who* we are must be central questions if we hope to change our actions in the direction of just, sustainable planetary living. It is useless to censure people for their actions when the roots of those actions lie in deep, unexamined assumptions. The problem lies in our theologies and our anthropologies. The problem, as many have pointed out, is a "spiritual" one, having to do with our *will* to change. We already know more than enough about the disaster ahead of us—having more knowledge (or technology) will not solve the problem. Only changing human wills can do so.

But is this possible? It is not sufficient "to know the good" in order "to do the good." While the Greeks believed this, St. Paul knew better, and most of us think Paul is the better realist. So why bother with new theologies and anthropologies? Aren't they just more "knowledge"? Yes and no. Yes, because obviously they fall into the category of knowledge, but no, because it is a peculiar kind of knowledge, the deepest possible kind—who we are and who God is. If we change these basic assumptions, our behavior may change as well. To be sure, it will not happen necessarily, easily, or universally, but it can and might happen. Or to put it negatively, unless *another* option becomes available to us, we have nothing to choose but the conventional view of God and ourselves, a view that is destructive of ourselves and our planet.

Who Is God?

If we are in agreement that the understanding of God is not a description but an interpretation and that interpretations can influence our behavior, then let us look at a major model of the relationship between God and the world that has been traditional and is still current in much Western theology. We recall that our task in this essay is to trace the movement over the past century toward a model of God that expresses both divine immanence and divine transcendence in the most radical way. Such an understanding of God would encourage us to love both the world *and* God, or more accurately, to love the world *in* God. We are reaching for a doctrine of God that tells us that loving the world *is* loving God.

THE TRADITIONAL DOCTRINE OF GOD

The classical view certainly does not do this. The First Vatican Council (1869–70) expresses the God-world relationship that, with some variations, is a common one in major creeds of various Christian churches since the Reformation and which lies behind the traditional creation story.

> The Holy, Catholic, Apostolic, Roman Church believes and confesses that there is one true and living God, Creator and Lord of Heaven and earth, almighty, eternal, immense, incomprehensible, infinite in intelligence, in will, and in all perfection, who, although He is one, singular, altogether simple and unchangeable spiritual substance, must be pure and distinct in reality and essence from the world, most Blessed in Himself and of Himself, and ineffably most high above all things which are or can be conceived outside Himself.[5]

Given this view of the God-world relationship—one of total distance and difference—the story of creation and providence follows. That story, in its simplest form, claims that an absolute, all-powerful, transcendent God created the world (universe) from nothing for entirely gratuitous reasons. God did not need creation nor is God internally related to it: it was created solely for God's glory. Unfortunately, creation "fell" through the pride of one of its creatures—human beings—making it necessary for God to initiate a reversal of creation's downfall through Jesus Christ, who atones for the sins of all human beings. In this story creation and providence are part of one coherent, historical, all-inclusive drama in which *God is in charge* from beginning to end, creating all things and saving them through the atoning blood of his own Son.

This mythic story focuses on God's actions—God is the protagonist of the world drama—and its purpose is to answer Why not Where questions. The story speaks to our concerns about why the world was made, who is in charge of it, why it is no longer harmonious, and how it is made "right" again. This story does not speak to our interest in the world or how we should act toward our neighbors. Human beings are, in fact, minor players in the classic Christian story of creation and providence. Moreover, the action does not occur in our physical neighborhoods, the actual spaces and places we inhabit, but over our heads, as it were, in the vast panoramic historical sweep of time, with its beginning (creation), middle (redemption), and end (eschatology). In each of these events God is totally in charge; we, at most, like good children are grateful to our all-mighty, all-loving Father and try to follow his will. Even when sin and evil divert the drama from its triumphant course (and cause us to lose faith and hope), the Lord of history will prevail, the King will be victorious.

What is left out of this story of creation is creation itself, that is, "the neighborhood," the lowly, concrete, particular—and fascinating, wonderful—details of physical reality. It is about history, not geography: about God's action through the sweep of time, not about our life on planet earth. In fact, the story does not seem to be *about* creation, but about a God whose "spiritual substance . . . is to be declared really and essentially distinct from the world." This God does not inhabit creation; in fact, the assumption behind this creation story is that spirit and matter are entirely distinct and in a dualistic, hierarchical relationship. God, and all things spiritual, heavenly, and eternal, are perfect and exalted above all things material, earthly, and mortal, with the latter being entirely different from the former and inferior to it. It is difficult to overstate the importance of this assumption—the dualistic, hierarchical relationship of God and the world—for it encourages not only an understanding of salvation as the escape of individuals to the spiritual world, but also justifies lack of attention to the flourishing of this world. If God is spirit and creation is matter, then God does not occupy the earth and we need not attend to it either. But what if spirit and matter were not entirely different; what if all life—God's and ours, as well as that of all others on earth—was seen to be on a continuum, more like a circle or a recycle symbol, than like a dualistic hierarchy? What if spirit and matter were intrinsically related, rather than diametrically opposed? Would not this make a difference in how we thought of *where God is* and *where we should be*? Would it not turn our eyes to the earth, whether we were searching for God or trying to understand where we belong?

The traditional model of God and the world does have the advantage of underscoring divine transcendence. It sees the relationship between God and the world as one in which the divine, all-powerful king controls his subjects and they in turn offer him loyal obedience. It underscores the "godness" of God, for the monarchical imagery calls forth awe and reverence, as well as vocational meaningfulness, since membership in the kingdom entails service to the divine Lord. The continuing power of this model is curious since contemporary members of royalty scarcely call up responses of awe, reverence, and obedience, but its nostalgic appeal, as evidenced in the gusto with which we all sing Christmas carols that are rife with this imagery, cannot be underestimated. Any model that would attempt to criticize it ought to look carefully at the main reason for its attraction: it underscores and dramatizes divine transcendence. In other words, it accomplishes one of the tasks of a model of the God-world relationship: it emphasizes the power and glory of God.

Nonetheless, this model has several problems, the first being that the model of God as king is "domesticated" transcendence, for a king rules only over human beings, a minute fraction of created reality. The king/realm model is neither genuinely transcendent (God is king over one species recently arrived on a minor planet in an ordinary galaxy) nor genuinely immanent (God as king is an external superperson, not the source, power, and goal of the entire universe). Moreover, a king is both distant from the natural world and indifferent to it, for as a political model, it is limited to human beings. At most, nature enters this model only as the king's "realm" or "dominion," not with all the complexity, richness, and attention-grabbing qualities of the living, mysterious creation of which we are a part. Moreover, the hierarchical nature of the model encourages human beings to act like kings in relation to the rest of creation: we are to subdue and dominate it.

The king-realm model would not be so harmful if it were not also hegemonic; that is, for many Christians it (along with the father-child model) literally *describes* the divine-world relationship. It is not for them a model—that is, one good, useful way of talking about the God-world relationship (while admitting there are other ways)—but *the* one and only way. Both of these favorites, the king-realm and the father-child model, exclude the natural world, they exclude the neighborhood we need to pay attention to. Models are dangerous as well as helpful and necessary, for they only allow us to see what they want us to. If the God-world relationship is not expressed in models that include the natural world—God's love for it and our responsibility for it—then, we ignore it: the "world" will mean the human world, either personally or politically. What model of God and the world might help us to see loving God and the world *together*?

THE WORLD AS GOD'S BODY

We take as our text Augustine's words expressing his sense of the God-world relationship.

> Since nothing that is could exist without You, You must in some way be in all that is; [therefore also in me, since I am]. And if You are already in me, since otherwise I should not be, why do I cry to You to enter into me? . . . I should be nothing, utterly nothing, unless You

> were in me—or rather unless I were in You 'of Whom and by Whom and in Whom are all things.' So it is, Lord. So it is. Where do I call You to come to, since I am in You? Or where else are You that You can come to me? Where shall I go, beyond the bounds of heaven and earth, that God may come to me, since He has said: 'Heaven and earth do I fill.'[6]

If God is always incarnate—if God is always in us and we in God—then Christians should attend to the model of the world as God's body.[7] For Christians, God did not become human on a whim; rather, it is God's nature to be embodied, to be the One in whom we live and move and have our being. In Christianity, the God-world relationship is understood in light of the incarnation; hence, creation is "like" the incarnation. Jesus Christ is the lens, the model, through whom Christians interpret God, world, and themselves. The doctrine of creation for Christians, then, is not different in kind from the doctrine of the incarnation: in both God is the source of all existence, the One *in whom* we are born and reborn. In this view, the world is not just matter while God is spirit; rather, there is a continuity (though not an identity) between God and the world. The world is flesh of God's "flesh"; the God who took our flesh in one person, Jesus of Nazareth, has always done so. God is incarnate, not secondarily but primarily. Therefore, an appropriate Christian model for understanding creation is the world as God's body. This is not a description of creation (there are no descriptions); neither is it necessarily the only model; it is, however, one model that is commensurate with the central Christian affirmation that God is with us in the flesh in Jesus Christ and it is a model that is particularly appropriate for interpreting the Christian doctrine of creation in our time of climate change. Its merits and limitations should be considered in relation to other major models of the God-world relationship.

The world as God's body is appropriate for our time (as well as being in continuity with the Christian incarnational tradition) because it encourages us to focus on the neighborhood. It understands the doctrine of creation not to be primarily about God's power, but about God's love: how we can live together, all of us, within and for God's body. It focuses attention on the near, on the neighbor, on the earth, on meeting God not later in heaven but here and now. We meet God in the world and especially in the flesh of the world: in feeding the hungry, healing the sick—and in reducing greenhouse gases. An incarnational understanding of creation says nothing is too lowly, too physical, too mean a labor if it helps creation to flourish. We find God in caring for the garden, in loving the earth well: this becomes our vocation, our central task.

Climate change, then, becomes a major religious, a major Christian, issue. To be a Christian in our time, one must respond to the consequences of global warming.

Another implication of the model of creation as God's body is that it radicalizes both God's transcendence and God's immanence. This model has been criticized by some as pantheistic, as identifying God and the world. I do not believe it is. If God is to the universe as each of us is to our bodies, then God and the world are not identical. They are, however, intimate, close, and internally related in ways that can make Christianity uncomfortable, when it forgets its incarnationalism. But we Christians should not shy away from a model that radically underscores both divine transcendence and divine immanence. How does it do so?

In the world as God's body, God is the source, the center, the spring, the spirit of all that lives and loves, all that is beautiful and true. When we say "God," that is what we mean: we mean the power and source of all reality. *We* are not the source of our own being; hence, we acknowledge the radical dependence of all that is on God. This is true transcendence: being the source of everything that is. Our universe, the body of God, is the reflection of God's being, God's glory; it is the sacrament of God's presence with us. The most radically transcendent understanding of God is, then, at the same time the most radically immanent understanding. Because God is always incarnational, always embodied, we can see God's transcendence *immanentally*. Meeting God is not a momentary "spiritual" affair; rather, God is the ether, the reality, the body, the garden *in which we live*. God is never absent; God is reality (being); everything that has being derives it from God (we are born of God and reborn by God). The entire cosmos is born of God, as is each and every creature. We depend on this source of life and its renewal absolutely. We could not live a moment without the gifts of God's body—air, food, water, land, and other creatures. To realize this is an overwhelming experience of God's transcendence; it calls forth awe and immense gratitude. Yet, at the same time, as Augustine puts it, God is closer to us than we are to ourselves. Where can we go where God is not, since God fills heaven and earth: "I should be nothing, utterly nothing, unless You were in me—or rather unless I were in You . . ." The God whom we meet through the earth is not only the source of my being, but of all being. We see glimmers of God in creation (God's body) and we see the same God more clearly in Jesus Christ, the major model of God for Christians.

A further implication of our model, then, is that is allows us to meet God in the garden, on the earth, at home. We do not have to go elsewhere or wait until we die or even be "religious." We meet God in the nitty-gritty of our regular lives, for God is always present in every here and now. This implication underscores that since God is here in our world, then surely it is indeed our neighborhood, our planet and its creatures, that we should be caring for. The significance that the transcendent God is with us cannot be overestimated as we struggle to care for the earth. It means that we are not alone as we face the despair that creeps over us when at last we acknowledge our responsibility for climate change. We do not face this overwhelming problem on our own: God is with us as the source and power of all our efforts to live differently.

THE INCARNATE GOD

At the outset of this essay I mentioned that a passion for the world and a passion for God is the litmus test of a Christian doctrine of God. The reason this is so is that Christians do not start talking about who God is "in general," but always in relationship to the message, life, and death of Jesus of Nazareth. What does the story of Jesus tell us about God? Most essentially, it tells us that God does not "exist" in another world; rather, "God" is what/who makes this world go round. "God" is knowing that I owe my life to Something, Someone other than myself. What we learn from the life and witness of Jesus is that the questions "Where is God?" "How great is God?" "Is God with us here on earth?" are not abstract, useless questions but at the heart of what Jesus tells us of God. "God" is not, on this reading a distant, minimal, supernatural being but, rather, God is another name for "reality," for the reality that actually creates, fuels, sustains, and saves all life. The lives of saints witness to this God at both the macrocosmic and the microcosmic levels. At the macrocosmic level God is the Yes that the scientific story does not give us—God is not only the source of life but its direction toward flourishing. At the microcosmic level God is also the Yes that helps each of us get out of bed in the morning and keep going. "God" is the plus in life, the "extra" that makes life worth living. "God" is why the earth is not flat and sterile, why it shines with glory. "God" is that specific Something/Someone that keeps us from sinking every day, who lifts us out of the pit of despair. "God" is everything and anything that is good, true, and beautiful. Does this mean that God is everything and therefore the world is nothing? No, but God is the Yes (however small) to all the big No's—the No to slavery, to starvation, to market capitalism, to war, and to climate change. Is God, then, merely human hopefulness? No, because folks who protest these No's do not believe that hope comes from themselves, no matter how dedicated their efforts. Rather, hope comes *to* us. We are not the source or strength of any of our efforts toward justice and sustainability. At most, we can try to move our narrow egos out of the way so that we can become channels of God's loving power for saying No to all that diminishes life and Yes to all that promotes it. We are the receivers, the listeners, the admirers, the grateful ones. We live within a world "cupped" within the hands of God, who is all things good, true, and beautiful. We did not create any of this and we cannot live apart from What/Who did.

Starting with the most immediate, personal, and daily experiences of that Something/Someone beyond us but within whom we live from breath to breath—what I read as the story of Jesus and the experience of our saints (and know from my own spiritual journey)—embraces both the beauty and the suffering of the world. These experiences are not a "foundation," a claim to truth about the theology that follows. On the contrary, they are a recognition that all statements about God rest on the shaky sands of human experience, but nonetheless, such experiences *are* intimations of God. Neither beauty or suffering is sufficient alone: beauty and suffering are both routes to God, the beauty of the world that causes us to exclaim with wonder and gratitude just for another day in this glorious place and the suffering of millions of individuals and species, human and nonhuman, both by accident and by intention that likewise causes us to exclaim, but now in horror and unbelief, that such waste and cruelty are possible. "God," then, is first of all not a "being" (no matter how great) but the slow (or sudden) experience that makes us aware that we are not alone—and that we are living in the world of Yes. Julian of Norwich's enigmatic words reach out trying to express this: all will be well. The Christian Easter attempts to say the same thing: all it says is that while we do not know how or what will be "well," we know that it will be. It simply says that a Yes rather than a No rules and empowers the universe. This is all we need to know: it is the witness against our deepest fear—that despair, hatred, indifference, and/or malevolence is at the heart of things. We see glimmers of the Yes in the tiniest forget-me-not flower hidden under a mountain rock as well as in a piece of bread shared with a hungry person. This, not a "being" of any sort, is "God."

The Kenotic God

So we begin our sketch of a Christian doctrine of God not with the creation of a world separate from God, but with the history—the "face" of Jesus of Nazareth, his message, actions, and especially his cross. Here, Christians, those who base their lives on faith in Jesus as a limited but persuasive revelation of God, claim that the first thing to say about God is self-emptying love. Jesus' whole life was a lead-up of total giving to others, culminating in the cross where he sacrificed his life, not for the atonement of humanity's sins, but as a witness to the totally unexpected and overwhelming gift of God's own self as the answer to our questions about who we are and how we should live. The cross of Jesus tells us that God's own life is also our life (for we were made in the "image of God" to live as God lives). And the most important characteristic of God's life is "love." Here, we have the one word that we use to talk about God that is not a metaphor; that is, every other word we use to express the divine reality is something drawn from our world and used—stretched—to function somehow for God. Thus, when we call God Father or Mother or the body of the world, and so forth, we are taking meanings that we understand and substituting them for the silence that inhabits God-talk. We do not know how to talk about God, so we use metaphors from ordinary life. But with this one word—love—we make a statement that is open, blank, unfilled: we need God to define what "love" means. And this, I believe, is where "faith" enters: "faith" is not belief that God "exists," that God is a "being" (even of the highest sort). Rather, "faith" is the willingness to turn to the "face" of Jesus of Nazareth for intimations of what "love" means.

And here we find a strange thing. Rather than the traditional story of an absolute, all-powerful God who relates to the world by controlling and demanding its allegiance, we see God as the one who relates to the world in a new and astounding way: as self-giving love for the well-being of all creatures. The Christian tradition has called such total self-sacrificing love "kenotic" (after the Greek word for "emptying"). We have hints of this kind of love in the saints, sometimes in mother love, and here and there even in the biological world where give and take, reciprocity, sacrifice, and even hints of altruism emerge (as we have seen), but it is in the story of Jesus that Christians find both the fulfillment and the paradigmatic expression of this countercultural love.

But the kenotic theological story does not stop with Jesus—it points to God in God's self. The doctrine of the Trinity—that seemingly abstract and often irrelevant notion that God is "three in one"—becomes central at this point. This is the case because Christianity is not Jesus-worship; it is not about him, but about God, and not just about how God relates to the world but how God is in God's self. Thus, the doctrine of the Trinity—a subject that has often been used to illustrate the esoteric irrelevance of the Christian view of God: How can "one" be "three"? "Do Christians believe in three gods"? becomes the center of a profoundly immanental understanding of divine transcendence. That is to say, rather than a conundrum to baffle people about who God is, the doctrine of the Trinity clarifies and deepens our understanding of God, if it is seen as the "face" of Jesus, as we have suggested. A wide range of theologians agree. Julian of Norwich, writing in the Middle Ages, does not mince words concerning this connection: "Jesus himself, as she sees him bleeding on the cross, is the source of her understanding of the Trinity."[8] Centuries later, John Haught, an evolutionary theologian, claims: "At the center of Christian faith lies a trust that in the passion and crucifixion of Jesus we are presented with the mystery of God who pours the divine self-hood into the world in an act of unreserved self-abandonment."[9] And Jürgen Moltmann adds: "The content of the doctrine of the Trinity is the real cross of Christ himself. The form of the crucified Christ is the Trinity."[10]

This is the first and most important point to make about a kenotic theology: our understanding of who God is comes not from "above," from an external or general source, from the common misunderstanding that "everyone knows who God is," which is often the opening comment of conversations about the nature of God. For instance, when scientists and theologians gather to discuss "God," an assumed generic view often prevails on the side of the scientists: God is a static, transcendent, distant, all-powerful superbeing dwelling in another world. If, however, the question of who God is starts with what Jesus did in his life, teachings, and death, we have a very different view, one in which, as Grace Jantzen says of Julian's view, ". . . since the revelation of God in Jesus is a manifestation of the totally self-giving suffering of love, this is also the most important fact about the Trinity."[11] Hence, it makes all the difference "where we start" to talk about God.

Moreover, it also makes a difference what we understand the work of Jesus to be. If it is primarily a sacrificial atonement on the part of an all-powerful God, then the Trinity is likely to be seen as the mechanism for this transaction: thus, as in Anselm's view, the Son, the "second person of the Trinity," sacrifices himself for the sins of his brothers and sisters in order to save them from divine punishment by the "first person," with the Spirit, the "third person," conveying the benefits to the faithful. Here the focus tends to be on the "persons" of the Trinity and their connecting tasks or functions. Thus, the Western understanding of the Trinity, deeply influenced by Augustine, underscores the "oneness" of God, with the three "persona" (traditionally called the Father, Son, and Holy Spirit) as functions, aspects, or modes of the divine oneness. The tendency is to see the Trinity as one substance with three natures in contrast to the Eastern view which claims that outside of the Trinity there is no God, no divine substance. The Eastern Christian view underscores the "threeness" of the divine, and in particularly, the *relationality* of the three. The result of these different emphases is that the Western understanding of God verges on an "individualism" for both God and humanity, while the Eastern view focuses on the process of giving and receiving. The first sees both God and humanity as "substances," separate beings, while the second sees them as "relationships," reciprocal processes of give and take. In other words, the

Western view of the Trinity supports a paradigm of God and the world as both characterized by static, individual substances or essences while the Eastern view assumes that life—for both God and the world—is a process in which relations are more important than entities.

The implications of the process view are significant. Here, "love" is not a property or characteristic of God, some attribute added on to God, but "love is the supreme ontological predicate," of both God and of us human beings, who are made "in the image of God."[12] In other words, we choose self-emptying love or nothing; we are not created beings who then choose love, even as God is not "God" who then decides to love. Rather, who God is and who we are is defined by love, by the self-emptying action of one into the other, of God into the world and of all parts of the world into each other. What it means to be a human being is simply to *choose* to be what one is: a participant in God's very own life of love. Thus, poetically, the Eastern view sees the inner life of God as a "eternal divine round dance" in which there is no inferior or superior, no first or second, but an eternal self-emptying and refilling of each by each. Here we see the glimmers of mutual reciprocity evident at all levels of evolution epitomized in the Godhead itself, now understood (for Christians who see God in the cross of Jesus of Nazareth) as the very nature of reality. The Eastern view of the Trinity is more suited to the task of conveying immanental transcendence, that is, radical self-emptying love as the heart of the divine, than is the Western view, although many, including Augustine with his view of that God is lover, beloved, and love itself have attempted to emphasize kenotic love.

A second implication of starting with the incarnate self-emptying love of Jesus, epitomized in the cross, is a different view of divine power. The tendency of monotheistic religions (Judaism, Christianity, and Islam) to provide support for the current radical individualism of Western culture, a view that as we have seen undergirds human domination of nature among other things, is aided by unqualified monotheism: as God dominates the world, so human beings, made in the image of God, should dominate the natural world. This view has supported centuries of human exploitation of nature, culminating in our current human-induced global warming from excess greenhouse-gas emissions. It is impossible to overemphasize the significance of monotheism's contribution to this customary stance of human beings, as it is often the unspoken assumptions of "who we are in the scheme of things" that has more influence than any explicit statements of "who we *should* be in the scheme of things." Thus, a radically different understanding of divine power—one in which "God" epitomizes total self-emptying openness to others, all others—is not only an indictment of the common view of power as control, but also a paradigm of "letting be" so profound and so inclusive that we are speechless to suggest what it means.

Buddhism's *sunyata*, the "God" beyond God; the mystic's prayer to free us from our desire to possess God; the statement by a Christian theologian that "the Godhead is profound and utter claimlessness"; and Meister Eckhart's suggestion that there is no God beyond the distinctions of the Trinity are all attempts to address this speechlessness. In this understanding, God "gives up" all names and properties, wary of all attempts to reach to the "emptiness" of God, acknowledging the breakdown of all human attempts to say what cannot be said—that "God" is *God*. Ursula LeGuin, the science-fiction novelist, published a nice piece in *The New Yorker* magazine some years ago in which she imagined Eve deciding to "unname" the animals, a first step toward overturning the exceptionalism of human beings in "naming" others, from the yak to God. LeGuin notes that "Most of them [the animals] accepted namelessness with the perfect indifference with which they had so long accepted and ignored their names." As she leaves Adam (who is wondering where his dinner is?) to join the other animals, Eve notes how difficult it is to name (and thus possess others): "My words must be as slow, as new, as single, as tentative as the steps I took going down the path away from the house, between the dark branched, tall dancers motionless against the winter shining."[13] May our words, before all else, "unname" those, including God, whom we have so glibly named and thus sought to control.

Thus, in summary, in the kenotic theological paradigm, there is continuity all the way from evolution to God and vice versa: one "reality" that is characterized at all levels by various forms and expressions of self-emptying. Hence, beginning with the incarnation of God in Jesus Christ, Christians believe that we have a paradigm of God, humanity, and the world that does not validate raw unilateral, absolute power at any stage or level of reality; rather, the inverse is the case. For "what makes the world go round" is mutual, interdependent sacrifice and self-emptying. Thus, one moves from this reading of the incarnation to an understanding of the creation of the world as God's gift of pulling back and giving space to others that they might live (but as the "body" of God, not as separate beings) and an understanding of human life as itself part of the divine life, but as its "image." We live by participating in God's very own life (since this is the only reality there is), but not simply as parts of God; rather, human life is learning to live into the relationality of God's own life, which is one of self-emptying love for *others*. Such a theology is not pantheistic (the identification of God and the world), but panentheism (the world as living—finding its source and fulfillment—*within* God's very self, the dance of self-emptying love that desires the flourishing of all life). It is a sacramental vision, in which the world is a reflection of the divine in all its trillions of individual life-forms and species; thus, as Gerard Manley Hopkins reminds us, "The world is charged with the grandeur of God," not as one shining explosion, but in all its tiniest parts, even the intricate workings of a mosquito's eye. The motto here is "*Vive la différence.*" We human beings are the one life-form that does not fulfill its role as being a bit of God's grandeur simply by existing; rather, we, made in the image of God, must grow into the fullness of that reflection of God by willing to do so. And, according to the kenotic paradigm, this is what "salvation" is—not release from punishment for our sins, but a call to relate to all others (from God to homeless persons and drought-ridden trees) as God would and does.

Some Concluding Thoughts

What have I learned in the seventy or so years since I first "woke up" at seven years old? First of all, I have learned to slow down and pay attention. In Jericho Park where I walk every morning I often stop and take in the sights, sounds, and smells of the trail, rejoicing in the present moment. I have learned to appreciate the sacrament of the present moment, how every bit of creation mirrors and indeed "rings out" that unique aspect of the divine that one is. What I have learned and rejoice in is that we do not live in two worlds, but in one: we live here and so does God! The world lives within, for, from, and toward God every minute of every day. Hence, we do not live now on earth away from God, but always, whether in life or death, we all live within God. Death is not to be feared nor is it the only time we meet God. God is the milieu of earthly existence and "heaven" is here and now. To live in heaven, one must practice the presence of God, but that is not impossible since we are constantly, everywhere and always, surrounded by God in our earth, God's body. Whether in pain or beauty, backache or a walk in Jericho, I live within God. My death will be a seamless transition to living more fully within God.

Let me reflect on this statement more fully. It began when I was seven years old and "woke up" for the first time. All my life since then I have been going in and out of being awake. Sometimes I was not able to stand the terror of it, and escaped as many others have into unconsciousness. Being truly awake means being objective, realistic, "facing the music." That is, it means facing death—one's own and the death of everyone and everything else. "Not being here" is the first revelation of being awake: everything one cherishes (including oneself) will *not be here* some day. No matter how powerful, how beautiful, how important, how noble, it will all pass away—and the question haunting the awakened ones is, *where* does it all go? Does it slide into nothingness, into nonbeing, or is there an alternative; namely, that everything lives forever within God, within love, within the mutual cosmic dance of self-emptying give and take?

To say Yes to this alternative is, I think, what "believing in God" means. It means that waking up, acknowledging one's radical contingency, is not just a cruel joke, but an invitation to participate consciously in the cosmic dance of self-giving love one to another, of accepting life as a gift, living that gift joyfully and gratefully, and then passing it along to others. One goes from the active to the passive stage of this dance. This means one must "let go" of the active phase, be willing to step back and let other dancers lead. However, one still plays a part—a part similar to a "nurse log," a tree that has fallen down and now allows oneself to serve as nutrients for others to have their turn to grow in the sun. As Teilhard says in his prayer on death, in the passive stage one allows God to part the fibers of one's being so as to bear each of us away within the divine self. So, "waking up," becoming a conscious human being, is an experience of both terror and beauty. One experiences the astonishing beauty of the world (from plankton to penguins, including human beings) along with the horror of losing it all. However, "believing in God" means that we all continue as a part, a nurse log, in the cosmic dance of self-giving love.

Notes

1. Annie Dillard, *An American Childhood* (New York: Harper Perennial, 1988), 11.
2. Pierre Teilhard de Chardin, *Writings in Time of War*, trans. Rene Hague (London: Collins, 1968), 14.
3. Karl Barth, *The Epistle to the Romans*, 2d ed., trans. Edwyn C. Hoskyns (London: Oxford University Press, 1953), 10.
4. Pierre Teilhard de Chardin, *The Divine Milieu* (New York: Harper & Brothers, 1960), 62.
5. First Vatican Council, "Dogmatic Constitution concerning Catholic Faith," in *The Sources of Catholic Dogma*, ed. Heinrich Denzinger, trans. Roy J. Defarrari (St. Louis: B. Herder, 1957), 443.
6. Augustine, *Confessions* 1.2, trans. F. J. Sheed (Indianapolis: Hackett, 1993), 3–4.
7. See McFague 1993 for an interpretation of this model. For a comparable development of the economic as well as the science/cosmological sides of the issue, see esp. McFague 2001, 2013.
8. Grace M. Jantzen, *Julian of Norwich: Mystic and Theologian* (London: SPCK, 1987), 109.
9. John F. Haught, *God After Darwin: A Theology of Evolution* (Boulder: Westview, 2000), 48.
10. Jürgen Moltmann, *The Crucified God: The Cross of Christ as the Foundation and Criticism of Christian Theology*, trans. R. A. Wilson and John Bowden (New York: Harper & Row, 1974), 247.
11. Jantzen, *Julian of Norwich*, 110.

12. See John D. Zizioulas, *Communion and Otherness: Studies in Personhood and the Church* (London: Darton, Longman and Todd, 1985), 46.
13. Ursula LeGuin, "She Unnames Them," *The New Yorker*, January 21, 1985.

Index of Names and Subjects

Abbey, Edward, 111
Anselm, 261
anthropocentric/-ism, xi, xxii–xxiii, 37, 45, 53, 135, 153, 162, 214, 215, 248
anthropology, xii, xiv, 48, 140, 142, 143, 145, 179–80, 192–93, 195, 208, 211, 227, 233–35, ch. 19 (passim), 252
anthropomorphism, 75, 86, 91, 135, 248
Apostles' Creed, 25
Aquinas, Thomas, xxv, xxvi, 49, 82, 90, 137
Aristotle, 57–58, 86, 104, 175
Arius, 29
arrogant eye, 107, 113–17, 119, 121, 128, 134
Athanasius, 243
atonement, 52–55, 174, 197–98, 253, 260, *see also* redemption, salvation; sacrificial/substitutionary, xii, 174, 198, 261; theories, 30, 55, *see also* deification
Auerbach, Erich, 20
Augustine, xix, xxv, 4, 29, 49, 51–52, 82, 90, 108, 136, 168, 182, 205, 255–57, 261, 262
autobiography, xii, xix–xx, 155

Barth, Karl, ix, xxi, xxvi, 17, 82, 195, 247, 249
Berry, Thomas, 122–23
Bethune-Baker, J. F., 29
Birch, Charles, xxviii
Black, Max, 78
Bonhoeffer, Dietrich, xix, xxiii, xxvi, 152–53, 205
Borg, Marcus, 205
Bornkamm, Gunther, 7
Buber, Martin, 116, 218

Bultmann, Rudolf, 34
Bunyan, John, 5

Calvin, John, 211
capitalism, market, xi, 141–42, 144–45, 151–52, 204, 244, 258
Catholic, xxi, xxvii, 108, 208
Christ, xix, xx, xxii, xxiii, xxvi, xxviii, 26, 27, 29, 30, 52, 53, 55, 64, 73, 77, 82, 99, 108, 137, 152, 162, 169, 182, 193, 195, 197–98, 202, 208, 211, 212, 232, 239, 243, 245, 253, 256, 257, 261, 263. *See also* Jesus
Christianity/Christian faith, xxi, xxii, 22, 25, 26, 28, 30, 39, 44–49, 64, 69, 81, 83, 85, 86, 91, 99, 100, 103, 121, 128, 130–33, 135, 137, 140–43, 149–52, 161, 168–70, 174, 181, 207, 235, 244, 246, 250, 256, 257, 260, 262
Christian(s), xi, xix, xx, xxii, xxiii, xxvi, xxvii, xxviii, xix, 22, 25, 26, 53, 57, 59, 75, 107–9, 113, 116, 117, 119, 124, 127–33, 135–37, 139, 141–42, 150–52, 161, 168, 182, 195–99, 203–5, 208, 211, 212, 219, 227, 232, 244, 255, 256, 257, 259–60, 262, 263
Christology, 17, 25, 73, 127, 174, 195, 198, 208, 227; economic ecological, ch. 16 (passim)
church, xxviii, 26, 30, 46, 74, 88, 108, 127, 151, 204, 253, *see also* community; models of, 55–60
climate change, xii, 134, 139, ch. 11 (passim), 155, 156, ch. 18 (passim), 244–46, 247, 250–51, 256–58. *See also* global warming
Code, Lorraine, 115, 118

community/-ies, xxvii, 55, 74, 97, 101–5, 132–34, 144, 146, 150, 153, 156, 172, 186, 190, 192, 202, 204, 205, 208, 213, 236, *see also* church; Christian, xxvi, 57, 59, of friends, 56–58; individuals-in-, 217–18, *see also* Trinity
community-of-care ethic, 127, 132
concept(s)/conceptual language, 8, 9, 15, 25, 26–28, 30, 34, 37, 51, 71, 76–78, 80–83, ch. 7 (passim), 98–99, 136, 162, 176, 189, 190, 212, 251
consumer culture/-ism, xi, xxiii, xxvi, xxviii, xxix, 134, 139–41, 143, 148–50, 152, 208, 215, 223, 229
cosmology/cosmological, xi, xiv, xxii, xxiii, 130, 141, 179–80, 191, 197
creation, xv, 11, 12, 26, 27, 42–45, 55, 62–64, 97–98, 115, 128, 153, 156, 161–62, 169, 179, 185, 196–98, 212, 214, 218–21, 224, 228–32, 234–35, 239, 241, 244, 253–57, 259, 263; common story of, x, 61, 95, 98–99, 179–80, 182, 184–88, 191, 193, 197, 219, 253–54
creed(s), 8, ch. 3 (passim), 88, 253. *See also* Apostles' Creed, Nicene Creed
cross, xxviii, 35, 39, 41, 162, 167, 170, 174–76, 195, 197, 206–7, 238–39, 242, 244, 259–62
Crossan, John Dominic, 149–50, 171, 202–4, 206

Daly, Mary, 135–36
Dante, 4
Day, Dorothy, xii, xix, xxv–xxvi, 3, 155, 160, 163, 205, 241, 244, 245
deification, xxviii, 30, 195, 197–98, 201, 206, 218, 242–43. *See also* salvation
Derrida, Jacques, 88
Descartes, René, 8, 100, 117
Dickinson, Emily, 109

Dillard, Annie, xx, 111–12, 123, 188, 207, 248
disciple(s)/-ship, vii, xiii, xix, xxviii, 54, 152, 202, 205, 207, 242, 244–46
Donahue, John, 72
Donne, John, 4–5
Dostoevsky, Fyodor, 245

ecology, 107, 140, 141, 146, 172, 233, 247, 250; deep, 117, 189–92
economics, xii, xiv, xxix, ch. 11 (passim), 156, 160, 162, 171, 173, 192, 211, 213, 221, 223, 225, *see also* capitalism, market; ecological, xi, ch. 11 (passim), 157–58, 198, ch. 16 (passim), 213, 215, 217, 219, 221, 223, 224; neoclassical, ch. 11 (passim), 201, 204, 213, 221–22
ecumenicity, 141, 146
Edwards, Jonathan, 48
Ehrlich, Gretel, 111
Eliot, T. S., 5, 18, 77
embodiment, x, 8, 15, 36, 37, 38, 52, 56, 57, ch. 5 (passim), 95, 98, 99–105, 107, 115, 117, 135, 153, 155, 161, 163, 182, 184, 196, 237, 238, 244, 245, 246, 256, 257. *See also* incarnation
Emerson, Ralph Waldo, 117
ethic(s), x, xiv, 22, 40, 45, 55, 63, 79, 97, 98, 107, 121, 130, 205, 222, 246; of care, environmental, 120–21, 134, 191, 192, *see also* community-of-care ethic; of God as friend, 55–60; of rights, 120; of sustainability, 129, 134, 146, 147–49, 152
eucharist, 46, 55, 99, 108, 151, 170, 204, 245,
evil, xxvi, 47–54, 95, 151, 196–98, 204, 220, 239, 254. *See also* sin
Exodus 33:23b, ch. 5 (passim)
experience, ix, xxi, xxv, xxvi, 8, 9, 22, 26, 28, 35, 38, 44, 76, 77, 79, 81, 82,

86, 89, 91, 92, 95, 100–105, 162, 168, 172, 207, 211–14, 218, 222, 223, 231, 241, 248, 257, 259, 265

faith, xix, xxii, 6, 15–16, 25, 29, 42, 43, 73, 81, 82, 89, 92, 93, 95, 99, 105, 128, 130–32, 140–41, 167–70, 202, 207, 212, 214, 217–19, 232–34, 237–40, 244, 250, 254, 259–61
feminism/feminist thought, x, 33, 83, 100, 101, 104, 109, 117–19, 122, 135–36, 168, 191, 214, 249
food, 35, 38, 44, 46, 108, 129, 150–51, 155, 159–63, 187, 190, 198, 203–204, 220, 231, 241, 244–46, 257
Francis of Assisi, 108–109, 127, 130, 135–36
Friedman, Thomas, 156
Frye, Marilyn, 114–15
Funk, Robert, 15, 19, 77

Gandhi, Mahatma, 157
Genesis, 11, 98, 128–29, 179
global warming, xii, 134, ch. 11 (passim), 156, 229, 234–35, 238, 257, 262. *See also* climate change
God: *see also* love, of God/divine; love, God as; model(s), of God; Spirit, Holy/of God; Trinity; as Being-itself, 34, 37, 216, 231, 232; as father, x, 33, 35, 39, 41, 42, 44, 56, 75–76, 77–78, 83, 86, 87, 91, 92, 260; as friend, x, 33, 34, 35, 38, 39, 40, 41, 44, 55–60, 75, 86, 91, 176, 242–44; kingdom/reign of, 22, 26, 28, 30, 69, 72–74, 81, 149–50, 171–73, 203–206; as lover, 33, 34, 35, 38, 39, 40, 41, 44, 47–55, 56, 58, 75, 86, 91, 176; models of, xii, ch. 4 (passim), 75, 92; as mother, 33, 34, 35, 38, 39, 40, 41–47, 56, 58, 75–76, 78, 86, 87, 91, 92, 176, 260; reality of, xxiv,

xxvii, 231–32, 236–39; as Subject, 129–30; traditional doctrine of, 253–55
"God's Grandeur" (Hopkins), 3, 5, 9–12, 14, 227–30, 239–40
Gould, Stephen Jay, 95–96
Griffin, Susan, 189
Gustafson, James, 179

Hartshorne, Charles, 36
Haught, John, 261
Hegel, G. W. F., 34, 101, 195
Herbert, George, 5
Heschel, Abraham, 124
Hick, John, 157
Hildegard of Bingen, 108
hope, xi, xv, 6, 70, 104, 106, 196, 201, 212, 218, 227–30, 232, 233, 235–40, 254, 258
Hopkins, Gerard Manley, 3, 5, 9–12, 13, 14, 15, 108, 227–30, 240, 264
"house rules," xxix, 143, 148–51

immanence, x–xxii, xxv, 11, 17, 33, 34, 37, 39, 61–63, 97, 115, 140, 153, 214–16, 218, 236, 248–49, 253, 255, 257, 260, 262. *See also* transcendence, immanental
incarnation/-alism, x, xii, xix, xxii, xxiii, xxv–xxix, 23, 62–65, 73, 107–8, 110, 112, 136–37, 153, 157, 160–61, 181, 195–98, 208, 212, 215, 218, 220, 223, 224, 230–32, 237–39, 241, 244, 246, 250, 256–59, 262–63
Irenaeus, 230, 242, 243

Jantzen, Grace, 261
Jeffers, Robinson, 156, 157, 190
Jeremias, Joachim, 17
Jesus, xii, xiv, xxvii, xxviii, 4, 17–20, 22–23, 26–27, 29–30, 41, 46, 52–56, 62–63, 69–77, 82, 121, 137, 149–51, 155, 161–63, 167, 169–77, 182, 197–98, 201–9, 211, 219–21, 232,

238, 241–44, 253, 256–63, *see also* Christ; as parable of God, 22, 25, 26, 30, 72–76, 82, 167–68
Johnson, Elizabeth, 135–36
Jonas, Hans, 117
Julian of Norwich, 196, 205, 230, 232, 237–38, 239–40, 259–61
Jülicher, Adolf, 17
justification, 81–82, 131–32, 137

Kant, Immanuel, 100, 101, 185
Kaufman, Gordon, ix, xxii, 34–35, 85, 90
Keck, Leander, 72
Keen, Sam, 3, 4, 5, 8, 12–16
kenosis/kenoticism, xii–xiv, 155, 157–63, 241–46, 247, 259–65
Kierkegaard, Søren, 5, 22, 249
King, Martin Luther, Jr., xix, 205

LaCugna, Catherine, 218
language, 3, 14–16, 20, 22, 26–28, 29, ch. 3 (passim), 35, 37, 39, 69–71, 74–77, 80–81, 86–92, 107, 118, 121, 155, 171, 176, 185, 218, *see also* concept(s)/conceptual language; credal, 27–30; for God (God-talk), viii, 3, 4, 5, 6, 12, 13, 14, 26, 39, 74–76, 87, 135–37, 249, 251, 260; for humans, 12, 251; metaphorical, 8–9, 12, 14–15, 22–23, 26, 37, 69–70, 77, 89, 92; theological, vii, x, 12, 15, 33, 76, 77, 92
LeGuin, Ursula, 83, 263
Leopold, Aldo, 111, 189–92
Lewis, C. S., 42
Lopez, Barry, 111
love, 6, 7, 39, 50, 55, 70, 116, 160, 161, 176, 190, 206, 211, 213, 229, 232, 233, 236, 239, 240, 260; agape, 41–47; agential model of God's, 214, 216–17, 224; deistic model of God's, 214–15, 249; dialogic model of God's, 214–15; divine/God's, x, xix, xxvi, xxvii, xxviii, 7–8, 33, 40, 42, 43, 45–48, 53–54, 56, 95, 162, 197, 206, 212–17, 219–21, 223, 229, 231, 236–40, 245, 249, 255, 256, 260, 262; eros, 42; for God, xxii, xxv, xxviii, 107, 127–29, 155, 157–58, 160, 205, 225, 245, 253; God as, xii, xxiii, xiv, xxv, xxvii, 153, 160, 175, 211, 212, 213, 214–17, 218, 224, 230, 232, 236, 238, 241, 259–60, 262; kenotic, xii, 160, 161, 241–46, 259–60, 261–62, 264–65; monarchical model of God's, 214–15; for nature: *see* nature, love of; for others/world, xxv, xxviii, 40, 48, 55, 56, 65, 107, 128–29, 131, 134, 155–57, 159, 160, 162, 174, 205, 206, 225, 242, 253, 264; organic model of God's, 214–17, 224; parental (maternal/paternal), 28, 40–47, 242, 260; philia, 42, 58; self-, 50, 53
loving eye, 107, 113–17, 119, 128–30, 132–33, 135, 137, 191
Lugones, Maria, 122
Luther, Martin, 168

Marcuse, Herbert, 14
Mechthild of Magdeburg, 230
metaphor(s), ix–x, 3, 6, 8–10, 12, 13–15, ch. 2 (passim), 26, 28, 29, 33, 36–38, 42–43, 45, 47, 55, 61–64, 69, 70–74, 76–83, ch. 7 (passim), 99–101, 105, 117, 135–37, 151, 155, 161, 167, 169–71, 175–76, 211, 215–16, 220, 227–28, 230, 239, 241, 260; dominant, 77, 80, 82–83; map or hike, viii, 122–24; personal, 34–40, 76; root-, 26, 30, 77, 81–82
metaphorical thinking, 70–73, 78, 83, 87
Midgley, Mary, 185
Milton, John, 5

model(s), x, xi, 26–27, 77–82, ch. 7 (passim), 100; classic, 61; defined, 77–78, 88; ecological, xi, 61, 118, 128; ecological economic, xi, ch. 11 (passim), 157–58, 198, ch. 16 (passim), 213, 215, 217, 219, 221, 223, 224; of God, 27, ch. 4 (passim), 175; organic, xi, 61, ch. 8 (passim); parental/familial, 28, 42–47, 76, 255; patriarchal, x, xi, 39, 83, 255; reason for adopting, 101–6; scientific, 78–79; triumphalist/royal, 35, 39, 45, 214–15, 255
Moltmann, Jürgen, 99, 261
Mother Teresa, 205
Muir, John, 189
Murdoch, Iris, 109, 110–11, 113, 116
mysticism/mystic(s), 34, 36, 127, 157, 162, 195, 199, 212, 231, 237, 263
mythology, 54, 174, 175

nature/natural world, xi–xii, xxi–xxii, xxvi, 10–11, 17, 37, 49, 95, 100, 102, 107, 108, 113–14, 117, 119, 122–23, ch. 10 (passim), 139, 141, 142, 144, 145, 148, 153, 157–59, 173, 181, 183, 185, 189–92, 212, 217, 221, 222, 228–29, 240, 255, 262; love of, ch. 9 (passim), 127, 128, 130, 139, 157; spirituality, xi, ch. 10 (passim); theology of, ch. 8 (passim); writing about, 111–13
Nelson, Richard, 190
Nicene Creed, 25–27, 30, 77, 85
Niebuhr, H. Richard, ix, xxi, 216
Nineham, Dennis, 85, 91

objectivity, 111, 116–17, 142
Ogden, Schubert, 37
Ong, Walter, 18–19

panentheism, xi, xxi, 61, 107, 195, 216, 247, 249, 264

pantheism, xi, 64, 216, 223–24, 232, 249, 257, 264
parable(s), ix–x, 4, 6–9, 15, ch. 2 (passim), 25–26, 28, 30, 41, 69, 72–77, 81–82, 167, 170–72, 174–76, 202, 205; *see also* Jesus, as parable of God; as metaphors, ch. 2 (passim), 69, 70, 72, 73, 76; of the Prodigal Son (Luke 15:11-32), 5–9, 10, 13, 15, 74; of the Wedding Feast (Matt. 22:1-10), 17, 20–22, 149–51, 203–4
"The Peach-Tree Monkey" (Keen), 3, 5, 12–16
Perrin, Norman, 18, 23
Plato, 104, 116, 117, 175
power, xxviii, 11, 35, 39, 41, 42, 44, 46, 48–51, 54, 72, 75, 97, 102, 104, 134, 161, 162, 168, 169, 176, 214, 216, 230, 231, 254, 263; divine/God's, xii, xix, xxv–xxvii, 12, 38, 40–43, 54, 63, 75, 89, 90, 92, 153, 162, 167, 175, 195, 197, 207, 215, 216, 218, 223, 228–31, 236, 238–40, 249, 253, 255–63
Protestant(s), xxi, 41, 42, 130, 136, 208, 217; Principle, xxi; prophetic witness, xxvii; sensibility, 70, 73–74, 82

Rahner, Karl, 29
Ramsey, Ian, 29
remythologizing, 33, 86, 89, 93, ch. 8 (passim), 131, 219, 224
resurrection, 26, 35, 40, 55, 174–77, 197, 206–8, 220, 238–40
restraint, vii, 157, 163, 244
revelation, xxiii, xxiv, 54, 99, 100, 105, 110, 112, 211, 259, 261, 265
Ricoeur, Paul, 81
Rubenstein, Richard, 4, 5, 8
Ruether, Rosemary Radford, 173
Russell, Letty, 168

sacrament(s), 52, 54, 55, 62, 103, 136, 190, 223–24, 230, 257, 264
sacramental thinking/sacramentalism, xxvii, 10, 69, 71, 72, 108, 127, 135–37, 208, 229–30, 264
salvation, xiv, xxv, xxvii, 26, 40, 50, 48, 52–55, 56, 82, 97, 152, 153, 161, 162, 167–69, 172–76, 181, 195, 197–98, 218, 224, 225, 254, 264, *see also* atonement; as deification, xxviii, 197–98, 206, 243, *see also* deification
sanctification, 131–32, 137
Schleiermacher, Friedrich, xxvi, 34, 82, 168
Schweichert, Russell, 113
Scotus, Duns, 12
Sellar, Anne, 122
sin(s), xiv, xxv, xxviii, 26–27, 41–42, 47–55, 60, 78, 88, 131–32, 151, 157, 160, 169, 170, 172, 174–75, ch. 14 (passim), 195–98, 201–2, 204, 206, 207, 221, 214–15, 221, 224, 253, 254, 260–61, 264; against humans/us vs. us, 182–84; against nature/us vs. it, 189–93; against other animals/us vs. them, 184–89
Smith, Adam, 144
Snyder, Gary, 190
Soelle, Dorothee, 212
Spelman, Elizabeth, 122
spirit, 47, 61, 172, 185, 221, 254
Spirit, Holy/of God, 25, 26, 35, 61, 88, 189, ch. 15 (passim), 215–17, ch. 18 (passim), 249, 254, 256–57, 261
spiritual/-ity, xxvi, 7, 45–47, 50, 78, 107, 123, 131, 132, 151, 153, 155–60, 180, 181, 183, 199, 204, 205, 222, 230, 233, 251–54, 257, 259; nature, xi, 97, chap. 10 (passim)
subject-object(s) model, xi, 111, 112, 115–19, 121, 122, 127–28, 130, 217

subject-subject(s) model, xi, 107, 111, 112, 115–23, 127–37, 214, 217, 242–43
suffering(s), xxviii, 51–53, 59, 64, 137, 153, 191, 195, 197, 203, 233, 249, 259, 261

table fellowship, 41, 56, 167, 170, 172, 174–76
Teilhard de Chardin, Pierre, xxvii, 5, 36, 95, 98–99, 157, 205, 247–50, 265
Teresa of Avila, xxv, 205
theodicy, 51–52
theology/-ies, vii, xix–xxi, xxvi, 4, 12, 14–16, 27, 46, 69, 74, 75, 76, 79, 83, 85–86, 88, 98, 130, 141, 153, 155, 160, 162, 167–70, 198, 209, 181, 208, 212, 225, 241, 243, 247, 252, 259; constructive, xx, 86, 88–91; feminist, x, 33, 168; hermeneutical, 89; incarnational, 108, 110, 112, 160, 181, 232; kenotic, xii, 155, 160–63, 261, 264; liberation, 109, 168–73, 204, 224; metaphorical/heuristic, xiii–xiv, 4, 28, 30, 37, 39, 57, ch. 6 (passim), 86, 88–93, 167–68, 176; natural, 97–99, *see also* nature, theology of; systematic, x, 9, 15, 77
Tillich, Paul, xxi, 34, 41–42, 85, 90
Tolstoy, Leo, 18
tradition(s), 9, 13, 14, 15, 25, 34–39, 45, 46, 50, 62, 70, 74, 76, 80–83, 88–91, 93, 97, 99, 100, 103, 104, 108, 120, 133, 156, 157, 168, 205, 214, 224, 235; Christian, 4, 15, 46, 49, 62, 75, 76, 82, 83, 86, 97, 103, 107, 135, 167, 172, 180–81, 90–91, 103, 107, 135, 167, 172, 180–81, 197, 212, 217, 218, 231, 256, 260; Jewish/Hebrew, 62, 75, 103, 181, 217; Judeo-Christian, 20, 34, 38, 45, 47, 75, 89, 90
transcendence, x, xi, xxii, 17, 50, 61, 69–70, 113, 115–16; of God, xxi,

xxv–xxvii, 39, 61–64, 97, 153, 214–16, 218, 248–49, 252–55, 257–58, 260–61; immanental, x, xxii, xxv, 17, 33, 63, 140, 215, 257, 260, 262
trinitarian formula/model, 25, 26, 29, 218, 227, 242
Trinity, xii, 42, 88, 160, 218–19, 227, 228, 232–33, 242–44, 260–62; as creator, liberator, sustainer, 218–23

Via, Dan, 8

Walker, Alice, xxi, 110, 111, 124
Watts, Alan, 191
Weil, Simone, xii, 110, 155, 160, 163, 241, 242, 244, 245
Wheelwright, Philip, 9
White, Lynn, 142
Wilder, Amos, 18, 20
Williams, Rowan, 241
wonder(s), xx, xxi, 44, 51, 62, 64, 110, 111, 112, 186–89, 213, 234, 259
Woolman, John, xii, xix, 3, 5, 155, 160, 163, 205, 241, 244, 245
world, xi, xii, xxii, xxiii, xxiv, xxv, xxvi–xxix, 6, 8, 10–12, 14, 16, 18, 21, 25, 27, 35, 45, 49, 51, 54, 55, 56, 58, 59, 60, 63, 71, 73, 74, 75, 79, 82, 90–93, 95, 100, 104, 108–15, 117–23, 127–28, 130, 136, 127, 141, 144, 147, 150–51, 153, 155–57, 160–61, 171–72, 175–76, 181–82, 195–98, 202, 204–8, 212–13, 219, 221–22, 224, 229, 236–40, 248–50, 255, 259–60, 265; and God, vii, viii, x, xii, xxi, xxii, xxiv, xxvi–xxviii, 12, 26, 27, 33–41, 45, 48, 50, 52, 53, 55, 56, 59, 61, 64, 69, 85–86, 88, 90, 97–99, 108, 131, 140, 150, 152, 153, 157, 160–62, 167–68, 170, 175–76, 195–96, 207–8, ch. 17 (passim), 228–32, 235–40, 242–43, 247, 249–50, 252–58, 260–64; as God's body, vii, x–xii, 40–41, 45, 48, 50, 51, 53, 55–56, ch. 5 (passim), 86, 100, 140, 161, 181, 215–17, 223–24, 230–32, 247, 249, 255–58, 260, 264; and humans, viii, xiii, xxiv, 36, 40, 50, 53–56, 59, 64, 70, 77, 80, 99, 101–4, 122–23, 144, 146, 157, 161–62, 169–72, 174, 179, 188, 191, 196, 202, 205, 207, 231, 234, 239, 241, 242, 249, 253
Wyschogrod, Edith, 244

CPSIA information can be obtained at www.ICGtesting.com
Printed in the USA
LVOW13s0436170913

352574LV00004B/12/P